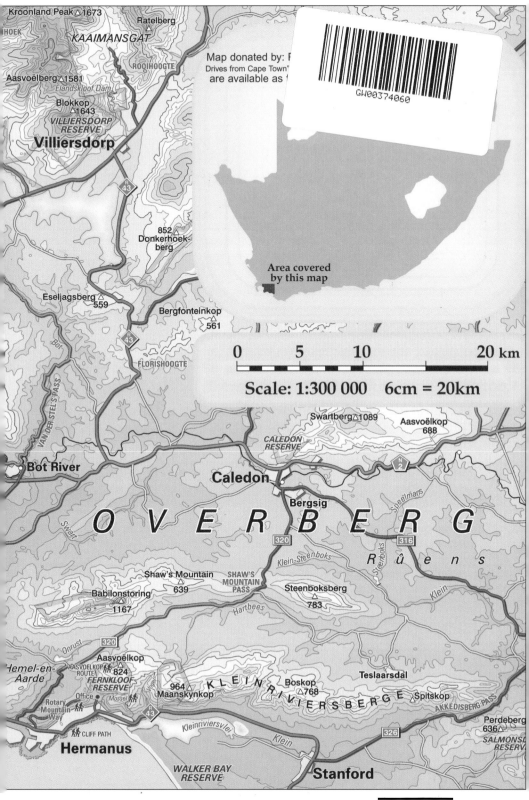

Kroonland Peak △1673

Ratelberg

HOEK

KAAIMANSGAT

ROOIHOOGTE

Aasvoëlberg △1581
Elandskloof Dam

Blokkop
△1643

*VILLIERSDORP
RESERVE*

Villiersdorp

43

852
Donkerhoek-
berg

Eseljagsberg △
559

6 43

Bergfonteinkop
△
561

FLORISHOOGTE

VAN DER STEL'S PASS

Bot

0   5   10   20 km

Scale: 1:300 000   6cm = 20km

Swartberg △1089   Aasvoëlkop
688

*CALEDON
RESERVE*

N
2

Bot River   **Caledon**

Bergsig

O V E R B E R G

Swart

320   316

Klein-Steenboks   *Rûens*

Steenboks

Steelmars

Shaw's Mountain
△
639

SHAW'S
MOUNTAIN
PASS

Steenboksberg
△
783

Klein

Babilonstoring
△
1167

Hartbees

320

Onrust

*Hemel-en-
Aarde*

Aasvoëlkop
AASVOELKOP
ROUTE △ 824
*FERNKLOOF
RESERVE*
Office ●

Rotary
Mountain
Way

CLIFF PATH

Hermanus

Mossel

43

964 △
Maanskynkop

K L E I N R I V I E R S B E R G

Boskop
△768

Teslaarsdal

Spitskop

AKKEDISBERG PASS

Perdeberg
636△

*SALMONSD
RESERV*

Kleinriviersvlei

Klein

326

*WALKER BAY
RESERVE*

Stanford

STELLENBOSCH
TO
HERMANUS

Thamnea uniflora

Mimetes hottentoticus

Klattia flava

Metalasia cymbifolia

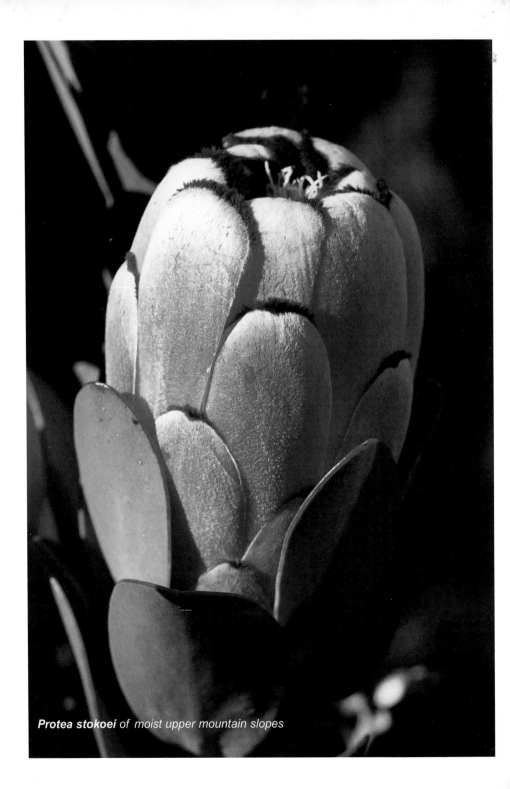

Protea stokoei of moist upper mountain slopes

STELLENBOSCH TO HERMANUS

South African Wild Flower Guide 5

second revised edition

including Kogelberg and Hottentots Holland

Text by: ANNE BEAN and
         AMIDA JOHNS

Photographs by: AMIDA JOHNS & others

Illustrations by: WENDY HITCHCOCK

Published by the
Botanical Society of South Africa
2005

These guides are produced through the co-operation of members of the public and private sector and their dedication to the conservation of our floral wealth. The publication of this volume has been made possible by contributions from the following bodies: the Botanical Society of South Africa, Hermanus Botanical Society, the Cape Tercentenary Foundation, the Western Cape Nature Conservation Board, the South African National Biodiversity Institute and many private individuals living in the area covered by this publication. The Publications Committee of the Botanical Society that has promoted this series consists of representatives from the Botanical Society of South Africa, the South African National Biodiversity Institute, the Western Cape Nature Conservation Board and several botanists.

Second edition, first impression 2005
Botanical Society of South Africa, Cape Town

© Copyright Text: Anne Bean and Amida Johns
© Copyright Photographs: Amida Johns and Anne Bean, Dr John Manning, Dr Charles Boucher,
Mr William Liltved, Mr Graham Duncan, Dr E.G.H. Oliver, Prof. Peter Linder,
Dr Anthony Verboom, Mr Giorgio Lombardi, Dr. Colin Paterson-Jones,
Mr Louis Mostert, Mr Gerald Hoberman retain their own copyright.
© Copyright Map: Peter Slingsby

English editing: Dr David McDonald, R. Geary-Cook

Design and production: Lynette Barnard, Alvin Horlin - Fairstep, Cape Town
Photo-reproduction: Hans Hnilicka, Riccardo de Klerk, Garth Lategan - Fairstep, Cape Town

Reproduction: Thomas Schrick - Fairstep, Cape Town

Printed and bound: Associated Printing

ISBN 1-874999-58-9

Front cover: Palmiet River valley, Kogelberg Nature Reserve   Amida Johns
Back cover: *Mimetes argenteus,* Hottentots Holland Nature Reserve   Amida Johns

FOREWORD

Ministry of Environmental Affairs and Development Planning
Ministerie van Omgewingsake en Ontwikkelingsbeplanning
I-Ofisi yoMphathiswa weMicimbi yeNdalo esiNgqongileyo
noCwangciso loPhuhliso

The First Edition of the South African Wild Flower Guide No. 5: Hottentots Holland to Hermanus was published in 1985. Since then a considerable amount of research has been conducted in the Cape Floristic Region and our knowledge of the ecology has been greatly enhanced. Photographic and printing techniques have also improved remarkably, making it possible to greatly improve the production of images of Cape fynbos species in the Second Edition of South Africa Wild Flower Guide No. 5, now titled " Stellenbosch to Hermanus". This book captures the essence of the "heart" of the Cape Floristic Region and will hopefully inspire future generations of citizens of the Western Cape, other parts of South Africa and abroad to appreciate and celebrate the immense floral wealth and beauty of the Stellenbosch to Hermanus region and promote its conservation.

It is with pleasure that I recommend this book as a very worthwhile contribution to the promotion of the conservation of biodiversity in the Cape Floristic Region and an encouragement to enjoy the natural wonders of this special region.

Tasneem Essop
Provincial Minister of Environmental Affairs and Development Planning

Private Bag x 9086, Cape Town, 8000   Tel (+27 21) 483-3915   Fax (+27 21) 483-6081
Privaatsak x 9086, Kaapstad, 8000   Tel (+27 21) 483-3915   Faks (+27 21) 483-6081

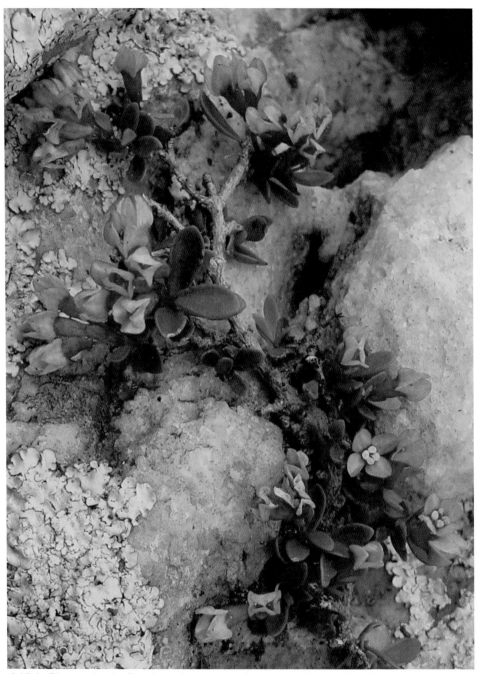

*A Klein River endemic, **Brachysiphon rupestris**, growing in a rock in a lichen covered rock.*

ACKNOWLEDGEMENTS

This second edition of a field guide to the flowers of the region from Stellenbosch to Hermanus is based loosely upon that entitled "Hottentots Holland to Hermanus", published in 1985 by the Botanical Society of South Africa, with changes in text, species and in the land area it treats. The opening up of the Kogelberg Nature Reserve to the public subsequent to 1985 has given an opportunity to include some of the unique plants seen on the trails in this area in addition to almost all those illustrated in the first edition. Lastly, 20 years has seen huge advances in photographic technology to yield the quality of these illustrations, which are all taken anew for this edition.

We are indebted to the Hermanus Botanical Society, whose members, and botanical mentor, Dr Ion Williams, by having cared for, housed and documented the botanically complete herbarium of Fernkloof and the coastal flora of Hermanus, provided an invaluable resource. I thank them all. We also made much use of other local herbaria, and thank Tony Xaba for allowing free rein in the Harold Porter Botanical Gardens' excellent herbarium, Caroline Joubert for accompaniment down many a species identification road; Pat Runnalls and company for their hard-earned species list of the Helderberg area, and to Mark Johns for his support. Dr Koos Roux and his patient and obliging Compton Herbarium staff at the South African National Biodiversity Institute, Kirstenbosch have personally helped us with this second edition.

The interval between 1985 and 2005 has seen an astonishing outpouring of publications on the Flora of the Cape and of South Africa that have been vastly helpful to the authors. It would be impossible to exaggerate how much time has been saved by that useful Conspectus of the Cape Flora by Peter Goldblatt and John Manning. (Ed 2), Strelitzia 9: (2000). We are grateful to all those who contributed to this work. Numerous checklists and other compilations helped particularly in establishing distribution details.

THE SLIDES AND DIGITAL IMAGES
A few additional slides were generously supplemented by Dr John Manning, Dr Charles Boucher, Mr William Liltved, Mr Graham Duncan, Dr E.G.H.Oliver, Prof. Peter Linder, Dr Anthony Verboom, Mr Giorgio Lombardi, Dr Colin Paterson-Jones, Mr Louis Mostert and Mr Gerald Hoberman. Peter Slingsby's map was on our wish list from the start, so we thank him most gratefully for this gift to the Botanical Society. Christine Wakfer supplied several digital images.

THE LINE DRAWINGS
Wendy Hitchcock has provided many line drawings and been more than willing to depict important details. For her contributions and friendship we are most grateful.

COMMENTS ON THE TEXT
The text was written initially by Anne Bean, then amended, expanded and edited by Amida Johns. The text of the Fabaceae was checked by Dr Anne Lise Vlok, the petaloid mono-cotyledons by Dr John Manning and the Ericaceae by Dr E.G.H. Oliver. The nomenclature conforms with Plants of Southern Africa by Germishuisen and Meyer (Strelitzia 14) 2003 and the Conspectus of Cape Plants by Peter Goldblatt and John Manning. Any remaining errors are those of the authors.

9

*A post fire display of grasses and **Aristea** in the Kogelberg.*

CONTENTS

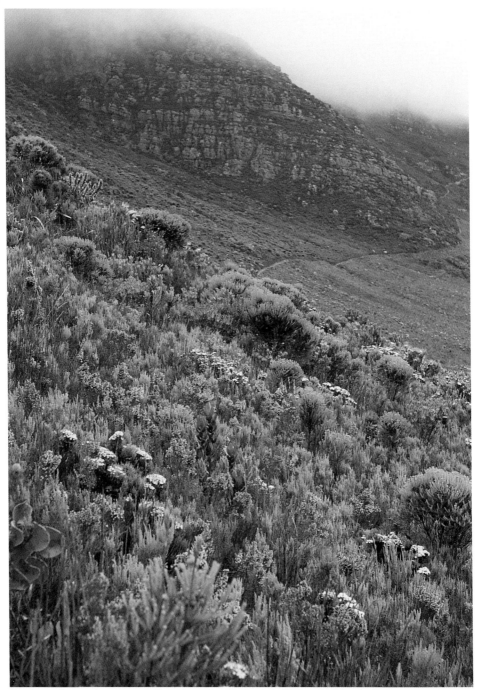

Lush southern slope vegetation along the Hottentots Holland hiking trail.

INTRODUCTION

This rugged, largely treeless and windswept south-westerly corner of the African continent is the heart of the fynbos and is one of the richest floral areas in the world. Whereas the natural major stresses to life in the fynbos are frequent strong winds and long periods without rain in summer, our area suffers least. Being close enough to be cooled by the sea, it also receives reliable rainfall in winter and equally dependable clouds misting the upper slopes in summer to support seeps and bogs and keep rivulets running all summer. Although no one has yet done a tally of plant species in our area, the Fernkloof nature reserve has recorded nearly 1500 species of flowering plants, and Kogelberg is presently listed with 1650 species. The species turnover from Jonkershoek to Somerset West, to Hottentots Holland, to Kogelberg, to Onrus Mountains and lastly to Klein River mountains is considerable, despite there being many species common to all. There remain species still to be discovered botanically, so it would not be too far-fetched to estimate the final figure above 2000 species.

There is no season when this shrubland of heaths, reeds, proteas and jewel-like scatterings of bulbs and herbs is not worth walking through, with its diversity, friendly texture and comparative lack of spines.

Not only is this wonderland botanically incredibly rich, but the scenery is also magnificent. From the blue or silvery False Bay and the restless, cold Atlantic ocean to the west and south, where the Southern Right Whale comes inshore to calve each winter, to the 1300 m high peaks of the Hottentots Holland and Kogelberg Biosphere and Klein River mountains soaring out of the ocean, breathtaking views can be seen almost anywhere along the hiking trails and roads.

TRAILS AND WALKS

User ethics
Hiking is restricted to constructed footpaths. Shortcuts destroy the vegetation that protects the underlying soil, quickly turning into erosion gullies. Take rests on a durable surface, such as rock or the bare ground of the path. Objects in nature derive much of their beauty from their surroundings and never look quite the same back home … so, load your camera, not your pack, let photos, drawings and memories be your souvenirs.

Snow falls and lies briefly on the highest slopes, and early morning frost crackles underfoot; the extra nip in the air is enough just to add to the exhilaration of an early start. The moderate climate invites many hikers armed with sunhats and sunblock in the warm dry summer weather and raingear and warm woollies in the cool wet winter. But be warned: in summer a cold front with thick enveloping mist can strike the mountains almost without warning. Many are the tales of hikers losing their way and not a few die of hypothermia in these conditions, so always be prepared with warm clothes, rain gear and extra high calorie foods, and take note of weather forecasts before your departure.

A large range of trails and scenic drives wend their way through the spectrum of habitats, plant communities, geological forms and scenery that make up this special area. Walking and hiking provide some of the best ways to get to know and enjoy the flora found here.

Hottentots Holland

The majestic mountains between the Sir Lowry's and Franschhoek passes from the 30 000 ha expanse of the Hottentots Holland Nature Reserve. Always public land, this mountain landscape received formal recognition as a Nature Reserve in the 1970's – one of the most secure statuses under environmental law. The primary objective of this category has been to conserve the precious water, flora and fauna associated with this mountain fynbos ecosystem. Unlike its mostly transformed lowland counterparts, the diversity of fynbos found in the mountainous areas of the Cape Floral Region is relatively well represented and protected in a series of reserves along the Cape Fold Mountains – the Hottentots Holland is a vital link in this chain.

Entrance to the reserve is at the Nuweberg office, approximately 11 kilometres off the R324 from Grabouw to Villiersdorp. All trails begin here and permits are required and obtainable from Cape Nature's office. Hiker numbers are limited so advanced booking is recommended.

The well-known Boland hiking trail traverses these wilderness mountains offering excellent views, splendid wildflowers and an opportunity to experience the great outdoors. Two separate overnight huts make it possible to hike the 43 kilometres of trail through this pristine mountain fynbos. Variations in biophysical conditions of soil and altitude account for much of the change in habitats and thus plant communities and species to be found en route. The trail begins with a short, stiff climb from the Reserve parking. Levelling out to pass the Sphinx at about 1000m, fields of the pink Four Sisters Heath, *Erica fastigiata*, may be seen covering the shallow, white soils in the summer months. Derived from the quartzitic sandstone of the Peninsula Formation (see Geology) that forms the spectacular mountain scenery, this geological base dominates the mountains of the reserve. The major peaks, Somerset-Sneeukop and Victoria Peak rising to some 1590m, remain overpoweringly in view. The path soon crosses a wet kloof, dense with trees of *Protea lacticolor*. In contrast the underlying soil here is brown and clayey. This marks the crossing of the Cederberg shale band – the other notable component of the mountain geology – as it erodes into the streams that source the Palmiet River, some 60km from its outlet at the sea. The long-tubed *Erica longifolia* puts on a colourful display along this band. Other commonly encountered plants along the trail en route to the first overnight hut include the blombos, *Metalasia cephalotes*, the buchu, *Adenandra acuta*, the restio, *Ceratocaryum argenteum*, as well as large sprawling plants of the pea, *Psoralea asarina*. Once at the Landroskop huts you can rest while admiring the panoramic view.

The second leg of the walk follows the road down alongside the kloof carrying the headwaters of the Riversonderend River. Seen flowering in late summer, *Erica jacksoniana* is a special local endemic to the Hottentots Holland Mountains. En route the mountainside is densely dotted with the berg palmiet sedge, *Tetraria thermalis*, as well as species of pea, *Podalyria montana* and *Liparia myrtifolia*. Some notable clumps of the mountain cypress, *Widdringtonia nodiflora*, an ancient gymnosperm genus of cedar, are encountered before you cross the suspension bridge. This hanging thoroughfare allows access over Boegoekloof, an aptly named ravine dense with heavily scented boegoe/buchu of the citrus family, *Rutaceae*. Particularly abundant is the real buchu, *Agathosma crenulata*. Once on the other side fine plants of the icon of these mountains, the silver leafed *Mimetes argenteus* and the beautiful *Protea stokoei* are seen. This wet mountain fynbos on the south facing slopes is an ideal and characteristic habitat in which to find these species.

14

The rugged snow-capped Somerset Sneeukop and adjacent peaks.

Instead of following this route down from Landroskop hut, an additional 16km circuit offers the fitter and more adventurous the chance to escape deep into the wilderness of these mountains. The path heads upwards to skirt the boulder-strewn upper 'restio herblands' across Somerset-Sneeuwkop, passing species such as *Cliffortia grandifolia* and *Liparia myrtifolia*. At 1400m you also see the magnificent high altitude *Protea grandiceps*, and mountainsides covered with *Spatalla setacea*. Keep your eyes open for other botanical treasures along this upland track. At the top neck of Boegoekloof you may either exit out via the Jonkershoek Valley, joining on to the Panorama Trail, or continue down the kloof itself – a wet gully full of the tall, willowy restio *Cannomois virgata* and trees of *Empleurum unicapsulare* and waterwitels, *Brachylaena neriifolia* – to cross the suspension bridge and on to your second night's rest. From Pofaddernek to the huts the shale band descent is rich with geophytes including *Aristea major*, *Watsonia borbonica* and *Lanaria lanata*- especially conspicuous after fire. The rocky outcrops around the huts are home to the fan-leafed aloe, *Aloe plicatilis* that gives the name to one of the huts, Aloe Ridge.

The final stretch of this trail takes you back to the reserve parking along the lower eastern slopes overlooking the fruit orchards of the Vyeboom valley and views of Theewaterskloof dam. This fertile Bokkeveld shale (see geology) valley, like the Elgin basin, has largely been transformed by agriculture. Only remnant patches of its unique Coastal Renosterveld and transitional fynbos vegetation remain. It is home to rare endemics such as *Leucadendron elimense subspecies vyeboomense*. Landowners have formed conservancies – a co-operative environmental management agreement – to conserve patches of this threatened habitat. An alternative exit route takes you northward to the Franschhoek Pass – the northernmost extent of the reserve and this guide.

Huts have cold water and toilets. All hikers must bring their own food and sleeping bags. The mountain weather is unpredictable so clothing for all weather conditions is required. More detailed maps of the routes are obtainable. Permission from the reserve management is required for alternative routes. Routes, numbers and frequency of access are restricted to limit environmental impact.

Jonkershoek

Behind Stellenbosch lies one of the most beautiful valleys in the Cape. Flanked on all sides by rugged pinnacled sandstone peaks, the Jonkershoek Valley is one of the Cape's hidden wildernesses. The most popular hikes here are the circular 17 and 18 kilometre Panorama and Swartboskloof routes which contour around the back of this watershed, famed for receiving some of the highest rainfall in the Western Cape.

The Panorama trail starts from the carpark at Witbrug with a tough 4km ascent over rounded granite hillslopes. Favouring these deep, brown soils are dense stands of *Protea neriifolia* and *Cannomois virgata* interspersed with scattered clumps of the cedar, *Widdringtonia nodiflora*, the cone-bush, *Leucadendron daphnoides*, as well as *Leucospermum lineare, Brunia noduliflora* and the occasional tall *Aspalathus globosa*. This strenuous start levels out at 800m to track below the sandstone cliffs for a further 4km, passing through Bergriviernek with spectacular views down Assegaaiboschkloof and onto the Dwarsberg plateau, dense with restios. A very steep 2,6km descent down Kurktrekker-nek joins on to the waterfall route and back to Witbrug.

The Swartboschkloof route starts before Witbrug and traverses the northern aspects of the valley. This fan-shaped kloof with its abundance of restios and grasses and emergent protea trees, gives the impression of a grassland landscape. The lower slopes are dominated by the taller *Protea repens* and *Protea nitida* with shorter tussocks of *Restio perplexus*. Other conspicuous species

Granite hills below the sandstone cliffs of the Jonkershoek valley

include *Rhus angustifolia, Cliffortia cuneata* and *Phylica pubescens* with *Erica hirta* particularly abundant.

In the various forested areas along the rivers there are tree species such as the african holly, *Ilex mitis*, the rooiels, *Cunonia capensis* and wild almond, *Brabejum stellatifolium*. The piles of boulders forming the screes are supported and stabilized by forest trees as well as the more shrubby Kliphout, *Heeria argentea*. This is where *Aloe mitriformis* may be seen. From here the path zigzags up onto the contour path that tracks around to join the Panorama trail in exiting down Kurktrekker.

The waterfall route may also be walked separately as a single return track. Also starting from Witbrug it passes alongside the Eersterivier, yellow with tall *Cyclopia maculata* in the early summer, taking one to the First and Second Waterfalls. The steep and dangerous ascent to the waterfall itself is closed to hikers.

Helderberg

Situated up the southern flank of the dramatic Helderberg mountain, this local authority nature reserve offers a number of circular trails of increasing distance. Colour coded, they range from 3 to 18 kms and traverse mostly over the Malmesbury shale hills that surround the base of Helderberg Peak. Here tall trees of *Protea coronata* together with other shrubs form a dense vegetation.

Well-tended lawns with roaming bontebok make this a favourite weekend picnic destination. The reserve has an interpretive centre which identifies common flowering species on a weekly rotation. Be warned that many plants in the immediate vicinity of the parking area do not occur here naturally, so may not be identifiable from this book. Indigenous plants are also for sale at the nursery.

Kogelberg Biosphere Reserve

Proclaimed in 1999, this reserve is managed in accordance with the internationally accepted principles of a biosphere reserve. It is a 100 000 ha expanse of natural vegetation, plantation, orchards, towns and marine environment. The aim of the reserve is to link conservation and development under the guiding principle of sustainable utilisation. In other words this type of reserve focuses on man, living in, and using, the natural resources of the environment in a way that sustains the ecological systems on which the resources depend.

The Kogel Bay coast forms the western extent of the Kogelberg Biosphere Reserve.

The reserve is structured according to three different but associated zones of utilisation and transformation of the natural environment. The strictly protected inner core zone is the most undisturbed and biologically rich area. Here priority is given to natural ecological processes. Recreational activities that do not impact heavily on the environment, such as trail hiking and kayaking, are encouraged, as is non-manipulative research.

A middle buffer zone, of mostly private land, acts to 'buffer' or help protect the core from the adverse effects of development. This zone also assists in the maintenance of viable plant and animal populations. Sustainable utilisation of natural products, and eco-tourism initiatives that support the ecology of the area are encouraged here. The third zone is the transition area or 'zone of cooperation'. This includes towns, farmland and plantations where the natural environment is intensively utilised and transformed. Conservation knowledge is applied here to support the biosphere. A biosphere reserve ensures that the environment lived in is healthy and pleasant while providing natural produce as well as opportunities for employment, recreation, education and tourism.

The **Kogelberg Nature Reserve**, together with Steenbras Mountain Catchment area, make up most of the core area – a 30 000 ha expanse of mountains endowed with the most exceptional quality fynbos. In keeping with the biosphere concept, outdoor recreation if limited and of the primitive kind. Off-path walking is strictly prohibited to prevent trampling of sensitive habitats and rare plant populations.

A drive out to the Kogelberg Reserve office, between Betty's Bay and Kleinmond – the start of all the trails – takes one along the spectacular R44 coastal route. Screes of geologically old rock-falls are strewn on slopes that mask rounded Malmesbury shale hills. A number of parking areas along the way allow one to appreciate the dramatic sea and mountain scenery as well as some of the unique plants of the area.

Restricted to these slopes the white flowered *Leucospermum bolusii* fills the air with its strong sweet scent in the early summer months. Passing over the Rooiels River estuary and on to Betty's Bay the coastal forelands stretch out in a mosaic of rocky shores, dune wetlands and sandy flats – its vegetation fast disappearing under housing development. Water pooled between the mountain and coastal dunes supports a dense, wet vegetation dominated by *Berzelia lanuginosa*, the swamp daisy *Osmitopsis asteriscoides*, with *Erica perspicua*, *Psoralea pinnata*, scattered clumps of *Mimetes hirtus*, and even the rare *Witsenia maura*.

*The Kogelberg lower reaches of the Palmiet River and **Mimetes cucullatus.***

18

Erica patersonia emerges as yellow 'mealie cobs' amongst the restio fields, notably *Elegia filacea*, of the drier sandy flats.

The turn off to the Reserve office at Oudebosch is shortly before the Palmiet River bridge. Taking its name from the nearby forested kloof, Oudebosch is nestled in a band of shale where the vegetation turns bright yellow in the spring months with the flowering 'en masse' of the conebushes Leucadendron xanthoconus and Leucadendron microcephalum. From here a short circuit family walk takes one along the lower reaches of the Palmiet River.

This meandering gentle stream turns into a roaring, white-water river in winter. The banks are fringed with pristine riparian vegetation dense with the restio *Cannomois virgata* and the palmiet, *Prionium serratum*, as well as trees of the wild almond, *Brabejum stellatifolium*, riverine yellowwood *Podocarpus elongatus* and *Metrosideros angustifolius*. On the mountain slopes the blue woody Irid, *Nivenia stokoei*, contrasts sharply with the russet fields of *Restio bifarius* with its heavily pendulous male inflorescences. The route crosses numerous sidestreams thick with water-loving species. *Restio dispar, Erica macowanii, Leucadendron salicifolium, Grubbia rosmarinifolia, Pseudobaeckea africana* and the ferns *Todea barbara* and *Blechnum capensis* are all found here.

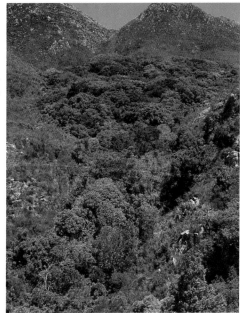

An alternative short, stiff walk from Oudebosch to Harold Porter Gardens provides a mosaic of fynbos, forest and sea views. An initial short ascent up Oudebosch kloof takes one through patches of Afromontane forest. Interlocking crowns of real yellowwood, assegai and cape beech filter the light for the tree saplings and ferns of *Pteridium aquilinum* that cover the floor. Here the cape tree fern, *Cyathea capensis,* prefers the riverside. Persisting amid a sea of fynbos the forests are found where the erodable Cederberg shales have produced rich soils and a kloof that protects it from fire. On leaving the forest a transition zone of forest margin plants including *Cliffortia heterophylla* and tall trees of *Protea mundii* is seen, and the valley fills with the scent of the coffee bush *Brunia albiflora* and *Psoralea aphylla*, as one follows the stream down the zigzag path into the Harold Porter National Botanical Garden. Before you descend, look out for the endemic dwarf species of *Penaeaceae, Sonderothamnus petraeus*, in rock crevices.

A forested mountain kloof surrounded by fynbos.

The highlight of any visit to this area would be the 24-kilometre Kogelberg Trail that traverses the heart of the Reserve. The rewards of walking this trail are unparalleled. The track begins by following the Oudebosch forest route but branches westward, past stands of the sticky, long-tubed *Erica thomae*. Then it's on to the wet, lush southern slope vegetation of Platberg. *Brunia*

19

stokoei is particularly abundant downslope, as is *Liparia vestita*. Also keep an eye out for another woody Irid, *Klattia stokoei* entangled amidst the vegetation of the more shaded and wetter sections of the trail.

The path levels off onto a plateau covered with *Erica fastigiata* and *Leucadendron gandogeri*. Wet seepages are yellow and pink with *Erica campanularis* and *Erica intervallaris*. A downhill track descends back into the Palmiet valley along the Louw's River Gorge.

If you don't want to climb but want the views afforded by height, Perdeberg provides a wonderful amble along six kilometers of jeep track that takes you to Perdeberg peak, with views over the coastal area and the Palmiet river valley. The vegetation is predominantly a mix of ericas and restios such as *Erica massonii* and the tall reed, *Restio egregius*. This is also *Nivenia* country. Here the other endemic species, *Nivenia levynsiae*, prefers the shelter of rocky outcrops. The trail exits out at the Kleinmond Nature Reserve, down through moist southern slope vegetation and onto the Cederberg shale band plateau that winds it way out of the Kogelberg valley. Stands of the unmistakable bright red *Erica pillansii* can be seen here in the autumn months.

An extension of the Perdeberg Trail offers the only overnight hike in the area, the Highlands Trail. This takes you through the zones of the Biosphere. Starting on farmland, the path leads down to Rooisand – a remaining patch of Southwest Coast Renosterveld and transitional fynbos on the west banks of the Bot River vlei. Here *Xiphotheca reflexa*, *Hermannia angularis* and, after fire, many of the geophytes such as *Satyrium pumilum*, may be seen. Then it's on to sandy flats and over the coastal barrier dunes of Strandveld, where many of the dune species may be seen. The trail finishes for the day with a walk along the beach to the hut in Kleinmond. The second leg of the walk is a round trip up to Perdeberg. This is a general overview of the landscape. A more detailed hiking map is available on booking.

Kleinmond
Wedged between the houses and the sea is a corridor of fynbos on coastal sandstone rock. The vegetation is often subjected to intense, salty sea spray – a feature tolerated by the species growing here. A leisurely easy path skirting the coastline explores this environment where *Coleonema album*, *Metalasia muricata*, *Phylica ericoides*, *Othonna dentata*, *Ruschia macowanii* and *Polygala myrtifolia* are intermingled with splashes of the lovely red geophytes, *Gladiolus priorii* and *Gladiolus cunonius*.

The west bank of the Palmiet River estuary affords another coastal amble through the whole spectrum of coastal vegetation types including dunes covered with thickets of *Sideroxylon inerme*, *Rhus* and *Olea*, walls of *Psoralea pinnata* of the coastal wetlands and a coastal variation of mountain fynbos with *Serruria adscendens*, *Pseudopentameris brachyphylla* and fields of *Edmondia sesamoides* and *Elegia persistens* in the summer months of the first few years after fire. The sandy flats are where *Lachnaea densiflora* and *Berzelia abrotanoides* can be found.

An energetic alternative to these coastal explorations is an ascent up Sandown and Three Sisters peaks – the mountain ridge that forms the backdrop to Kleinmond town. The middle southern slope of this ridge is again the continuation of the shale band and the vegetation is richly proteaceous. Dense stands of *Protea compacta* extend down onto the sandy flats below.

20

The coastal mountains from Hangklip to Betty's Bay.

Betty's Bay

An extensive band of natural dune vegetation occurs along the coastal zone from Betty's Bay to Pringle Bay only intermittently interrupted by rocky shelves. On the sands closest to the sea *Ehrharta villosa, Tetragonia decumbens, Dasispermum suffruticosum, Ferraria crispa, Senecio elegans, Trachyandra divaricata* and *Nemesia versicolor* are characteristic. A more dense scrub with *Osyris compressa* and several *Rhus* species soon covers the dune and merges into a dense thicket of *Sideroxylon inerme,* together with *Cussonia thyrsiflora, Olea, Cassine* and *Asparagus* species, *Tetragonia fruticosa* and *Knowltonia vesicatoria*. The tall showy dune orchids, *Satyrium carneum* and *Bonatea speciosa* flower here during early summer.

The Harold Porter National Botanical Garden is one of eight gardens within the South African National Biodiversity Institute. Primarily a garden to grow and display plants of the area, it also provides numerous short walks through intact communities of coastal mountain fynbos, to forested kloofs and over rivers thick with riparian vegetation. Both Disa and Leopard Kloof have scenic waterfalls at their upper reaches. Expertly created dune and wetland habitat gardens – with many typical plant species – aim to interpret these environments to the visitor. As well as providing local plants for sale, a restaurant and gift shop, the gardens hold numerous events during the year, the favourite being their summer concerts held in the new year.

Brodie Link Reserve

When under threat from development, this property was bought by WWF-SA through funds made available by the Brodie family. Called a 'link' reserve it forms a corridor of sandy flats and coastal mountain fynbos from the Hangklip Mountain through the flats of Betty's Bay to the mountains of the Kogelberg Nature Reserve. A walking trail crosses the Reserve between Betty's Bay and Pringle Bay. Among the threatened species the Brodie Link protects are *Protea angustata, Erica patersonia,* and the orchids, *Acrolophia bolusii* and *Disa venusta*.

Fernkloof Nature Reserve   Frank Woodvine

Fernkloof, founded in 1957 and managed by the Overstrand Municipality, is rightly considered the gem of Hermanus. On its approximately 2 000 ha no fewer than 1 500 flowering plant species naturally occur, occupying a range of ecological niches from sea-level to its highest point at 824m. A considerable network of trails covering some 50km gives easy access generally, with a few steeper gradients providing a challenge. Many of the paths were badly damaged in the floods of the southern Overberg region in April 2005 when Hermanus received some 200mm of rain in 24 hours – so the paths need negotiating with care. Adjacent to the entrance gate is the Botanical Centre, built with funds raised by the Hermanus Botanical Society, which from the outset has made an outstanding contribution to the reserve's progress over the years. Pride of place goes to the herbarium where some 5 000 named plant specimens are housed. Managed to a high standard, it has gained international recognition and is referenced as `HER' in the Index Herbariorum, a rare achievement for a small community. A well-stocked nursery carries a wide range of indigenous plants while a comprehensive map shows all the trails and gives a wealth of relevant information.

Starting at the western end of Rotary Way Mountain Drive a 6 km contour path traverses the southern aspect of this ridge over grey and brown weathered sandstone en route to the reserve entrance. Initially, the vegetation reflects the too frequent fires that have occurred and now only scattered specimens of the formerly common krepelhout, *Leucospermum conocarpodendron*, remain. Soon dense stands of proteas such as *P. compacta, P. repens* and *P. longifolia* dominate. At the foot of Buff Rock, look out for the lanky shrub *Anisodontea scabrosa*, with its pink hibiscus-like flowers. Where Elephant Path crosses, *Leucadendron tinctum* is profuse, its leaves flushing red and yellow at the tips of the branches.

An aerial panorama of the Hermanus coast and mountains.   Gerald Hoberman

Adenandra brachyphylla and *A. uniflora are* common. Members of the citrus family, *Rutaceae*, oil-glands on the leaves emit a distinctive individual smell when crushed and their delicate petals earn them the common name of china-plant.

These southern slopes are rich in proteaceous species. Look out for *Serruria heterophylla*. On sandy slopes above the suburb of Hermanus Heights, the keen eye will be rewarded with a glimpse of botanical rarities such as, *Liparia splendens, Protea angusta* and *Sonderothamnus speciosus*, all hugging the path on a 100m stretch.

Near Klipspringer is found the shy, blue-flowered *Viola decumbens*, the only member of this cosmopolitan family found in the fynbos, alongside the near endemic *Erica ecklonii*. On the shaded rocky ground the spreading *Sutera hispida* and the daisy, *Thaminophyllum latifolium* with well-spaced rounded petals occurs. Emerging from shade, the open slopes have the delicate caledon bluebell, *Gladiolus bullatus* in spring and the widespread patrysbos, *Leucospermum truncatulum*. Approaching the Visitor Centre, no fewer than five species of the carnivorous genus *Drosera* line the path.

At the Visitor's Centre the path skirts the southern slope of Lemoenkop to Waterkloof and the Rockfill Dams, the major water supply for Hermanus until the late 1970's. Climbing the steep short section to regain the path, digress to walk the dam wall and look up into the kloof which supports a fine patch of Afromontane forest. In addition to typical species such as cape beech, rooiels and assegaibos the rarer white-pear *Apodytes dimidiata* is found. Watch out for the head-high blister bush, *Peucedanum galbanum*, fortunately not common, which can provoke severe skin irritation when the plant is bruised. More common is tontelblaar, *Hermas villosa* with its 1 m long stem bearing clusters of globose flowers and carrot-scented leaves at ground level. At Droekloof is the rare member of the *Asteraceae Thaminophyllum latifolium*. Rounding the shale banded Mount Cyclopia, bell-shaped flowers of *Roella incurva*, dark-spotted within, crowd the slopes from October to March. Ericas include salt-and-pepper *Erica imbricata, E. sessiliflora* and *E. tenella*. Where streams trickle off the mountain, strips of forest hug the banks and here iron martin, *Laurophyllus capensis*, the only member of the genus, occurs.

Finally, the path emerges onto the R43, the Hermanus- Stanford road, where, ideally, you will have a car awaiting you. As a diversion, cross the road and take the path along the bank of the Vogelgat River to the bird-hide, where in summer migrant waders flock on the mudflats formed as the river enters the estuary. Along the length of the Contour Path, several link-up trails give the option of dropping down to the suburbs of Hermanus or upwards to the network of trails at higher altitudes.

To access the higher reaches, a clearly signposted path leads from the Jeep Track to Galpinkop and on to Aasvoëlkop. From the visitor centre this is roughly a 2 hour walk to Galpin hut. Of the 74 species of *Erica* collected in Fernkloof to date, on this walk several may be seen in flower regardless of the time of year. Sticky-tubed species include *E. massonii*, the bottle-heath, *E. retorta* and loveliest of all, the impressive pride of Hermanus, *E. aristata*, locally profuse but confined to an area between Hawston and Hermanus. *E. lanuginosa* nestles in rocky outcrops whilst the rarely encountered *E. holosericea* with its soft pink flowers prefers open ground.

Where the path forks at White Rock, there are a few specimens of the regally named *Paranomus sceptrum-gustavianus*. Taking the left fork leads to a bubbling perennial stream, alongside which is a small colony of the bizarre vlieëibos, *Roridula gorgonias*. Another endemic family is represented by *Grubbia rosmarinifolia* and nearby is *G. tomentosa*. Where the path reaches a T-junction, the right hand path southwards takes you to Galpin Hut, half-hidden amongst the sheltering rocks.

Galpin Hut is maintained by the local botanical society as a facility for its members. A small side path to the peak offers a bench where one may sit and drink in the stunning view of Walker Bay and the sprawling expanse of coastline. The observant person will spot the brilliant red blooms of *Crassula coccinea* in mid-summer and the blue tubes of *Selago serrata*, both equally at home clinging to rocky outcrops.

The Hermanus mountains stretching to the distant Kogelberg.

A path ascends gently round Sculptured Corner of Platberg and on to Aasvoëlkop. Along the way are tall specimens of *Liparia vestita*, attractive with its densely hairy silvery branches. Turning sharply eastward, the path winds over a large exposure of tillite which forms most of the northern slope of Platberg down to the kloof below where it meets the ascending Cederberg shale band. Below, is that most beautiful of valleys, aptly named Hemel-en-Aarde, Heaven and Earth, by early missionaries, now given over largely to agriculture, due to its fertile soils.

A path allows a return to Galpinkop or alternatively you may opt to continue to Aasvoëlkop, at 824 m the highest point in the reserve. Before the final ascent the band of Cederberg shale is crossed with a host of typical plant species. The peak itself is sandstone. Tackling this is worth the effort for the panoramic views. Southwards the expanse of Walker Bay merges with the ocean. To the east, Vogelgat Private Nature Reserve merges with the provincial reserve of Maanskynkop, giving 3 contiguous reserves which together form an alien-free expanse of pristine mountain fynbos. Looking inland, Babilonstoring at 1 168m is the dominant peak. Retracing one's steps to the Galpinkop junction and continuing along the southern face of Platberg. Passing Banksia ridge, one may be rewarded with a sighting of *Erica banksii,* flowering in late summer and growing only on south facing rocky outcrops. A 4-way signpost near Galpin Hut provides 3 options of returning to the Jeep Track, each with its attractions.

A coastal walk along the Cliff Path is an alternative to a mountain hike. Along its entire 10 km length, from the New Harbour in the west to the Kleinriver in the east, the Cliff Path offers spectacular scenery, floral richness and possibly the best shore-based whale watching in the world. The almost complete exclusion of fire for decades on this narrow strip of land between buildings and the sea has transformed the vegetation in places from fynbos to *Rhus* dominated coastal scrub on shallower soils and emerging forest on deeper soils. Despite this, bulbous geophytes, dependent on fire or disturbance to stimulate flowering, are still plentiful.

Near the New Harbour the striking cliff lily, *Gladiolus carmineus*, autumn-flowering, thrives on rocky windswept cliff-faces buffeted by salt spray. Tall bushes of *Coleonema album* thrive here as does *Chrysanthemoides monilifera, Cotyledon orbiculata, Lachenalia rubida*, and the arum lily, *Zantedeschia aethiopica* on marshy ground, the tubers of which provide a feast for porcupines, still common on this narrow coastal strip. The path turns inland for a few hundred metres along the main road and is regained at Mollergren Park. At De Gang the tubular drooping flowers of hangertjie *Erica plukenetii*, provide nectar for 3 species of sunbird, the fynbos endemic orange-breasted sunbird, the lesser double-collared sunbird and malachite sunbird. The confusingly similar *E. coccinea*, bearing a wide range of flower colours, is also prominent. Tearing one's eyes

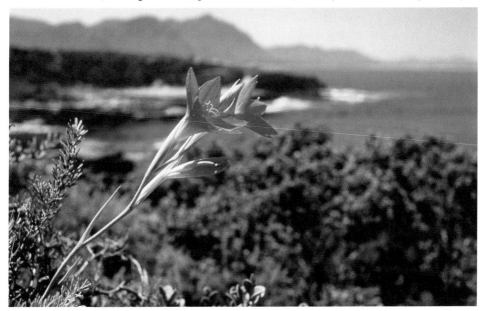

*Hermanus rocky coast with the beautiful **Gladiolus carmineus**.*   Anne Bean

away from the captivating views of rocky cliffs, sandy coves and marine life, at Sieverspunt look out for the large green orchid, *Bonatea speciosa*, the only member of the genus occurring in this area. On marshy patches, the *Gentianaceae* is represented by both Christmas berry, *Chironia baccifera* and *Orphium frutescens*. Near Kwaaiwater, *Gladiolus cunonius* is common.

The wooden footbridge over the Mossel River was destroyed by the floods of April 2005, but it is not unusual to come across a family of Cape Clawless Otters in the vicinity of the river mouth or in the adjacent sea. Return to the main road for a short distance. Small copses of milkwood, *Sideroxylon inerme* have survived in the face of increasing development between the river and Grotto beach, a kilometre to the east. At Grotto Beach the path winds through a forest of large, ancient milkwood. Emerging on to the coast, the dunes are anchored by the wind-pollinated shrub, *Passerina vulgaris* and the sour fig, *Carpobrotus acinaciformis.*

A small yet informative brochure, " Guide to the Cliff Path of Hermanus ", is available for a small fee and will add immeasurably to the enjoyment this loveliest of all walks has to offer.

Vermont Coastal path

Although vegetation may not be as diverse as on the Hermanus Cliff Path, Vermont offers a short, comfortable stroll along an excellently maintained path, in places virtually at the high tide mark. Starting at the car park at the tidal pool, the path winds amongst wind shaped rocks and patches of wild sage, *Salvia africana-lutea*, a 2 m tall shrub with densely packed aromatic leaves. One also encounters *Carpobrotus acinaciformis* forming a dense carpet alongside the sprawling sweet-scented *Pelargonium capitatum* and clumps of khoi bedding, *Helichrysum crispum*. The hardy sea lavender, *Limonium scabrum* of the statice family, peeps from beneath sheltering rocks and sturdy boardwalks carry you over marshy patches full of arum lilies.

On entering the sign-posted Vermont Nature Reserve the trail improves to a wide, well gravelled track flanked by dunes. Wind-pruned *Rhus* species intermingle with stunted milkwoods and bitou, *Chrysanthemoides monilifera*, which lend support to scramblers such as haakdoring, *Asparagus aethiopicus* and dronkbessie, *Solanum quadrangularis* of the potato family.

The path ends at the foot of the steep sandy slopes of well known Brekfis Baai, where a board-walk leads upward to the small parking area at Geelvink Close.

CLIMATE AND GEOLOGY

Climate

The climate of the area is classified as a Mediterranean type with warm dry summers and cool wet winters. In winter successions of cold fronts bringing rain and snow sweep in from the northwest. Between these fronts the weather breaks into sparkling clear days. Rainfall varies from its highest at the head of the Jonkershoek Valley at 3 000 mm per annum to around 1 000 mm along the coast. From the Kogelberg northwest through the Hottentots Holland Mountains the rainfall is strongly seasonal with markedly more rain falling in the winter months. This diminishes eastwards with the Klein River Mountains being less clearly seasonal. Here the contrast between winter and summer rain is not as well-defined, the summer months being somewhat wetter.

Snow is common on the more inland high peaks of the Hottentots Holland Mountains. Hikers are warned to take note of weather conditions when planning a trip. The coastal mountains seldom receive snow due to the moderating effect of the sea.

With the change to summer, the wind shifts to southeast with fair amounts of moisture coming from clouds formed over the coastal mountains. Summer temperatures average 28 °C and tend to be cooler at the coast. Occasionally temperatures soar to 40 °C and hikers run the risk of heat exhaustion. The dry and windy conditions of summer make this the most hazardous time for fires. Natural fires that result from lightning strikes occur mostly during the late summer months. In a single thunderstorm event at the end of March 1991 the mountains of the Kogelberg area were ignited by 11 strikes resulting in five days of continuous burning. The range and extent of fires depends on weather conditions, the age of the vegetation i.e. how flammable it is, as well as management strategies and resources. Although fires are an integral part of the ecology of fynbos, if they occur outside the natural cycle and season they can be catastrophic. Please be careful and only make fires where fireplaces are provided.

A crystal clear day follows snow in the Hottentots Holland mountains.

Geology

The evolution of the landforms we see today began some 1000 million years ago (mya) when Africa lay at the centre of the great supercontinent Pangaea, later breaking up into Gondwana and a northern part. From this time two major cycles of deposition, mountain building and erosion have ensued. It is from the latter cycle that the present landscape of the area encompassed in this floral guide, has been so distinctly shaped. The deposition and consolidation of the layers of the Cape rocks – the Cape Supergroup – began around 450mya, to be deformed 200 million years later by an episode of folding and faulting of gigantic proportions.

The underlying layers were thrust upwards into almost vertical folds to form impressive mountains – reputed to have reached up to three kilometres into the sky! With subsequent continuous weathering and erosion these mountains have been reduced to the mere vestiges we see today. The topmost or youngest strata of this Supergroup – the Witteberg and Bokkeveld groups of shale, have been washed from the mountain tops and are now found only as the fertile rolling hills of the Elgin, Vyeboom, Bot River and Caledon valleys. The more erosion-resistant sandstone and quartzite of the Table Mountain Group have persisted as spectacular mountains with high vertical cliffs and jagged peaks. Within this group the older, more basal Peninsula Formation is of quartzitic sandstone. It built the Hottentots Holland mountain block and the coastal aspects of the Kogelberg and Hermanus mountains as well as the rocky coastline. The inland aspects and peaks have been formed from more recent deposits, mostly sandstones of the Nardouw Subgroup.

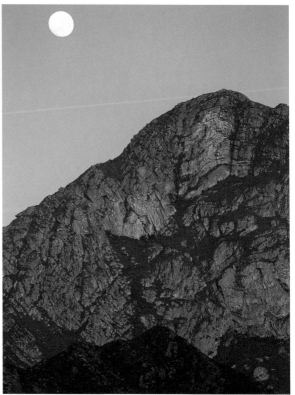

Sandwiched between the Peninsula Formation and the formations of the Nardouw Subgroup is a layer of tillite, the Pakhuis Formation, followed by a band of shale, the Cederberg formation. The tillite is the result of a glacial episode that interrupted the deposition of the two sandstones some 400mya and may be identified in the landscape as blocks of rock with inclusions of scattered faceted pebbles.

The more erodable Cederberg shales have tended to form the kloofs and smoothly weathered slopes of the mountains – notably around Oudebosch in the Kogelberg Nature Reserve. These bands have also formed the obviously rounded grassy peaks of Victoria and Emerald Dome in the Hottentots Holland range. The formations of rock strata take their names from where the typical layer was described – the 'type' location.

Layers of sandstone.

Oldest, but not as dominant in the area as the rocks of the Cape Supergroup, are the Granites of the Stellenbosch intrusion found on the western rolling foothills of the Hottentots Holland and Jonkershoek Mountains. The granites originated around 550mya as igneous upwelling into the existing Malmesbury sediments. Granite weathering produces typical rounded rocks, as opposed to the rugged formations of Sandstones so noteworthy in the Cederberg. It also gives rise to a coarse grained, deep and fertile soil favoured for cultivation.

In contrast, the most recently formed landscapes – within the last 75 000 years are found within the Bredasdorp group and comprise the uncompacted sand dune barriers along the coast from Hangklip to Gansbaai, as well as the semi-consolidated windblown marine sands found further inland behind these dunes – most notable at Walker Bay. Acid sandy soil, also of relatively recent origin, flanks the west bank of Bot River, extending to Kleinmond, as well as the coastal plains at the foothills of the mountains of Betty's Bay and Hermanus to Stanford. This is mostly the weathered product of Table Mountain sandstone. In places organic matter has accumulated, resulting in a dark and peaty soil. Sand in this area is extensively mined for building.

Scree – fallen rock – covers most of the lower slopes of the mountains. Extensive deposits are seen in the road cuts from Gordon's Bay as well as along all the coastal mountain slopes. Along the Hottentots Holland Mountains and Jonkershoek Valley, scree is found in conjunction with the granites and, less commonly, the Malmesbury shales. Scree deposits originate from the Cenozoic period, about 65 million years before present.

The two broad dominant groups of rock type, shale and sandstone, give rise to the major differences in soil type, habitat type and, ultimately, vegetation type in the region. The shale soils – generally found in the low-lying areas – are yellowed, clayey and richest in plant nutrients. The other – that derived from the sandstones – is white, coarse sand of low nutrient status. Granite soils are also yellowed and richer but are generally coarser grained or 'loamy'.

HABITATS

The area covered by this guide falls into the fynbos natural vegetation region, in which two vegetation types occur, fynbos and renosterveld. Most of the plant species that have been included in this guide come from the fynbos, which holds some two-thirds of the species diversity. The fynbos is characterised by a predominance of members of the protea, erica and restio families and is generally found on the sands of low plant nutrient status soils of the Table Mountain Group sandstones. Fynbos is not, however, restricted to this base and may occur on richer clay soils where the rainfall exceeds 700mm per annum. Below this it grades into renosterveld.

The lower foothills of the inner Jonkershoek valley have deep granite soils that support a lush protea-rich fynbos. Helderberg too has this variation of fynbos but here the rich soils are derived from the Malmesbury shales that encircle the dominant sandstone-capped peak. Amidst the ragged sandstone mountains themselves it is the Cederberg shale band that gives rise to assemblage of plant species characteristic of richer soils.

The dominant sandstone mountain fynbos shows a high variation in plant species and their communities. This is related to habitat conditions such as moisture availability, which in turn is related to altitude, aspect and ground water upwelling, giving the mountains their well-known floral diversity. Higher areas are generally more moist, receiving extra water from orographic clouds, as are south facing slopes that are often shaded for significant periods of the day, especially in winter. Here the vegetation tends to be a heathland dominated by ericas and restios. This is especially so in the Hottentots Holland mountains. The Kogelberg mountains, over-looking the coast, however, often retain their protea dominance. Leucadendrons, characteristic of lower slopes, can extend to the summits. North-facing slopes are exposed to the full force of the summer sun and the vegetation often has a large proportion of restios, ericas and further inland Asteraceae. Each of the three main groups of mountain covered in this guide, the Hottentots Holland/Jonkershoek/Helderberg, Kogelberg and Klein River have different assemblages of plant species as well as having their own local endemics.

Like the mountains, the coastal areas from Gordon's Bay to Hermanus have a range of species exclusive to their unique habitats. There are restio dominated sandy flats, depression bogs dense with *Bruniaceae*, Asteraceous Dune Fynbos to dune thickets and rocky sandstone shelves and cliffs. The development of non-fynbos coastal thicket vegetation depends on the exclusion of fire and the build up of a fire resistant community of plants, something akin to the mountain forest patches.

The forests, found as isolated patches, are mostly confined to the sheltered mountain kloofs where they are protected from fire. They are best-developed where the soils are rich and deep. On open slopes below sandstone cliffs, especially from Helderberg to Jonkershoek, boulders of rock scree protect discrete pockets of forest.

Renosterveld is the dominant vegetation type of the valleys between the mountains. Widely cultivated, these fertile lands now support only small remnant patches of this vegetation in its natural state. It is distinguished from fynbos by the dominance of the renosterbos *Elytropappus rhinocerotis* and occurs where rainfall is below 400mm per annum. Transition communities to fynbos form a mosaic of vegetation types notably in the Elgin basin and Rooisand. The most diverse groups of plants in renosterveld are undoubtable the geophytes, seen at their best after fire.

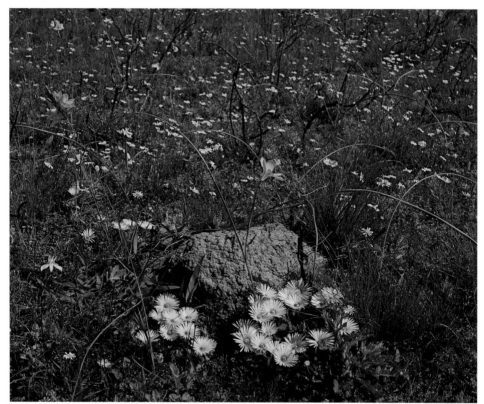

Post-fire geophytes on Rooisand coastal renosterveld.

ECOLOGY AND ORIGINS

Where did our flora arise?

The earliest years. Some of the earliest fossil flowering plants on earth have been discovered on parts of the fragmenting Gondwanaland supercontinent of c. 113 mya, and the first proteaceous fossils found in our region are dated to c. 96 mya when there was widespread sub-tropical forest in a warm damp climate. By about 65 mya *Proteaceae, Restionaceae, Rosaceae* as *Cliffortia*, and *Ericaceae* appear in our admittedly very sparse fossil record. The earth at this time lacked any ice caps or sheets so ocean levels were high enough for shorelines to lap the bases of the Cape mountains, which were themselves quite a bit higher than now.

Summer drought begins. From c.16 mya ice sheets formed on Antarctica, and by c. 4 mya the associated system of the Benguela current gave rise to a Mediterranean climate of winter rains and summer droughts which has remained since then at the Cape. Accompanying climatic change, there is evidence of widespread fire, and by 4 mya, almost total loss of the hitherto widespread forests, and fynbos came to dominate. In this last period there have been at least 10 cycles of greater or lesser ice in Antarctica, with concomitant changes of ambient temperatures and rainfall, and in our area associated coastline fluctuations of up to 200 km further south and 200 m lower than at present, with at times heavy frosts in the valleys and winter snow widespread on the flanks of the mountains, and perhaps lying for protracted periods on the peaks. Throughout this whole 113 my, however, the Cape escaped the destructive ice sheets of the northern hemisphere.

While much is conjecture, it seems that at the commencement of the harshest recent periods the fynbos itself underwent much loss and change in genera and species. While the most ancient members of the fynbos flora, *Proteaceae, Bruniaceae, Grubbiaceae, Penaeaceae, Roridulaceae* and *Stilbaceae*, survived the climatic fluctuations of the last 70 million years by escaping to mountain refuges such as the Kogelberg, the bulk of modern fynbos is believed to have arisen quite recently with the surviving genera spawning hundreds of species into what must have been an emptier, less competitive environment especially on the newly exposed coastal slopes and lowlands. Some of these large Cape genera include: (species in brackets), *Aspalathus* (245), *Disa* (162), *Erica* (c. 650), *Ruschia* (138), *Phylica* (133), *Agathosma* (c.150), *Oxalis* (129), *Pelargonium* (125), *Senecio* (113), *Cliffortia* (106). It is no wonder that these are some of the more difficult groups to name correctly.

The human factor. Humans have been here for at least 500 000 years, (and maybe evolved here), using fire to transform fynbos for their purposes for at least a few thousand years. Latterly, 2000 years of herding with increased use of fire for grazing have speeded up the transformation. Now fynbos is dominated by plants with life strategies tuned to fire.

Fynbos and soil

Fynbos evolved in the Cape on soil deficient in almost all the nutrients required to sustain plant growth, due to the low mineral status of the underlying rocks. Nutrient shortages force fynbos plants to husband their chemical resources most carefully. Almost all the mineral resources of any fynbos area are held within the combined living plant bodies in the newer plant tips, roots and flowering shoots, and most of those minerals originate from the ash of the previous fire. Some species shunt minerals from older to newer growths, or hold on to the same crop of leaves for 6 years or more.

The problem of obtaining enough nutrients is answered by special "proteoid" roots in proteas which proliferate just below the soil surface as dense coral-like growths. These roots can be damaged by trampling. 75% of the rest of the higher fynbos plants form a special relationship with soil microorganisms on their roots, called mycorrhiza, using the extra-efficient chemical processes of microbes to harvest and translocate the chemicals to the host plants. As these microbes may also protect the host plants by keeping soil pathogens like *Phytophthora* at bay, anything such as artificial fertilisers which damage the soil microflora is problematical.

It is easy for plants to make carbohydrates in the Cape environment, as sunshine and water are only transiently limiting. Carbon is an abundant and nowadays increasing resource. Although production of nitrogen-based plant proteins and hence soft tissue growth in fynbos is limited by low nitrogen availability, a surplus of carbohydrates is easily photosynthesised. This is then diverted into secondary non-nitrogenous compounds to support resprouting buds in underground stumps, bulbs, corms or tuberous storage organs, to build sturdy fireproof seed-stores, to reward pollinators with copious sugar-rich nectar, or on the other hand to create distasteful, poisonous alkaloids and coumarins, or repellent tannins and natural oils etc. So copious is the oil content of many fynbos plants that they are inflammable even when first picked. It is the aroma of these oils which makes walking through fynbos so characteristically memorable.

Pollination and seeds

Pollination. The transfer of pollen to stigmas to ensure that seeds will set is fraught with problems for fynbos plants. Pollen is the most nutritious food available, full of concentrated accessible proteins which are expensive for plants to produce in this nitrogen-poor landscape and a too attractive and very fine food for animals. Releasing it into the wind as is done by some Ericas, a few Leucadendrons, and almost all *Restionaceae* and grasses is imprecise and haphazard, so most flowering plants seem to have been pushed along the road of animal pollen carriers. Although this involves much less pollen, the plants must motivate and reward animals to carry it by the promise of either nectar or a part share in the pollen, as well as advertising their whereabouts. This has resulted in a marvellously diverse, intricate and precise process and set of structures in both animal and plant which can only very briefly be touched upon here and of which only the very first stories have yet been told. Pollination ecology is still a wide open field for the amateur naturalist.

The bird pollinated plants.
Birds have little or no sense of smell so bird pollinated flowers have no scent, but tend to be conspicuously brilliant red or orange to us, as birds' colour vision is much like that of humans. Birds have long, strong beaks so flowers store the nectar reward of comparatively weak but copious nectar in deep sturdy tunnels. Because local birds mostly perch to feed, flowers have to be accessible at perch levels provided by plants.

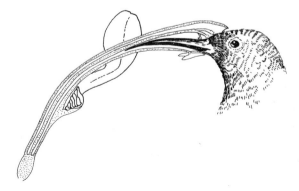

Sunbird and **Gladiolus cunonius.**

Contrast this with hummingbird technique, which entails hovering at the mouth of a flower like a hibiscus or fuchsia and not perching, so these plants provide no landing platform. The target for the bird is nectar; the pollen is a dusty superfluity carried inadvertently by the bird from flower to flower, thus fulfilling the plant's needs as well as its own. The nectar is stored away inaccessible to raiders. The curve of flower matches bird's head and beak very well, while stamens and stigma are placed best to intercept the bird's pollen-clad movements.

The heady maiden moth on **Aspalathus nigra**.

Moth pollinated flowers advertise themselves in the twilight and dark by means of pale colours and pervasive sweet scent. Their concentrated nectar reward is hidden in deep tunnels accessible only to very long very thin tongues where it is safe from raiders. *Gladiolus liliaceus* (see page 116) is a unique case: brown, drab, scentless and unattractive by day, it transforms into a glory of perfumed lilac at night and back again by day, presumably pouring out its nectar in time with these changes. The heady maiden moth is an exception among moths in that it is both colourful and goes about its feeding during the day.

Most *other insects* have colour perception strongest in the ultraviolet, blue and yellow range and absent in the full red part of the spectrum, and such insect flowers confine themselves to this colour range. If attracting flies or wasps their scent tends to be more or less repellent to us humans, the extreme being the rotten meat smell of *Stapelia*, with its shallow open dish-like flowers. Others of cup or bell shape entice honeybees with only moderately long mouthparts. They may employ sweet scent as a subsidiary advertisement, and are usually massed together to alert many bees quickly. However some solitary bees specialise in an oily reward found in some orchids and a *Tritoniopsis* in the Kogelberg. They have specialised hairy front legs to insert into floral tubes and have few competitors. Other flowers entice long-tongued daytime insects, concealing the nectar reward at the base of very narrow bore tubes where it is inaccessible to short-tongued creatures. Many peas attract carpenter bees (see p. 205).

The summer butterfly-flower group are brilliant red, confounding all generalisations about insect colour vision. A diversity of plant species in many families rely on the same very active, strong-flying butterfly, *Aeropetes tulbaghia,* the Table Mountain beauty, which is perhaps uniquely attracted to red, whether clothing or flowers.

Pollination by mammals such as the striped and namaqua rock mice, is found in low growing proteas with bowl shaped, yeasty scented flowers that offer much sweet nectar.

All insects have a life cycle which involves a juvenile stage. Sometimes this is known. In the case of long-tongued flies the whereabouts and details of their life history is unknown, and until it is discovered, conservation of not only the flies but also their larvae is uncertain.

Seed protection. Seeds are provided with such a rich starter pack of nutrients from the parent plant that they need to have special protection if they are to survive predation. Just lying around where they are shed is a hopeless strategy, yet this is apparently just what heaths do. They

33

shed their tiny seeds onto the ground beneath the parent, without much further ado. In theory, tiny seeds should not have a long life expectancy. Yet some fires in ancient forestry plantations trigger an astonishing reappearance of what are regarded as rare heaths, many decades after the disappearance of the last parental stand. We clearly do not know very much about this at all. Some *Erica* seeds are endowed with a generous fatty, food store around the embryo, and some have given evidence of surviving on the dry plant for decades in plant collections, still plump and fresh. These are enigmas waiting for an enthusiast with patience and a long life expectancy to explore.

Serotiny. Many fynbos *Proteaceae* protect their seeds in sturdy, woody old fireproof flowering heads which only open after the parent plant is killed by fire, a trait called serotiny. Then the environment is swamped by such a huge supply of seeds that predators cannot eat all up before they grow. Only rarely is this trait seen in other plant families, but *Erica sessiliflora* is one and the daisy *Phaenocoma prolifera* and *Brunia albiflora* are others. In Australian Proteaceae and gums, and northern hemisphere pines there are further abundant examples.

Leucadendron platyspermum *ejects its seed.*

Leucadendron platyspermum (see page 164) is an extreme example. It holds its very palatable fruits in the cone until a fire kills the mother plant and the cones open up, catching rain in their reservoirs. Rain triggers germination, and the root of the palatable growing embryo forces the seed body out of the cone and into the light which causes it to turn green, and become unpalatable. By the time it falls out it can lie safely uneaten until the rootlet plunges into the earth to anchor the young plantlet.

Myrmecochory. About 20% of the plants in some 20 families provide edible fatty titbits, eliao-

Ants carry off their seed.

somes, on their seeds for ants. The ants swiftly carry such seeds underground, gripping them by the softest parts, which they then consume. Nibbled seeds are too smooth to carry, so they accumulate in safe ant haven burrows until after a fire. This is referred to as myrmecochory. Seeds of some *Proteaceae* are known to remain viable for decades in such hidey-holes, until a hot enough fire permits germination of plants. There is even a hint that some *Erica* seeds may have a fatty eliaosome. Could they be myrmeco-chorous?

The speed of spread of myrmecochorous plants is limited by ants which don't go far, so this keeps the plants local, as opposed to wind-borne seeds which disperse widely. For this reason and others, evolution in these local populations occurs particularly speedily in fynbos.

Moraea ramosissima protects its corms from the cravings of mole-rats with an entanglement of roots modified to grow upwards around the primary corm and its myriad cormlets as a stiff spiny basket. The moles, undeterred, drag the complex back to their burrows, scattering cormlets as they go in their efforts to access the difficult main corm. They get some of their meal, and the Moraea is spread about way beyond the parent plant.

Timing of germination. Most fynbos plants germinate only once the cool nights and rains of autumn set in. These trigger a proportion of seeds into growth, but many need more than this to get them going. It has been established that certain components of smoke from bush fires, including ethylene but now also known to include butenolide, active at minute concentrations of a few parts per trillion, get very many plants ready for growth so that once they are wetted they get going promptly and in large numbers. These chemicals also boost growth and flowering in geophytes which explains the floral displays after veld fires.

Moraea ramosissima
cormlets.

Fynbos and fire survival

Throughout prehistory fires have started from lightning, which still remains a main natural source, as for instance on one sultry late March night when 11 fires were started by lightning in the Kogelberg area alone. In the Cape most thunderstorms occur in late summer, hence most fynbos fires occur in the hot months. Rock falls are a less quantifiable cause, but were seen to start countless fires on the mountains behind Ceres during one powerful earthquake.

Nowadays the majority of fires, are caused by man and can be deleterious to vegetation. Fires in late summer, if not too frequent, do not cause harm to fynbos because fynbos is adapted to endure them. However, fires at other times are problematical. Fire frees up space into which seeds germinate or plants sprout. This post fire environment has more available nutrients re-introduced from the ash, much light, and temporarily fewer nibbling granivorous mice and ants for the new plants to thrive in. Many shrubs in our area are killed by fire, that is, they do not resprout from stumps but are killed outright. They produce masses of seeds, either stored in the

Fire consumes the ready fynbos.

soil or on the plants themselves, which give rise to large new populations. This single age-class population has no chance of back-crossing to earlier generations, so mutants – new forms – have a good chance of becoming established. Other species, resprouters, form more or less massive underground stumps called lignotubers from which new shoots arise. They tend to make rather small seed crops, the seedlings tend to be rather sparse, and they can back-cross with older survivors. Geophytes are a special class of resprouter with storage organs underground, extremely effective for surviving fire, many of whose dormancy coincides with summer drought and the fire season, so they are undamaged. They exploit the post fire conditions by flowering profusely and setting large quantities of seeds into the open surroundings.

Interval between fires. Fynbos becomes moribund if not burnt after a number of years. A fire interval between burns of between 10 – 25 years is best to ensure survival and maintain species diversity, the shortest safe time being determined as once 50% of the population of the slowest maturing species, usually *Proteaceae* shrubs, have flowered for 3 successive seasons (thus carrying a heavy seed load). Species like *Protea stokoei* only start flowering and making seed at 10 years so to ensure the survival of this species in the community all fires before 15 years need to be determinedly extinguished.

After 30 years the protea shrubs begin to collapse and die. In serotinous species the seeds do not survive the old age death of the plant and few seedlings appear in the old vegetation, and those that do usually don't reach maturation before fire finally does come. This results in the local extinction of the species from the community. The veld is considered too old when more than half of the protea overstorey is dead. Maturation generally occurs most swiftly in areas of highest rainfall and southerly slopes, and most slowly on dry northern slopes, although exceptions in both habitats occur. Sprouters can survive a higher fire frequency than seeders and are generally long-lived. However new plants cannot survive fire, and thus be recruited into the population, until they have developed a resistant rootstock. Short intervals favour these sprouters and smaller faster-growing daisies and peas and grasses to the detriment of larger shrubby species.

Post-fire display of **Pillansia templemannii** *in the Kogelberg area.*

Frequent fires are also detrimental to the nutrient balance of the landscape. Every fire results in much ash being blown away. As nutrients are in such short supply and increased fire frequency will lead to wind removing fertility away more frequently, it is more necessary to try to combat fires these days, when there is such a greatly increased likelihood of fires being started accidentally by man.

Season of burn. Season of burn and the associated fire intensity are important. Spring burns destroy the seeds of many species which have not yet ripened and fallen. Proteaceae seed is mostly ripe and ready to be shed in summer. Fires too early in summer mean the seeds of serotinous plants, especially the Proteaceae, have a long time to lie on the ground and be exposed to predation from animals before germination in the autumn, hence a smaller seedling recruitment. Good germination of some of the characteristic fynbos plants is favoured by the hot burns of late summer. Astonishing reappearances after decades of absence have been seen in *Proteaceae, Erica* and *Fabaceae* when the land is released from forestry plantations by hot summer wildfires. Late summer fires seem usually to be followed by marvellous geophyte flowering and seeding which indicates that geophytes along with most other fynbos organisms are attuned to this regime. Conditions which favour cooler fires may result in a thickening up of *Asteraceae* like *Stoebe*. This has to do with the intensity of the fire. Under cool conditions the shallow stored soil seeds of the daisies are not destroyed as they are in hot fires and thus germinate profusely. Cool fires also do not heat-stimulate the deeper buried seeds of many myrmecochorous species to germinate. Late autumn cool fires do however result in excellent regeneration of serotinous proteas, that now germinate as soon as they fall to the ground and may form dense stands. Cooler fires in late March or April may be undertaken by managers for alien plant control or fire protection as a trade off between safety and ecology and are regarded to be within a suitable zone for fynbos regeneration. Burning for ecological reasons such as senescence that would benefit from hot late summer fire has become increasingly unnecessary with the present increased fire frequency from accidental fires. Geophytes are particularly sensitive to out of season fires and may be destroyed if burnt during their growing season. They start to grow by the end of March in our area and fire removes the leaves before they have had time to rebuild the next food store underground. Again these plants are attuned to late summer fires during which time they are dormant underground waiting for the first rains. The magnificent post fire displays of *Watsonia borbonica* will not occur if burnt during the active growing period. Fires in winter destroy the year's flower crop.

That fires any time but late summer are inappropriate is emphasised by some tortoises which lay their eggs in November for hatching in April, thus neatly sidestepping the fire season. Birds too time their nesting to the same regime.

Fire and conservation

The marsh rose, *Orothamnus zeyheri*, named for its rose-like appearance and preference for marshy habitats was discovered in the mountains of the Kogelberg and subsequently described in 1848. More than a century later, in 1968, a total of only 10 plants were known to exist in their natural environment. At the time fire suppression was a routine management policy of the authorities entrusted with the care of mountainous areas and all fires were diligently extinguished. The last time the roses had seen fire was twenty years earlier, in 1945. After noting the good effect of a fire on the emergence of new plants of another *Proteaceae* species, *Serruria florida*, as well as the appearance of Marsh rose seedlings after the clearing of the vegetation through hoeing at one of the marsh rose localities, management began in the 1970s, a program of veld burning. Partitioned blocks of veld in the Kogelberg known to have had the rose were deliberately set alight.

The result was the appearance of hundreds of new plants that germinated from seed buried and stored in the soil and triggered to germinate by the fire. As a result of this fire, burning was incorporated as a management tool in rejuvenating the veld by initiating new generations of plants.

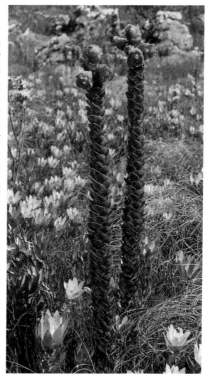

Orothamnus zeyheri.

With the overall increased incidence of fire due to accidental fires, a policy of fire suppression is now more common to maintain burning at an ecologically acceptable frequency and time of year, depending on the type of fynbos. Too frequent fires in some areas are now having a devastating effect, with slow-flowering species unable to produce enough seed for the next generation and so being eliminated from their local plant communities. The story of the Marsh Rose highlighted the role of fire in the ecology of fynbos and its influence in shaping this unique vegetation.

CONSERVATION

The fynbos vegetation is one of 25 global hotspots of plant diversity. With man's relentless assault on habitats set to continue, natural areas which still contain exceptionally large numbers of species have been selected as the focus of conservation efforts. The area covered by this guide covers the "hottest of the fynbos hotspots". Of the many threats to our corner the most urgent include:

-loss of lowland habitats with coastal
 development
-renosterveld land transformation;
-alien plant and animal invaders
-increased fire frequency;
-water extraction and alteration of
 natural water flow patterns;
-unsustainable flower harvesting and
 wildflower poaching;
and not as obvious, global warming.

What is being done? A biodiversity strategy and action plan termed CAPE, adopted in 2000 aims to conserve biodiversity in priority areas in the Cape region. International funding supports projects that address pressing conservation issues and promotes responsible eco-tourism. Landowners are encouraged to join

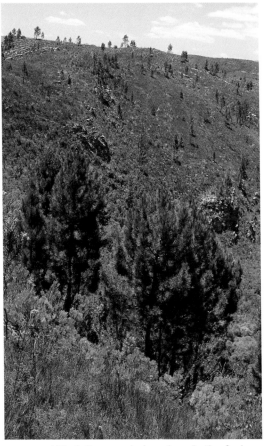

Wind dispersed pines invade the fynbos.

stewardship programmes where assistance is given by various organisations in the conservation of natural veld on their farms, especially surviving pockets of renosterveld.

The biosphere reserve aims to ensure that development takes into account the environment, as is the case for all development in the country, and which necessitates environmental impact assessment. New legislation requires that landowners clear their property of alien vegetation and an environmental court sits in this area dealing with related crime. Despite all this we are still losing habitats along with their dependent plants and animals at an alarming rate.

ABOUT THIS BOOK

THE CHOICE OF THE PLANTS ILLUSTRATED

The majority of the plants illustrated in this guidebook can be seen from hiking trails, public paths, roadsides and within the nature reserves of our area, with only a few remarkable species less frequently seen but distinctive of the biosphere reserve or the fynbos added for interest. The species chosen for illustration are selected to represent the range in form within its genus. The text species are either all the others in our area, or those most similar to the illustrated species.

CLASSIFICATION OF PLANTS, AND THEIR SEQUENCE

Species Plants are grouped into breeding populations called species, and each is given a two-part name in Latin: eg the small brown afrikander is *Gladiolus maculatus* . This is its full scientific name. Another glad which is similar in appearance to this but not identical could be any one of a number of other relatives, close to but not usually breeding with it. These will share the first half of its name, *Gladiolus*, but will bear one of many other distinct second names such as *debilis*, the small painted lady, etc. Every plant has a Latin name constructed like these, consisting of two parts, the generic and the specific names. The first word designates the genus and the second the species. Together they refer to a unique kind of plant, also referred to as a species.

Genus The name 'Gladiolus' is a genus name, this particular genus containing an assemblage of some 250 kinds of plant having a number of characters in common, especially in those of the flower, indicating a shared ancestor some million years ago. So species, (written and pronounced species, whether singular or plural), each with its own double name, are grouped into genera (genus, singular).

Families Genera can likewise be placed in larger assemblages called families. All the members of a family are believed to be descended from a common but even more remote ancestor and share many important characters in common. The family of the glads is the family named after a typical genus, the irises: the *Iridaceae* or iris-like plants. The family name is a feminine plural latin word always ending in –ae and nearly always-aceae. Most of our *Iridaceae* share the following common characters: they are mostly soft perennials often dying down seasonally each year. Their leaves, sword-shaped or narrower, are usually arranged in two rows. The flowers are bisexual with 3 + 3 petal-like segments and 3 stamens with anthers facing outwards. The ovary supports the flower from below, that is, it is inferior in position, and it has three joined chambers with a few to many seeds. In a separate part of this book a description of each family included in the text is given, arranged in alphabetical order, and the common names of each family given.

In the main part of this guide book all members of a family are grouped together in an uninter-rupted sequence. Families which are related will likewise be grouped near together. Within the families, genera and species are usually presented alphabetically unless alternative grouping facilitates species identification or the bulk of text forces re-arrangement.

Common names on the face of it are usually more accessible to the layman and some are easier to pronounce than some Latin names. Applied to families or genera they may be particularly helpful in recognizing groups of similar flowers e.g. the' grasses', the 'pea' family or the 'pincushions'. Use them if you know them, but be warned that one common name may apply to many species in different areas, and different species may share one common name. Common names are therefore less precise and also less handy when researching them in publications, as you cannot be sure that everyone is referring to the same plant as you.

THE SEQUENCE OF FAMILIES.

Guidebooks are sequenced in a variety of ways. They can be clustered according to month of bloom; they may be grouped according to colour of flower, (problematical in species with a range of flower colour. Both these arrangements disperse closely related species widely throughout the text. This is one of the biggest drawbacks to such arrangements. Otherwise, as in this guidebook, they are grouped according to what is believed to be their natural sequence, that is, those having a more or less recent common ancestor and sharing some of its characters being clustered together. In this way the grasslike families are grouped together; those having 3 + 3 flower parts together (the Monocotyledons) from page 66 while those with flowers counting in 4's or 5's are placed in separate sequences in the later pages.

PRIMITIVE AND ADVANCED CHARACTERS.

A flower. What indeed is a flower? It is believed to be the modified and specialised cluster of leaves at the top of a twig.

If those leaves were spirally arranged, then the ancient flowers had sepals, petals, stamens and carpels similarly arranged. In some extant flowers such as waterlilies, *Magnolia* and *Ranunculus* this can be seen if a flower is taken systematically apart from the outside in. In the waterlily after such a dissection, it is further obvious that each flower part grades insensibly into the next: sepals into petals, into stamens.

But most flowers seem to be derived from plants with leaves attached in that less common arrangement of circles, the outermost circle remaining leaflike and often green: the sepals; the next circle leaflike in shape but often brightly coloured: the petals; the next one or more circles being completely transformed into stalks bearing rounded or oval pollen chambers at the tip: the stamens. The innermost circle consists of one or more leaves folded and sealed along the length to guard the enclosed seeds from damage, the elements and predation: the carpels. There is little or no gradual transformation from one category to the next. A capacity to be transformed is still there, hidden in the DNA and awakened by plant breeders when, for instance they transform stamens into a bunch of sterile petals to create a `double' bloom.

 Regular or actinomorphic flower.

Flower symmetry The leaf units are arranged symmetrically in more primitive flowers so they have many planes of division in half. This is termed a regular or actinomorphic flower.

An irregular or zygomorphic flower.

Adaptations to animal pollinators have however driven many to a host of modern asymmetrical arrangements, allowing landing platforms, protection from rain, more precise placement of pollen or storage of nectar or oils, etc, so that there is only one way to slice such a flower to yield two equal halves, called zygomorphy or an irregular flower.

The evolutionary history of flowering plants is shrouded in mystery with but a few small windows revealed by scarce fossils. Even the identity and arrival of the first flowering plants in the fossil record is still debated and is mostly pollen which cannot be assigned with certainty to modern families. The first flowering plants appeared before the breakup of Gondwanaland which is dated variously as commencing with the rifting between Africa and South America about 150-130 mya. The sharing of many plant families like the Proteas and restios between several southern continents may therefore indicate a very early origin for these groups

Fragments of wood or pollen is often all that is vouchsafed in the fossil record. Among the earliest to be identified are the *Magnolia* group and the quite different wind-pollinated willow-like species. It seems that the stinkwood tree family and *Peperomia*-like plants were among the very earliest to appear, even before the well-known Monocotyledon and Dicotyledon lines were defined. It is interesting that we have both these archaic lines represented in the area of our book. Evolutionary history from then on is not along a single line, so it is not possible to place the families in our guide in a linear sequence and present the truth about their pedigrees. They are usually better presented in the form of a 3-dimensional branching tree, but this cannot be done in a book. We have chosen to follow a natural order currently accepted by most modern workers, and used in most of the Botanical Society's field guides, as this will allow comparison across a range of publications. This arrangement encapsulates what are believed to be those families containing plants with the most archaic features separately from those with largely modern characters. Below is a table of some archaic versus advanced characters. Note that some archaic and some modern features may be combined in one flower

Archaic characters	Advanced characters
Spiral arrangement of parts	- circular (whorled) arrangement
Parts not joined to each other	- parts joined to some extent to each other or to a different part
Large numbers of parts	- few units of each part
Actinomorphy/regular	zygomorphy/irregular
Ovary superior	- ovary inferior

The way in which these characters are combined delimits plant families. As your practice in naming and working with the guide increases, your growing understanding of family characteristics will help you to home in on your latest unknown more swiftly.

HOW TO USE THIS GUIDE TO NAME A PLANT

With Guide in hand and your plant in front of you, look for a likeness in the illustrations. Look for further details of structure in the supporting text, including flowering time and habitat. If all agree, you can fairly certainly award this name to your plant. If you are uncertain, reading through the descriptions of closely related species in adjacent paragraphs may help to clarify your thoughts. Careful reading of the generic description and perhaps even that of the family will further shed light on your unknown species. The plant descriptions are based on structures and characters on the living plant in situ, visible to the eye; a x 10 magnifying handlens (available from stamp shops and jewellers) will reveal delightful details with greater certainty, and is recommended to the enthusiast. Details of hairs and stamens are best seen in young parts and newly opened buds. Details of ovary and seeds are most easily detected as the flower withers and the pods swell. An old-fashioned razor blade permits thin slices to be made vertically to a flower to open it up and reveal its structure. Hairs and glands are often best seen if the object is held up to the light.

Defining characters. Characters to establish in your plant include the number of sepals and petals, whether they are joined into a tube, bell or other structure or free from one another, how many stamens and whether they are fastened to each other or to the petals etc., how many chambers in the ovary and whether the ovary is below the junction of the petals or above. These facts indicate quite clearly the family of your plant, which is a good place to start hunting for a name.

Identification is not always easy! Plants vary. Some have close relatives not illustrated in this guide. Your plant may be similar to but not identical to your best match. To aid in their identification, brief diagnostic characters of species deemed similar to the one that is illustrated may permit naming far more plants than only those shown. The number of species in each genus which has been recorded as growing in the area of this book is usually given. Whenever feasible, descriptions of all will be found under one or other of the illustrated species in the genus, so it may pay to read all before finally deciding on a name.

If you want to develop your expertise further, have a look at the dried specimens in the nearest herbarium and see if they correspond.

Aulax umbellata

42

SOME DISTINCTIVE FAMILY CHARACTERISTICS

Leaves opposite or whorled

Aizoaceae	Lamiaceae
Apocynaceae	Linaceae
Asteraceae (some)	Oleaceae
Crassulaceae	Rubiaceae
Dipsacaceae	Santalaceae
Gentianaceae	Scrophulariaceae

Leaves compound or deeply incised

Apiaceae	Sterculiaceae
Araliaceae	Zygophyllaceae
Asteraceae	
Dipsacaceae	
Fabaceae	
Ranunculaceae	

Leaves with stipules

Araliaceae	Rosaceae
Fabaceae	Rubiaceae
Linaceae	Sterculiaceae
Malvaceae	Zygophyllaceae
Rhamnaceae	Violaceae

Leaves gland dotted

Fabaceae (some)
Myrtaceae
Myricaceae, gold dotted
Rutaceae

Stamens fewer than 5

Cyperaceae	Proteaceae
Dipsacaceae	Scrophulariaceae
Iridaceae	Fumariaceae
Lamiaceae	Geraniaceae (some)
Oleaceae	Haemodoraceae (some)
Poaceae	Penaeaceae
Piperaceae	Stilbaceae

Stamens many

Euphorbiaceae
Malvaceae
Aizoaceae
Geraniaceae (some)
Myrtaceae
Ranunculaceae
Sterculiaceae

Petals/sepals± united

Apocynaceae	Proteaceae
Asteraceae	Rubiaceae
Boraginaceae	Scrophulariaceae
Campanulaceae	Solanaceae
Convolvulaceae	Thymelaeaceae
Crassulaceae	Menyanthaceae
Dipsacaceae	Oxalidaceae
Ericaceae	Penaeaceae
Gentianaceae	Plumbaginaceae
Lamiaceae	Stilbaceae
Lobeliaceae	

Ovary inferior

Amaryllidaceae	Myrtaceae
Apiaceae	Orchidaceae
Araliaceae	Rubiaceae
Asteraceae	Santalaceae
Dipsacaceae	Viscaceae
Hypoxidaceae	Bruniaceae
Iridaceae	Grubbiaceae
Lobeliaceae	Lanariaceae
Haemodoraceae (some)	
Aizoaceae	

Ovary with 2 or more separate carpels and styles

Aponogetonaceae	Ranunculaceae
Rosaceae	Crassulaceae

Mimetes argenteus in the mountain mist zone.

DESCRIPTION AND
ILLUSTRATIONS OF PLANTS

FAMILY DESCRIPTIONS

♣ *AGAPANTHACEAE* The *Agapanthus* family. An entirely South African family with one genus and 10 species occurring from the Cape along the eastern half of South Africa to Swaziland, Lesotho and southern Mozambique. They are mucilaginous perennial herbs with rhizomes, forming colonies, with strap-shaped, 2-ranked leaves and leafless flowerstalks bearing an umbel of showy blue or occasionally white flowers. Each flower has 6 tepals joined into a short tube at the base, 6 stamens and a superior, 3-chambered ovary with many winged seeds.

♣ *AIZOACEAE* (including *Mesembryanthemaceae:* vygies, ice plants and stone plants) A predominantly African family with a few representatives in Australia, consisting of 128 genera and c.1850 species. 43 genera and c.195 species are recorded in the South Western Cape. Only c.18 genera and 32 species occur in our area, none of them "stone plants". They are mostly extremely drought-adapted leaf-succulent herbs, but some are woody shrubs; they are most abundant in the harshest and driest parts of the winter rainfall region of South Africa up the west coast to Namibia and in the Karoo, so it is not surprising that they are only a small part of the flora of our climatically moist and moderate area. Flowers are of all colours except blue. All have paired leaves. With the exception of *Carpobrotus* which has a fleshy fruit, edible for humans, the rest hold their seeds in tough woody capsules most of which open only when wetted and may open and close repeatedly. The character of the fruits (capsules) is important in discriminating between genera. The flower has 5 fleshy sepals, a mass of fertile and infertile stamens, the outer broad and functioning as petals, some shielding and hiding the pollen-producing stamens, nectar and stigma. A relatively massive ovary with (1)-5-(many) chambers supports the flower from below, the stigma being stubby to long-lobed with the same number of lobes as chambers. Many are cultivated ornamentals.

♣ *ALLIACEAE* The onion family. A widespread family of 30 genera and c.720 species, represented in southern Africa by 2 genera and 21 species, and in our area by one genus and 2 species. The family survives the dry season by means of swollen underground stems and roots, or bulbs. The plants comprise a basal tuft of strapshaped leaves and long-stalked umbels of flowers protected in bud by membranous bracts. The 3+3 tepals and stamens surround a 3-chambered superior ovary with many seeds. A further exotic, unwelcome and persistent species, *Nothoscordum gracile*, the onion weed with its beautifully fragrant white flowers and characteristic (un-garlic-like) unpleasant smell of the leaves and especially the crushed bulb, is naturalized in the urban environment but probably not yet in the undisturbed veld. This weed is difficult to eradicate, spreading by seeds and copious bulbils.

♣ *AMARYLLIDACEAE* The *Amaryllid* or *Daffodil* family. A tropical to warm temperate perennial herbaceous bulbous family of 60 genera and c. 800 species, usually with leaves arising at ground level and usually several showy flowers arising in an umbel from an elongated, leafless stem. The flower stalk is always ensheathed by bracts which may be showy as in *Haemanthus*. The flowers have 6 tepals and 6 stamens (many in *Gethyllis*) and a 3-chambered inferior ovary, often followed by a capsule mostly with moist, variously coloured rounded slightly angled seeds which usually must be planted as soon as they are ripe, as they cannot be stored. *Cyrtanthus* has a dry capsule with winged papery seeds. Southern Africa has 18 genera and 280 species, (the Andes has the second largest number of species) with 7 genera and 13 spe-cies in our area. Many contain alkaloids and may be toxic to grazing animals; many are popular cultivated garden and pot plants e.g. Daffodils, bluebells, *Nerine*, *Clivia* and *Hippeastrum* (= "Amaryllis")

46

♣ *ANACARDIACEAE* The cosmopolitan poison ivy, pistachio, cashew and mango family of c.60 genera and 600 species, mostly woody trees and shrubs, represented in southern Africa by 13 genera (3 exotic) and c. 110 species, and in our area by 3 genera and 11 species. They have simple or compound leaves, without stipules, and clusters of small unisexual or bisexual flowers consisting of 3-5 sepals joined at the base, 3-5 usually free petals, 3-10 stamens and the floor of the flower mostly filled by a disc. The (1-) 3(-5)-chambered ovary usually matures only one seed per fruit. The well-known pepper tree, *Schinus molle*, and the sour plum, *Harpephyllum caffrum* belong to this family.

♣ *ANTHERICACEAE* **The grass lilies.** An old-world tropical family of 29 genera, 500 species, mostly in Asia and Australia, represented in southern Africa by 2 genera and c. 40 species. Herbaceous perennials with a rhizomatous rootstock and basal, spiral or 2-ranked non-fleshy leaves. The flowers, arranged in groups on a branched or unbranched stalk, have 6 tepals and stamens and an inferior three-chambered ovary.

♣ *APIACEAE* **The parsley and carrot family.** A worldwide family of usually aromatic and herbaceous, often tuberous rooted plants in 446 genera and 3540 species, of which 36 genera (8 naturalised) and 152 species, (15 naturalised) occur in southern Africa, and c. 10 genera and 25 species occur in our area. The usually bisexual flowers are rather insignificant, white, yellow or green, and clustered into a characteristic head known as an umbel, with the fruit 2-chambered and all the other flower parts in 5's. They are a source of fodder plants and foods, many spices, poisons such as hemlock, and perfumery. Several are ornamental garden plants.

♣ *APOCYNACEAE* incl. *ASCLEPIADACEAE* **The milkweeds,** largely tropical and subtropical worldwide with 480 genera and 4800 species, are represented widely in southern Africa by 90 genera and c.696 species, but are relatively rare in the fynbos. In our area 7 genera and c. 16 species occur, many creepers, but also succulent herbs and non-succulent perennial herbs. Many have a milky sap. Most have opposite, simple leaves. The bisexual flowers have 5 sepals, 5 joined petals and 5 stamens, and usually a 2-chambered superior ovary joined together and with outgrowths combining to make the identification of the parts very difficult. The seeds, contained within a characteristic two-forked long pod, are quite distinctive with their parachutes of silky hairs which aid wind dispersion. This family is of great economic importance, supplying timber, fibre, rubber, dyes, drugs such as strophanthin for the treatment of heart ailments, and cortisone precursors, and a host of cultivated ornamentals. Identification of the genera and species in this family requires an understanding of the very complicated structures within the flowers beyond the scope of a field guide.

♣ *APONOGETONACEAE* **The water hawthorn and wateruintjie family** consists of 1 genus and c.44 species in Africa, the East and Australia, of which 6 species occur in southern Africa and 2 in our area. All are aquatic, with leaves in tufts usually rising to the surface on long stalks. The flowers, borne on simple or forked stems are white, yellow, pink or red.

♣ *AQUIFOLIACEAE* **The holly family.** A cosmopolitan family of 2 (some say 4) genera and c. 400 species in subtropical and temperate forests, yielding timber, a tea: yerba maté; and ornamental shrubs and small trees, with only one species in southern Africa.

♣ *ARACEAE* **The arum lily family.** A pantropical family of c. 105 genera and 3300 species, most abundant in the new world, represented in southern Africa by 6 genera and 14 species of tuberous terrestrial or floating aquatic herbs, and in our area by 1 species only. The small flowers are crowded on a columnar spadix enfolded within a coloured spathe and give rise to berry fruits. Many species have starchy tubers poisonous to man due to their calcium oxalate crystals, which however are rendered edible after cooking. They have great value as a subsistence carbohydrate, such as taro and dasheen.

♣ *ARALIACEAE* A fairly cosmopolitan family of 59 genera and c.800 species especially well represented in the East, in southern Africa by 5 genera and 65 species of trees, shrubs, scramblers and herbs; and in our area by 3 genera and c.19 species. A diminutive cuplike calyx subtends 5 small petals and stamens, with a 2-chambered ovary below, followed by a fleshy fruit or two one-seeded fractions.

♣ *ASPARAGACEAE Asparagus* **family.** This family comprises one genus and c.120 species in Africa, Asia and Europe with 81 species in southern Africa, and c.15 recorded from our area. They are woody perennials usually with tuberous roots, leaves reduced to scales, the needlelike or leaflike "leaves" being actually reduced branchlets called cladodes, sometimes solitary, sometimes in clusters. The white starlike flowers, bisexual in contrast to the cultivated asparagus which is dioecious, have 6 tepals and stamens, and a 3-chambered ovary nestling in the floor of the flower, giving rise to a red or black berry.

♣ *ASPHODELACEAE* **The** *Aloe* **family,** comprising 15 genera and 780 species in the Old World, some in Australia and New Zealand, and 10 genera and 353 species in southern Africa, of which 5 genera and c. 25 species occur in our area. These plants have fibrous or tuberous roots, and mostly soft-textured above-ground parts although some develop woody stems and grow into trees. The flowers have 6 tepals, 6 stamens and a 3-chambered ovary below the flower parts (=inferior). Most are leaf-succulents, storing water in their leaves. There are many cultivated ornamentals, while Aloe products are important medicinally.

♣ *ASTERACEAE* **the daisy family,** an enormous group of herbs, shrubs, trees and a few climbers, in nearly 1535 genera and 25 000 species worldwide, of which 246 genera and 2305 species occur in southern Africa and in the Cape 121 genera and 1036 species. The flower form is of fragile miniature flowers = florets, borne upon a flat platform = receptacle, crowded together into a head = capitulum, surrounded below and held together by one or several rows of bracts, together called an involucre. The character of the involucre helps to determine the genus. Each floret has a corolla of 5 joined petals but no sepals, 5 stamens usually tucked within the tube of the petals, but sometimes the pollen-containing anthers just project. The ovary has one chamber with one seed inside, which is shed with its ovary wall cover as one unit, so therefore correctly termed a fruit, eg: the sunflower. The flowers may have all the petals of the same size and joined into a tube with free lobes: these are known as disc florets and the capitula termed discoid: in others, the outer flowers, (sometimes all), termed ray florets, the lobes are drawn out into a lopsided funnel with 1-4 lobes at the long tip, the remainder on the lowest part of the rim. Such capitula are called radiate. The florets may be male, female, bisexual or neuter and it is the way they are represented in one capitulum and details of their individual structure that helps to determine the genus. Finally, the heads may be single or grouped into larger masses.

♣ *BALANOPHORACEAE.* A wholly parasitic family of 18 genera and 120 species of moist upland tropical forests worldwide, represented in Southern Africa by two genera each with one species. In our area only the monotypic *Mystropetalon* occurs.

♣ *BORAGINACEAE* **The forget-me-not and borage family.** A worldwide family of 131 genera and 2500 species, especially around the Mediterranean, represented in Southern Africa by 17 genera (4 exotic) and 105 species, and in our area by 3 genera and 8 species. Bristly herbs or shrubs with simple leaves mostly with smooth edges, the flowers are usually nearly regular, with 5 sepals and petals joined into a tube, with 5 stamens attached inside the walls of the petal tube, a long thin style and in our species a superior ovary giving rise to a fruit of 4 nutlets. The family includes timber and fruit trees, dyeplants and some foods. *Echium plantagineum,* (not illustrated) known variously as 'Paterson's Curse' or 'Calamity Jane', found on road verges, overgrazed and ploughed land, is a 65 cm tall, widespread and abundant annual weed of European origin. It is often the most showy plant in agricultural environments making sheets of handsome purple-blue flowers fading pink, but it is a headache for environmentalists because it is difficult to eliminate in the veld. However it is viewed by beekeepers as a life-saving resource for bees in a world growing short of both bees and honey, now that extensive natural fynbos and gum plantations are gone.

♣ *BRASSICACEAE* **The cabbage family** of 365 genera and 3250 species is distributed throughout the world, mostly in the temperate Mediterranean and Asia. Those in Southern Africa number 14 genera and 153 species, enlarged by 20 exotic naturalised genera and 37 species; and in the SW Cape by 5 genera and 32 species, but only 17 species in our area. They are mostly annual and perennial herbs, with 4 sepals and petals, 6 stamens and 2 carpels, giving rise to a dry fruit with a papery divider between the chambers.

♣ *BRUNIACEAE* **The blacktips or *Brunia* family.** A family of twelve genera and 64 species of woody shrubs or trees with simple, often overlapping leaves, usually with a short stalk, and almost always tipped with a minute black wart or callus visible to the naked eye but better viewed with a x10 lens; minute flowers usually clustered into heads or groups of various sorts: round heads with projecting stamens in *Berzelia* and *Brunia,* spikes and panicles or single flowers in the rest. All except one species are confined to the Cape region of South Africa. One species occurs in Natal.

♣ *CAMPANULACEAE* **The bellflowers and canterbury bell.** C. 35 genera and c. 700 species of herbs, shrubs and a few trees, occurring worldwide mostly in temperate places; with 12 genera and c. 260 species in southern Africa, and 74 species in 6 genera in our area. Their leaves are usually alternate and without stipules, flowers regular and bisexual, petals joined to some extent but anthers not joined to one another, and ovary 2-5-chambered, inferior or half-inferior and maturing into a capsule. Many are cultivated garden plants.

♣ *CARYOPHYLLACEAE* **The carnation, catchfly and campion family.** A mostly cold-temperate family of soft plants, herbs or subshrubs, seldom shrubs, of 80 genera and 2200 species, represented in Africa by 22 genera (11 exotic) and 72 species (18 exotic). In our area there are c. 5 indigenous genera and 6 indigenous species, and 9 weedy genera and 14 weedy species. There are many cultivated ornamental herbs.

♣ *CELASTRACEAE* A family of woody plants widespread in tropical and temperate lands with 88 genera and 1300 species, represented in southern Africa by c.19 genera and 80 species, and in our area by 9 genera and 20 species. All but one here are large shrubs and trees. Some are cultivated ornamentals, *Catha edulis* of tropical Africa contains an amphetamine-like substance, khat, which confers temporary heightened endurance in those who chew the leaves.

♣ *COMMELINACEAE* **The spiderwort family.** A cosmopolitan family of herbs in warmer regions with 40 genera and 650 species, represented by 7 genera and 40 species in southern Africa, with only 2 species in our area. The short-lived usually blue or white flowers have 6 perianth segments and stamens, and a superior 3-chambered ovary with a few seeds in each. Many are ornamentals, some have edible tubers or leaves, one is a source of blue dye and others have medicinal uses.

♣ *CONVOLVULACEAE* **The bindweeds.** A cosmopolitan family of c. 55 genera and 1700 trailing, climbing and woody species in the warm regions of the Americas, but also in Australia, Africa and Madagascar, of which 16 genera and 115 species occur in southern Africa and 4 genera and c. 5 species are found in our area, including 2 species of dodder *(Cuscuta)*. Chief uses are as ornamental flowers and fruits (=wood roses), but the tubers of the sweet potato and leaves of others are foods.

♣ *COLCHICACEAE* An old world family with 17 genera and c.170 species, in southern Africa 12 genera and c.67 species, of which 6 genera and c. 14 species occur in our area. Geophytes with a corm or tuber, and flowers borne on a stiff, erect stem, with 6 tepals, 6 stamens, and a superior 3-chambered ovary with a 3-branched stigma.

♣ *CRASSULACEAE* **The stonecrop, houseleek and *Crassula* family.** An assemblage of mostly succulent but not tree-like herbs and shrubs in 35 genera and c. 1500 species worldwide excluding Australia and the w. Pacific, of which 6 genera (1 exotic) and 234 species (1 exotic) are recorded in southern Africa and in the area of this book, 3 genera and c.28 species. The simple leaves, lacking stipules, usually opposite and usually with water-excreting pores, may be in a basal rosette but also up the stem. The bisexual flowers are usually regular, with 4 or 5 sepals (-3-30), the same number of petals and same or double the number of stamens, and usually free and tapering carpels in the ovary equalling the sepals in number, a quite distinctive feature of the family. Many occur in very harsh, arid conditions but they are found in most habitats including aquatic ones, and are often an important constituent of the vegetation.

♣ *CUNONIACEAE* **The rooiels family.** A family of 19 woody genera and 340 species almost exclusively southern in distribution in South Africa, Australia, New Guinea and New Caledonia. Consisting of trees, shrubs or climbers with leaves paired or whorled and usually compound with stipules, the small flowers are almost always grouped in some way. Some are valued as timber trees, otherwise a few are cultivated ornamentals. In southern Africa 2 genera and 2 species occur, both in the area of this book.

♣ *CYPERACEAE* **Sedges** A worldwide family of 98 genera and c. 4350 species, of which 40 genera and 400 species have been recorded in South Africa and 29 genera and 206 species in the S.W.Cape. Almost all are perennials, with a tuft of basal leaves lacking a ligule, and usually solid stems, triangular in cross-section. The flower clusters are grouped near the apex of a usually unbranched stem, and have bracts of unequal length surrounding them, usually at least one, often more, overtopping the flowers. Characters used to distinguish between genera and species are mostly of a highly technical nature, not accessible to any but the expert. Although seemingly related to grasses, sedges are mostly unpalatable to animals except for a few with edible tubers. Others are used for thatching or basketwork, and *Cyperus papyrus* for paper-making, but on the whole, sedges are of only modest economic use.

♣ *DIPSACACEAE* **The teasel and Scabious family.** A small group of 11 genera and c.400 species of mostly ornamental herbs and subshrubs distributed between Africa and Eurasia. They are represented in southern Africa by 2 genera and 25 species, and in our area by perhaps two species of *Scabiosa* and three species of *Cephalaria,* very like *Scabiosa* but whose white heads have involucral bracts in several rows.

♣ *DROSERACEAE* **The sundews.** A family of 4 genera and 83 species of insectivorous herbs found on all continents except Antarctica, commonly growing in nutrient-poor bogs and wetlands; of which 2 genera and 21 species occur in southern Africa, 14 species of *Drosera* in the Cape and 8 in our area. The plants derive part of their food requirements by digesting insects trapped by the sticky glandular hairs covering the leaves. All are geophytes, most die down each year, but some are perennial.

♣ *ERICACEAE* **The heath family.** A cosmopolitan family of 140 genera and 4500 species of woody trees, shrubs and climbers and some epiphytes found almost everywhere except for most of Australia; of which 2 genera and 860 species occur in southern Africa, with one genus and c. 300 species in our area. Most prefer acid soils and form a symbiotic relationship with soil fungi called mycorrhiza. "The non-African species include berry-producing species – blueberry, cranberries and bilberries; *Gaultheria* produces wintergreen; the honey from some Rhododendrons causes a lowering of blood pressure extreme enough to cause dizziness: "mad honey poisoning"; *Kalmia* and some others are poisonous, and are referred to as "lambkill"; some *Rhododendron* leaf extracts are insect-repellent; *Rhododendron* with c.1000 species has long occupied pride of place after roses in horticulture with over 500 of its species in cultivation, and countless hybrids. *Erica* is an important source of nectar for honey.

♣ *ERIOSPERMACEAE* **The cottonseed family** is wholly African with 102 species in one genus, of which 11 are represented in our area. They are small geophytes whose only stems are inconspicuous leafless unbranched flowering stalks which arise, as do the leaves, directly from a subterranean tuber. Many species are hysteranthous, the flowers appearing in summer; the usually solitary leaves in an extraordinary diversity of forms, in the wet season. The stalked flowers have 6 tepals and stamens, and a superior 3-chambered ovary producing hairy white seeds: hence the common name

♣ *EUPHORBIACEAE.* **The rubber tree, spurge and milkweed family.** A near worldwide family of 313 genera and c.5000 species, many poisonous, it is represented in southern Africa by 50 genera and c. 484 species and in our area by 3 genera and c. 15 species. The largest genus, *Euphorbia*, with a milky latex, is represented by c. 8 species in our area, one, *E. caputmedusae*, a true succulent with coarse fleshy, lumpy sprawling stems tipped with a few deciduous leaves. *Euphorbia* has extraordinarily modified flowerheads in which usually one or a few pistils are associated with several stamens all surrounded by more or less ornamental petaloid bracts. Each pistil is actually a female flower, every stamen a male flower. *Clutia*, with about 70 species in Africa of which 7 occur in this area, has separate male and female plants, but quite usual flowers, each equipped with calyx, corolla, stamens or pistil.

♣ *FABACEAE* **The pea family,** the third largest family of flowering plants after the daisies and the orchids, occurs worldwide and comprises c. 650 genera and 18 000 woody and herbaceous species, of which southern Africa has 149 genera and c.1705 species and our area c.19 genera (and 2 weeds) and c.150 species (and 7 weeds). In our area most have compound leaves, (less often simple) usually with stipules. All except some exotics have the same basic pea-flower structure, adapted for pollination by insects or birds, consisting of 5 sepals and petals arranged with only one plane of symmetry, termed irregular or zygomorphic, 10 stamens and a pea-pod fruit. The roots of most if not all build up nodules to house soil organisms which fix nitrogen from the air. This feeds the host plant and when the roots die, surplus nitrogen remains behind in the soil which is used by other plants. The family supplies high protein legume food crops like soya and other beans, forage crops, like lucerne, ornamentals, tropical hardwoods, dyes and insecticides, thus equalling the grasses in importance in the world economy.

♣ *FRANKENIACEAE* A cosmopolitan family of 2 genera and 81 species represented in Southern Africa by one genus and 3 species. Found in temperate maritime habitats, they are of very little economic importance, and not much cultivated.

♣ *FUMARIACEAE* **Fumitories.** A north-temperate family of c. 17 genera and 530 species of mostly climbing annuals, represented by 4 genera and 9 species in southern Africa of which 2 genera and 3 species occur in our area. They have little except ornamental value. *Fumaria muralis* is a common weed of gardens and wasteland, introduced from Madeira.

♣ *GENTIANACEAE* **The gentian family.** A cosmopolitan group of 89 genera and 1200 species ranging from tall trees with huge leaves to minute annuals, represented in southern Africa by 9 genera and 70 species, and in our area by 3 herbaceous genera and c.15 species. Paired simple leaves, flowers with parts in 5's or 4's, 1-2-chambered ovary and many seeds, and in some species which are buzz-pollinated by carpenter bees, the anthers are coiled up like barley-sugar sticks and open by apical pores.

♣ *GERANIACEAE*. A family of 11 genera and 750 species found on every continent. In Africa it is represented by 5 genera and 290 species. Most are aromatic herbs or shrubs having leaves with stipules, usually simple but sometimes divided, 5 sepals, usually 5 petals but sometimes fewer, 15 stamens or fewer, and a 5-chambered superior ovary. Our largest genus is Pelargonium, with c. 220 species in Africa and the Middle East and c.31 in our area. Almost all are perennial, but several are summer-deciduous, dying down to a tuberous rootstock, and then sometimes hysteranthous, flowering ahead of the new leaves. They are distinguished (with one exception), by a hollow "flowerstalk", termed the hypanthium, at the base of which is located a nectary secreting nectar into the tube. The position of the nectar gland is clearly visible as a swelling on the outside of the flower stalk, while the length of the hollow portion is an indication of the length of the mouthparts of the pollinating insect: the range of hypanthium lengths in *Pelargonium* being a measure of the diversity of pollinators The long barbed shanks of the one-seeded fruits, tipped by backward facing bristles, coiled when dry, but straighten up when wetted, drilling the seedhead into the ground. Many are cultivated ornamentals while some provide essential oils, dyes and folk medicines.

♣ *GRUBBIACEAE* A family of 1 shrubby genus and 3 species entirely endemic to the fynbos of the S.W.Cape. The simple leaves are paired, and the groups of very small flowers arise in the axils of leaves, with 4 tepals, 8 stamens and an inferior 2-carpellate ovary. The mature fruits may coalesce into a compound fleshy berrylike structure. The family has no economic uses.

♣ *HAEMODORACEAE* The bloodroot or kangaroo-paw family. A largely southern hemisphere group characterised by an orange-red pigment seen most clearly in the underground parts of the plant, and made by no other plants. There are 13 genera and c. 100 species, found in Australasia and tropical South and North America – hinting at an ancient Gondwana lineage. 3 genera and 8 species occur in southern Africa and two genera and 6 species in the area of our book. The flower has 6 well-developed tepals, 3 stamens and a 3-chambered inferior or superior ovary.

♣ *HYACINTHACEAE* **The Hyacinth family.** A family of 46 genera and c. 900 species in N. America, Eurasia and Africa. In southern Africa 27 genera and c.400 species have been recorded, and of these only 4 genera and c.40 species occur in our area. They are bulbous geophytes with leaves arising mostly from the base and flowers grouped on an unbranched, leafless stalk. The flowers have 6 tepals and stamens, a superior 3-chambered ovary, a simple stigma, and unjointed flowerstalks.

♣ *HYPOXIDACEAE* **The Star lily family.** Eight genera and 220 species comprise this herbaceous cormous (or rhizomatous) family, which occurs in the southern hemisphere and coastal Asia. *Spiloxene* is the commonest genus to be found here but 2 others are recorded. Leaves appear with the flowers, the flowers have 6 tepals and no bracts, six equal stamens and a 3-chambered inferior ovary.

♣ *IRIDACEAE* Perennial evergreen or deciduous herbs, only rarely becoming shrubby. They are of worldwide occurrence mostly in temperate regions, with c. 65 genera and 1800 species, represented in Southern Africa by 32 genera and 1020 species, and in our area by c. 23 genera. They have rhizomatous or cormous rootstocks whose simple leaves with parallel veins are mostly arranged in a fan arising from the rootstock or stem. Simple or branching stems terminate in bisexual flowers. The flowers are long-lasting or short-lived, are grouped in various ways and are associated with bracts; they comprise 6 usually showy tepals, 3 stamens, an inferior 3-chambered ovary with 3 or 6 style-branches, and usually several seeds. Probably all are pollinated by animals, not wind, and their flowers are intricately adapted to attract pollinators, provide landing stages and reward them with food – in the form of pollen, nectar or oils. Many are important in horticulture and the cut-flower trade, many are poisonous and a hazard to stock in grazing lands, some are used in traditional medicine, and the corms of others were important foods for early man and may still be used as a food supplement in rural areas today. Lastly, the culinary luxury saffron comes from the stigmas of the autumn flowering triploid Crocus sativus of Greece.

♣ *KIGGELARIACEAE* A family of one dioecious shrubby tree species confined to southern and tropical Africa and occupying a large range of habitats, inside, and on the edge of forests and in rocky refugia wherever rainfall and shelter allow.

♣ *LAMIACEAE* The ubiquitous shrubby or herbaceous sage family usually with square stems and leaves in pairs frequently has a distinctive scent derived from volatile oils. The flowers are usually irregular, with 5 joined sepals and joined petals and 4 stamens, two long and two short (or only 2) arched under the top petals. The ovary develops into a distinctive group of 4 nut-lets within the calyx. Most are elaborately adapted to pollination by birds or insects. 252 genera and 6700 species worldwide are represented in southern Africa by 37 genera and 235 species, some naturalised, and by c. 5 genera and 9 species in our area. The family has medicinal and culinary importance: what would we do without lavendar, mint, basil, sage, rosemary and thyme? Many are popular garden plants.

♣ *LANARIACEAE* **The lanaria family.** A family confined to the Cape, with only one species of tufted perennial with a black rootstock, 6 tepals and stamens and a half-inferior 3-chambered ovary. It has no economic uses.

♣ *LAURACEAE* An extremely ancient, mostly woody plant group with 52 genera and more than 2000 species occurring all over the tropical and subtropical world. Some are of worldwide economic importance such as avocado pear, camphor, cinnamon, and the bay tree; here represented by only three genera, Ocotea, the valuable stinkwood timber tree, the parasitic devils tresses, and those described in the species text.

♣ *LENTIBULARIACEAE* **The bladderworts.** Cosmopolitan annual or perennial soft carnivorous herbs with special bladderlike traps to catch minute aquatic animals. 3 genera and c.245 species, represented in Southern Africa by 2 genera and 19 species, and only one species here in seeps and bogs. Miniscule bisexual irregular snapdragon-like flowers are borne a few together on leafless stalks. Neither cultivated nor of economic importance.

♣ *LINACEAE* The cosmopolitan **flax family** has 13 genera and c. 300 species of herbs and a few shrubs. Linum which produces linseed oil and linen is the most abundant and economically important. There are about 230 species of *Linum* world-wide, and 14 in South Africa, here all yellow-flowered, with 7 recorded in this area. In our species the flowers are regular and bisexual, with 5 sepals and petals, stamens, styles and ovary chambers with 1-2 seeds in each chamber. The petals are twisted in bud and often drop early.

♣ *LOBELIACEAE* A family of c. 30 genera and 1200 species of cosmopolian herbs and under-shrubs chiefly of the American tropics and subtropics, represented in southern Africa by 5 genera and c.134 species and in our area by 2 genera and 26 species. Characteristics are as for *Campanulaceae* except that the flowers are irregular and the stamens join together around the style. Most lack wood, many have milky sap. In some the corolla is split to the base, and the filaments typically arch through the split. The ovary is more or less inferior with 2 chambers and usually many seeds. Some have been used medicinally as narcotics and hallucinogenics, but others are regular standbys for pot culture and as bedding garden plants.

♣ *MALVACEAE* **(Including** *STERCULIACEAE)*. Recently several families have been incorporated into what has become this very large worldwide family of c. 240 genera and c. 2675 species, represented in southern Africa by 34 genera and 407 species, (some introduced weeds) and in our area by 11 genera and 57 species, of which 8 are weedy introductions. They have simple, stipulate leaves and most have a covering of stellate hairs which can be seen with a x10 handlens. Many have a circle of bracts on the flowerstalk just below the calyx, the 5 petals are twisted in bud and the often very many stamens can be joined into a hollow tube. The ovary has 1-many chambers, often breaking apart into segments.The family produces cocoa, cola nuts, timber, fibres, gum tragacanth and cotton.

♣ *MENYANTHACEAE* **The bogbean family.** A small cosmopolitan group of 5 genera and 40+ species of marshes and open fresh water, with 2 genera and 6 species in southern Africa and only 2 genera and 2 species here. Some are local foods or traditional medicines, ornamentals or serious weeds. They have simple leaves, 5 sepals, petals and stamens, a single style and 1-chambered superior ovary with many seeds.

♣ *MYRICACEAE* **The waxberry family.** A small group of 4 genera and c.55 species of aromatic shrubs found in the Americas, Africa, northern Europe and the far east. They have nitrogen-fixing root nodules, simple leaves with gold-spangled glands, small wind-pollinated separate male and female flowers on the same plant and warty, wax-covered fleshy fruits. There is one genus in S.Africa and 9 species of which 4 occur in this area. Some produce candlewax.

♣ *MYRTACEAE.* **The gum tree and myrtle family.** A family of woody shrubs and trees in 129 genera and 4620 species, found mostly in warmer parts of South America and Australia, represented in southern Africa by 9 genera, (6 naturalised) and c.34 species (13 naturalised) and in our area by forestry and weedy *Eucalyptus* and *Leptospermum* (Australian myrtle) and only one indigenous species. They have simple leaves without stipules, dotted with oil glands, and bisexual flowers, usually in clusters. The flowers have 4-5 sepals and 4-5 petals (sometimes lacking), many loose stamens, and a usually inferior ovary with one to many seeds. The family is economically extremely valuable, providing a large proportion of the world's building timber, edible fruit such as guava, abundant nectar for honey, spices such as cloves, bay rum and allspice, cultivated plants and cut-flowers.

♣ *OLEACEAE* A cosmopolitan family of trees, shrubs and climbers comprising 25 genera and c. 600 species, of which 5 genera and 22 species occur in Southern Africa and 2 genera and 4 species are recorded in our area. Here they are trees with pairs of simple leaves lacking stipules. The family is of great economic importance, supplying olive oil from olive trees cultivated since at least 3700 BC. The timber from *Olea* is the heaviest known, jasmine provides perfume oils, and several are ornamental garden plants. *Privet (Ligustrum)* is an invasive weed in forests from the Cape Peninsula east and north, with its fruits spread by birds.

♣ *ORCHIDACEAE* **The orchid and vanilla family.** A cosmopolitan family of c. 800 genera and 20 000 perennial epiphytic or terrestrial species worldwide, of which 52 genera and c.466 species occur in southern Africa and c. 15 genera and 110 species in our area. All the species in our area are terrestrial and most produce new leaves each year from a tuber or rhizome. The flowers have a complex structure relating to their pollination strategy, many being extraordinarily precisely evolved to accept visits from only a few pollinators. Each flower has 3 sepals and 3 petals borne above a 3-chambered, 6-ribbed ovary, the sepals often resembling petals, or the petals are much reduced. In many species the flower is resupinate: twisting on its stalk so that the third sepal, instead of being at the bottom of the flower, forms a hood at the top, the evidence of the rotation being a spiral twist in the stalk, visible in the ribbing of the ovary. The third petal is then at the bottom, as one looks into the flower, being known as the lip and often variously fringed, crested or lobed. Some have one or two hollow tubes called spurs for nectar or oils, arising from a sepal or petal. The seeds are short-lived, as fine as milled pepper, and in nature can only successfully give rise to new plants after forming an internal root association with a soil fungus (mycorrhiza). Most are difficult to grow, needing moisture yet detesting municipal water supplies. Most are conspicuous in the first flowering season after a veld fire and many flower only rarely in the absence of fire.

♣ *OROBANCHACEAE* **The broomrapes,** an entirely parasitic family of 15 genera and 210 species, mostly north-temperate Eurasian, but a few occur in both Americas, Australia and Africa. By some they are classified with the *Scrophulariaceae*. The tubular flowers are 5 lobed with 4 stamens, the ovary is superior and becomes a many-seeded capsule.They are curiosities; only a few are weeds of cultivation and reduce yields of crops. Southern Africa has 15 genera and c.93 species, of which 5 genera and 12 species occur here.

♣ *OXALIDACEAE* **The sorrels,** a group of about 6 genera and 775 species of small trees shrubs and mostly herbs with tubers or, (rare among dicotyledons), bulbs. Because they contain oxalates most are deemed to be poisonous yet a few have edible bulbs or tubers and another exception is the star-fruit of S.America, *Averrhoa* sp. Their distribution is mainly in the warmer parts of Africa but also in the Americas and Asia, with 2 genera and 270 species in southern Africa and c. 33 in *Oxalis* here. Almost all of the local species have compound palmate leaves. The white, yellow, pink, red or purple flowers comprise of 5 free sepals, 5 free petals, 10 stamens of two different lengths, and 5 styles of a third length arising from a superior ovary. The sepals and leaves may have tiny patches of coloured and slightly thickened tissue, known as callusses, towards the tips. Flowers and leaves close at night. Most bloom in autumn, and die down in the summer. They multiply by seed but also by bulbils, and some can become weedy, especially beyond our borders.

♣ *PIPERACEAE* **The pepper family.** An ancient family of 8 genera and 3000 species world-wide on the southern continents, Mexico, India and the Far East. By modern taxonomists placed with the waterlilies and the stinkwood family into an archaic group, pre-dating the mono-cotyledons and all the other dicotyledons due to the possession of many unique anatomical and other features. In our area represented by only one species out of 1000 in *Peperomia* worldwide.

♣ *PENEACEAE* The entire family of 7 shrubby genera and 23 species is confined to the fynbos area of the Cape. The neat leaves are opposite, mostly giving a 4-angled look to the stem. The flowers comprise a tube of joined sepals with 4 lobes at the top and the 4 stamens fastened within to the tube; there are no petals, and the superior ovary has 4 chambers.

♣ **PLUMBAGINACEAE The statice, plumbago and sea pink family.** A world-wide family of 27 genera and 650 species of perennial herbs, shrubs and climbers especially frequent in salty or dry habitats. The simple leaves usually have glands which exude water and calcium salts. Their flowers are bisexual and regular with the parts in 5's and the persistent often papery calyx is joined into a tube; in *Limonium* it acts as a seed parachute. Southern Africa has 4 genera and 24 species. Many of them are used as garden plants, and many are particularly successful in the dried flower industry; various folk remedies are derived from some of them.

♣ *POACEAE* **The grass family** is huge, with 770 genera and 9700 species worldwide, and c. 194 genera and 950 species in southern Africa. Approximately 206 species have been recorded in 63 genera in the Cape: c. 26 genera of grassy weeds have also naturalised themselves here. Grasses are of huge economic worth to man. From bamboo poles and thatching for building, to grazing for all domestic stock, to grains and sugar providing man with an abundance of carbo-hydrates, to aromatic oils, and for land reclamation by soil-binding species. The appearance of grasses was accompanied by the evolution of high-crowned teeth and the capacity for swift move-ment in grazing mammals, and it is likely that the huge herds of ungulates could not have evolved without grass. The identification of grasses is a specialised study with a complex vocabulary and involves the examination of very small or microscopic features which are beyond the scope of a field guide; only a few of the more conspicuous species or those playing an important ecological role have been included. All have stems round and hollow in cross section, with a ligule between the wrap-around base of the leaf and the free blade.

♣ *POLYGALACEAE*. The almost worldwide milkwort family of 17 genera and 950 species is represented in Africa by 5 genera and c. 211 species and in our area by 3 genera and 37 species. They are trees, shrubs and herbs with simple leaves and no stipules, 5 sepals, 3 petals in all local species, 7 or 8 stamens more or less joined into a tube, and a 2-chambered ovary, each chamber with one seed. The largest genus in the family worldwide is the non-spiny shrubby *Polygala*, characterised by having 2 of its 5 sepals much enlarged and brightly coloured so as to resemble petals, the lowest petal with a crest rather like a shaving brush, and 8 stamens. There are about 600 species worldwide, of which approximately 86 occur in southern Africa, and c.10 in this area. *Muraltia* has c.115 species of small, often prickly, shrublets of which c. 26 have been recorded in this area, most small shrublets less than 80 cm tall. They differ from *Polygala* in the absence of the shaving-brush crest, and in having only 7 stamens. Naming to species is vexingly difficult and has not been attempted in this work. *Polygala* is often mistaken for a pea.

♣ *PRIONIACEAE* **The palmiet family** A family wholly confined to the river systems of the Cape Province and Kwazulu-Natal, and consisting of one lone species of treelike shrub whose sturdy stolons at riverbed level subtend equally strong branched stems with layers of diaphanous water-absorbent bark and tough crowded leaves at their tips high above the water. The subtle protective capacity of this plant to control the potential damage done by sudden heavy deluges of rain characteristic of the Cape's weather systems is largely unrecognized by landowners. Most of the palmiet beds of the past have been deliberately destroyed, turning our rivers into turbulent rocky, muddy ditches alternating with dry sluits, resulting in the irreparable downgrading of our ecosystems, lowering water tables, carrying off valuable valley alluvium and increasing flood damage in our river valleys.

♣ *PROTEACEAE* **An ancient woody family** of southern hemisphere trees and shrubs evolving in Gondwanaland in the time of the dinosaurs, consisting of c. 75 genera and 1350 species, of which 16 genera (two Australian invaders) and 360 species occur in Southern Africa. Varying in habit from upright trees and shrubs to sprawling cushions or apparently stemless shrublets, single or multi-stemmed; if they have one stem they recruit only from seed after fire, but if they have several this indicates that they can also recover by means of shoots from a fire-resistant woody subterranean stump. Some are among the tallest members of the fynbos flora and if protected from too frequent fire, can form open canopy woodland although the opportunity to do this diminishes with every fire in the fynbos. The leaves are variously arranged and simple to much-divided and sometimes of two different forms on one plant, or between male and female plant in the dioecious species. The delicate flowers are grouped in a variety of ways into striking heads, often surrounded by showy leaves called bracts, and in addition, each flower arises in the axil of its own bract. In our genera each flower can give rise to only one fruit. The flowers have a unique structure of 4 perianth parts, the cupped tip of each housing one stalkless stamen. The one-chambered ovary has one permanently enclosed seed and a long, sturdy style, usually conspicuously knobbed, which scrapes the pollen out of the anthers and presents it to the pollinators. The cryptic stigma is in the form of a slit which only accepts pollen – from another flower - a day or so later after its own pollen has been dispersed. Pollinators are wind, birds, a range of insects, or small mammals. Many species protect their fruits from predation within fire-resistant closed bracts until the parent plant is killed by fire: this arrangement is called serotiny. Fruit dispersal is by wind, ants or small mammals.

♣ *PTERIDOPHYTES.* **The ferns.** This ancient group of land plants which appeared in the fossil record long before the flowering plants, evolved many devices to enable them to survive on land, such as sturdy upright build, water-proof surfaces, efficient root systems to absorb water from below, and effective internal mechanisms for moving that water upwards. Their Achilles heel, which gives away their lowly aquatic origin, is their sexual reproduction technique. The spores, blown in their millions in the air, give rise on a suitably damp surface to very delicate green liverwort-like small clumps of cells which make egg and sperm cells. The film of water present in such a habitat covers the plantlet and enables the sperms to swim to the eggs. Swimming sperms are a very ancient form of reproduction almost universal in algae, mosses and liverworts, relinquished only in the advanced cone-bearing plants, and only universally ab-sent in flowering plants. Fertilised eggs give rise once more to the fern plant with which we are all familiar, with its watch-spring unfurling leaves, "fern fiddles", its patches or clusters of spore-producing bodies, called sori with or without covers called an indusium, its usually much-divided leaf, and its archaic style of branching of veins or leaf blades which fork into two equal halves, known as dichotomous branching, and which can be seen in almost all ferns if the leaves are held up to the light. Dichotomous branching is almost unheard-of in flowering plants, but may be seen, for example, in a few species of *Aristea*. The vast majority of flowering plants have a branching style which gives rise to different orders of branches, larger and smaller, thicker and thinner. In the ferns there are c. 8550 species and 223 genera in 33 families, ranging from tall trees through sturdy perennials to delicate filmy ferns and free-floating aquatics. Many protect themselves from being eaten with toxic compounds, tannins, phenolics, glycosides and a host of others. They have worldwide distribution. Ours, like those of other continents, mostly have a much wider distribution than most of our fynbos plants, probably reflecting their much more ancient lineages and light wind-borne spores. Several have traces of a Gondwana distribution.

♣ *RANUNCULACEAE* **This large family** of predominantly northern distribution with repre-sentatives on all continents, consists of 62 genera and 2450 species of herbs, climbers and small shrubs, including some very popular garden plants; but it is poorly represented in Africa, with only 7 genera and 26 species. The structure of the flower in many species is archaic, with spirally arranged sepals and petals whose character transforms gradually one into the other, and may likewise continue to transform into stamens and several free carpels. Many species are very poisonous and a few are of medicinal importance. In our area only two genera and four species occur.

♣ *RESTIONACEAE* **The thatching reed and** *Restio* **family** These are rush and grasslike perennials, growing in clumps or tufts. There are about 28 genera and c. 400 species in southern Africa, Chile, Madagascar, Australia and New Zealand of which about 19 genera and 320 species are endemic to the Cape. They have wind-pollinated unisexual flowers borne on separate, often dissimilar plants which are best matched by comparing the sheaths on the stems. These wrap-around dry sheaths, which are split to the base and often drop off early, represent all that is left of the leaves. Generic markers include whether the stems are branched or simple, flat or round in cross-section, whether the sheaths persist or drop off, and the number of chambers in the fruit. The flowers are grouped together in spikelets usually in the axils of papery bracts at the top of green, almost invariably solid, rounded stems, (occasionally flattened or four-sided). Restios are ubiquitous in the Cape, almost taking over the place of grasses and even often forming extensive stands. Many resprout from fire-resistant crowns, greening up the landscape ahead of other vegetation after a fire. Distinguishing features of the species are largely technical, detailed and require a microscope or at least a x10 handlens to be seen. The flowering time of many species is unrecorded. Because of the high proportion of silica in their stems they make excellent, long-lasting thatching for roofs, but are also used for mats and brooms.

♣ *RHAMNACEAE* A family of c. 58 genera and 900 species of trees, shrubs and a few climbers of worldwide temperate and tropical occurrence. Southern Africa has 9 genera and 203 species, with 4 genera and 25 species in the Western Cape. The stipule-less *Phylica*, with 150 species in the Cape, Madagascar, St Helena and Tristan da Cunha, is represented in our area by 22 species, distinguished by rather minute structural characters inaccessible except with good magnification. A 5-lobed tubular calyx, usually hairy to shaggy on the reverse, supports in its mouth 5 much-reduced peg or spoon-like petals and 5 stamens, above a 3-chambered ovary with one seed inside each.

♣ *RORIDULACEAE* An entirely Cape family of two shrubby species with sticky glandular leaves which trap but do not digest insects. A bug lives here with impunity, feeding off the trapped insects; its droppings nourish the soil in which the host plant is rather weakly rooted. The family is related to the sundews and pollinated by bugs.

♣ *ROSACEAE* A family of 107 genera and c.3000 species represented on all continents, but with the greatest diversity in the northern hemisphere. Trees, shrubs and herbs with relatively simple old-fashioned floral structure, they are none the less of great economic importance providing most of the edible berries and fruits eaten around the world, as well as being of great horticultural distinction. 9 genera and c.140 species are found in southern Africa, the numbers enhanced by 9 exotic genera and 140 species; and in our area by c.4 genera and 44 species of almost no economic importance.

♣ *RUTACEAE* **The citrus and buchu family,** cosmopolitan with 156 genera and 1800 species of trees and shrubs, especially in the tropics, represented in southern Africa by 22 genera and 290 species, and in our area by 5 genera and c.32 species. Usually many parts of the plant are visibly dotted with oil glands which emit a diversity of distinctive scents often so typical that the species may be identified by them. In this area all are shrubs. The flowers have 5 sepals, petals, stamens, and 5 sterile stamens (=staminodes) in diverse forms from petal-like to minute pegs, and a superior 1-5 chambered fruit, in all but the 5-chambered *Adenandra* with a swelling or prolongation known as a horn at the top of each chamber. The bean-shaped seeds ripen to a shiny black with a waxy eliaosome body at one end, and are ejected by an elastic mechanism of the inner wall of the fruit to a metre or more. They are gathered and buried by ants, subsequent germination being triggered and encouraged by the smoke of a veld fire. The essential oils of some are exported for the flavouring and scent industry, and some are used in traditional medicine.

♣ *SANTALACEAE.* **The Sandalwood family** of 34 genera and 540 species of plants semi-parasitic on the roots of other plants, with simple leaves and clusters of small open-faced flowers, distributed worldwide except for the very cold parts of the northern hemisphere. Southern Africa has 5 genera and c. 200 species, of which 4 genera and 50 species occur in the South.Western Cape, and 3 genera and c. 37 species in our area. They are variously a source of timber, oil, edible fruits, tubers and tanning substances.

♣ *SAPOTACEAE* A pantropical family of c. 100 genera and 1000 species of trees and shrubs, predominantly in the tropics of the Americas; represented in southern Africa by 7 genera and 14 species, mostly in the lower altitude parts of summer-rainfall forests. Only one, the milk-wood, occurs in our area. All have a milky latex, simple, spirally arranged leaves, and clusters of flowers often arising on the trunks. They usually have up to 5 free sepals, 5 joined petals and 5 stamens, a superior ovary and berry fruit. The family produces latex for chewing gum and gutta-percha, tropical edible fruits such as star fruits, sapodilla plum and sapote and an edible oil, shea butter.

♣ *SCROPHULARIACEAE* **The snapdragon family**: a cosmopolitan assemblage of pre-dominantly herbaceous plants and some woody species, totalling 290 genera and 4500 species worldwide, represented in southern Africa by 80 genera and 760 species, and in our area by approximately 26 genera and at least 56 species. Naturalised species are c. 7, in 4 genera. There are comparatively few of economic importance save as ornamental garden plants, a few weeds and a couple which produce drugs, like digitalin. Their flowers have 5 sepals and petals, both joined into tubes of a variety of lengths, and the 4 or 2 functional stamens, fastened inside the corolla tube, are carefully placed to intercept animal pollinators. In most the 2-chambered ovary produces many seeds but in *Selago* and its allies only one per chamber.

♣ *STILBACEAE* An entirely Cape based, endemic family of 5 genera and 12 species, of which 4 genera and 6-7 species occur here. They are ericoid, densely leafy woody shrubs with a lignotuber, resprouting after veld fires. The leaves are usually whorled, thick, and with edges rolled under. The stalkless flowers, in spikes, have mostly 5 sepals and 5 petals joined into a tube with the 4-5 stamens attached inside the petal tube and a 1-2-chambered superior ovary with 2 seeds.

♣ *SOLANACEAE* A cosmopolitan family of often prickly shrubs, trees, lianes and herbs, especially important in the warmer parts of the Americas, comprising 90 genera and c.2600 species, represented in southern Africa by 4 indigenous genera and 42 species, and by 5 wide-ly naturalised genera. In our area occurs the indigenous spiny honey thorn shrub *Lycium afrum*, more typical of the drier, stony places up the west coast; the weedy, prickly stinkblaar poison apples, *Datura stramonium* and *D. ferox* important in local folk medicine volunteer in disturbed places. The family provides us with enormously important foods such as potato, tomato, brinjal, cape gooseberry, capsicums and chillies, and important drugs such as tobacco, atropine and insecticides, but also toxic alkaloids and hallucinogens. Our gardens would be much less handsome without the cultivated ornamental members of the family, such as *Petunia* and various "potato creepers" and "potato shrubs". The great cosmopolitan genus, *Solanum* has over 1700 species, many of them poisonous, containing such important plants as the potato, the tomato and tobacco.

♣ *TECOPHILAEACEAE* A family of 6 genera and 25 species occurring in California, Chile and tropical and southern Africa, of which 2 genera and 10 species occur in Africa, mostly in the South Western Cape. They are geophytes with annual above-ground parts and corms or tubers underground. While most are of little economic use, some are cultivated ornamentals and some have edible corms.

♣ *THYMELAEACEAE*. A family of c. 45 genera and 500 species on all continents except Greenland, and on many oceanic islands, represented in Southern Africa by 8 genera and 192 species, and in our area by 4 genera and c. 42 species. Most are shrubs with simple leaves and tough bark which tears into long strips. The flowers have a well-developed calyx with 4-12 petal-like lobes which, if present, are reduced to scale-like or fleshy lobes at the mouth of the calyx. There are 4-10 stamens attached inside the calyx tube and a superior ovary of one chamber with one seed. *Gnidia* has flowers usually arranged in terminal heads. In *Struthiola* the flowering spike is built up from flowers grouped 1-2 in the axils of the upper leaves; the flowers have only 4 stamens and the petals are surrounded by stiff hairs; *Passerina*, the only wind-pollinated genus in the group, has 8 stamens hanging out of the flower and no petals.

Lachnaea has no petals, instead, it has outgrowths from the inside wall of the flower tube below the stamens and the stigma is brushlike.

♣ *TYPHACEAE* **The reed-mace, cat tail or bulrush family** of cosmopolitan perennial marsh-herbs, consisting of one genus and 10-13 species, of which only one is represented in South Africa and in our area. This usually grows in dense stands in the moderately deep verges of ponds or slowly moving water and spreads and becomes denser in response to enrichment of the water with plant nutrients including waste products from sewage and gardening and farming operations. Then it is often seen as a threat by water managers, when in fact it is helping to lower the nutrient levels in the water by taking them up into its own growth, the water discharged below a bulrush stand being considerably purer and less enriched than above it. The key to controlling the spread of *Typha* is to lower the input of enrichment products to the water. Seed germination is promoted by an absence of oxygen in the mud in which the seeds lie.

♣ *VIOLACEAE* **The violet family,** widespread and particularly abundant in temperate climates, consists of 22 genera and 900 species, represented in southern Africa by 3 genera and 10 species. Only one species occurs in our area. *Viola odorata* is grown in France for its valuable perfume oil for perfumes and flavorings. Sugared violet flowers were once used as a delicious edible decoration on chocolates. A couple of species have poisonous roots with a very limited use in folk medicine.

♣ *VISCACEAE* **The mistletoe or birdlime family.** C. 7 genera and 450 species of parasitic plants of the old world, Africa, Madagascar and Asia; in southern Africa represented by *Viscum* with 17 species. They are shrublets with or without leaves, firmly attached to the stems of host plants, the minute flowers unisexual, borne on the same plant or separate plants, and fly or wind-pollinated. The berry, white, yellow or red, contains seeds with a sticky coating which adheres to bird beaks until rubbed off into bark cracks. Here fleshy clamps put out by the seed to stabilise it enable the embryo to establish an internal connection with the host. The berries are used by man as bird-lime to catch perching birds; and as a festive decoration in the house at Christmas: an ancient custom dating from Druid times.

♣ *ZYGOPHYLLACEAE* A predominantly tropical to subtropical family of shrubs, herbs and a few trees especially adapted to drier and saline conditions, consisting of c. 25 genera and 240 species of very diverse structure, with 8 genera and 55 species in southern Africa and 3 in this area. Elsewhere they produce valuable timber, essential oils for perfumery, edible fruits and some medicines.

PTERIDOPHYTA – The ferns

Todea barbara
grape fern

A large fern with a trunk-like rhizome upright to c. 60cm tall, and stiffly held arching fronds up to 2.5m long. The fronds are 2-pinnately divided with lobes divided almost to the base alternating upwards to a tapering apex. The sporangia, lacking an indusium, are scattered on the undersides of the lower leaflets. This large tree-fern-like species is confined to sandy seepage areas and streambanks of mountain slopes on quartzite and sandstone from the South Western and Southern Cape to the Chimanimani mountains, Australia, New Zealand.

♣ There is only one species.

Gleichenia polypodioides
coral fern, kystervaring

A trailing, much-branched widely creeping wiry fern with slightly scaly rhizome giving rise to widely spaced hairless fronds. The leafstalks are stiff, each frond being divided and redivided into equal divisions, the ultimate segments bearing broad-based triangular leaflets c. 3 x 2mm on either side of the midrib. The sori, situated towards the base of each, on its leading edge, are sunk into pits forming a blister on the upper surface. It is terrestrial or associated with rocks and is capable of piling up to form high heaps which smother young plantation pine trees in certain circumstances, and is favoured by high rainfall and frequent mists from the S.W. Cape to eastern parts of southern Africa to Tanzania, as well as islands in the Indian Ocean.

♣ There are 10 species, but only this one in our area.

Schizaea pectinata
curlygrass or cockscomb fern

A low-growing grasslike fern, with crowded, non-hairy, undivided thin fronds up to 30cm long. The fertile fronds bend into a horizontal terminal portion which carries a set of comb-like vertical divisions with sporangia on the inner surface. The identity of this unfernlike plant is clearly revealed when the young fronds unfurl in the manner of a watch-spring. It is most conspicuous in the first year after a veld fire. It occurs on well-drained poor sandy or quartzitic soils from the Western Cape to Port Elizabeth and up to Tanzania and Madagascar.

♣ There are 30 species, but only one other here, *S. tenella*, a much more slender form always associated with streams.

Cyathea capensis
tree fern

A sturdy tree capable of reaching 4.5m, with a bole 10-20cm across with dark, glossy tapering, pale-fringed-edged scales. The crown of the bole where the fronds emerge is filled with a mass of hairlike structures derived from much-reduced and transformed fronds. The fronds themselves have 50cm stalks, up to 2m long, with saw-like toothed blades made up of almost separate lobes, alternating up both sides of the midrib like a double-sided comb, hairless above but with scattered pale scales below. Each has usually only one sorus near the base, with an asymmetrical cover. It occurs in cool moist shady ravines on mountain slopes from the Cape Peninsula along the southern Cape coastal forests as far as Tanzania, favouring the sheltered high light intensity of breaks in the canopy where it can form extensive colonies.

♣ There are c. 600 species, but only this one in our area.

Lycopodiella cernua
nodding clubmoss

A leafy perennial herb with branched horizontal main stems rooting irregularly and giving rise to erect, well-branched fertile stems to c. 18cm. high. Spores are produced at the nodding branch tips in aggregations of sporangium-bearing leaves a little more tightly packed than on the sterile parts. It occurs on moist stream and road edges at lower altitudes from the Gifberg to tropical Africa and Madagascar. Three genera of clubmosses are probably represented in our area, modest descendents of world-wide giants of the Carboniferous flora of the Coal Measures of Europe and elsewhere; and amongst the most ancient of all our land plants.

Todea barbara

Gleichenia polypodioides

Schizaea pectinata

Lycopodiella cernua

Cyathea capensis

Pteridium aquilinum bracken

Sturdy upright plants 1m to c. 2.5m high with stiff hard hairless fronds 3 or 4 times divided. They arise singly from a subterranean rhizome which is densely brown hairy-scaly. The sterile and fertile fronds are the same shape, the continuous sori being tucked under the recurved indusium formed by the edge of the leaflets. Probably the most common fern worldwide, and including temperate and eastern tropical Africa, Madagascar, the Mascarenes, mostly in full sun, usually in well-drained sandy soils, becoming weedy where frequently burnt, and toxic to animals.

♣ There is only one species.

Histiopteris incisa

Quite large, soft-textured plants whose opaque hairless greyish fronds, c. 3m long and 1m broad, are 3-pinnately divided, with clearly visible veins which join up. They arise singly from a creeping underground scaly rhizome. The sterile and fertile fronds are the same shape, with continuous sori along the margin of the uppermost leaflets, covered by an inward-opening indusium formed from the recurved edge of the leaflet. It occurs in forest in strong light, in damp places from the South Western Cape to West Africa, Madagascar and southern temperate regions of the world.

♣ There is only one species.

Rumohra adiantiformis seven-weeks fern, leather-leaf, Knysna fern

Sturdy, spreading, thick, glossy and leathery fronds 25cm-1m tall, 3-4-pinnately divided, arise singly from a densely rusty-red scaly rhizome creeping on the surface of the ground. The circular sori placed in the lobes of the leaflets of all leaves are c. 2mm across and covered by a circular indusium which drops off at maturity. It is widespread on southern continents and islands, and in our area is to be found on the shady forest floor and margin or in boulder scree.

♣ There are 5 species, but only this one here.

Elaphoglossum acrostichoides tongue fern

A low-growing fern with simple fronds of two sizes, the smaller fertile. The non-sticky leaves arise singly from a horizontal creeping, dark to pale brown-scaly rhizome, growing on damp rocks of Table Mountain sandstone or on tree bark. The midrib projects below and the sporangia occur all over the underside of the fertile fronds to the midrib, This is the most common of the tongue ferns found in shady places on the Cape Peninsula, along the Southern Cape coastal belt, KwaZulu-Natal, in forest and to tropical Africa.

♣ A genus of c. 500 species with two others in our area. *E. conforme* has sticky young fronds and a midrib projecting above.

Blechnum capense deerfern

A sturdy dense fern with two kinds of fronds, up to 130cm long, arising from a thick brown-scaly rhizome. Each leaf has a row of short-stalked leaflets, with scalloped or toothed edge, each side of the glossy black or brown midrib. The fertile fronds are the same size or slightly smaller, but their leaflets are widely spaced and narrow, with sori almost all along their length, and a continuous, fringed indusium. It is a variable species occurring from the South Western Cape eastwards and north as far as Mozambique and Malawi. Here it is often a dominant fern on wet shaded stream-banks.

♣ There are c. 150 species, more or less worldwide, but in our area the c. 5 others have stalkless, smooth-edged leaflets.

Pteridium aquilinum

Histiopteris incisa

Rumohra adiantiformis

Elaphoglossum acrostichoides

Blechnum capense

65

CONIFEROPHYTA – The conifers

PODOCARPACEAE – The yellowwood family

Podocarpus elongatus
Breede River Yellowwood

A rounded shrubby dioecious tree to 6m when protected from fire, but on exposed sites stunted to almost prostrate. It is the dark tree in the foreground of the photograph. The grey-green leaves, arranged towards the ends of branchlets, are sub-opposite to spiral, up to 6 x 0.5cm but sometimes larger, and narrowly oval with distinctive longitudinal grooves especially below (visible to the naked eye) in which the stomata are sunk; these may be seen with the aid of a 10x lens. Male trees bear pollen-producing catkins, the females produce 1-2 seeds on a fleshy cushion which ripens from green to crimson as the oval seeds turn dark blue-green. It occurs on sandstone slopes along streams from the Bokkeveld Mountains to Swellendam, in the west of our area but not on the Klein River mountains. (Jan-May).

♣ *Podocarpus latifolius*, the broad-leafed yellowwood growing to 30m in forests and open mountain slopes also in the west of our area, has grey or purple seeds and longer leaves up to 13mm wide without the lengthwise grooves of the former.

CUPRESSACEAE – The cedar family

Widdringtonia nodiflora
mountain cypress

A resprouting shrubby tree usually below 6m these days, but capable of achieving a much greater height if the environment permits it, with evergreen scalelike leaves. Male cones are 2-4mm across and terminal, the female cones rounded, wrinkled and knobbly with 4 scales and winged seeds. It grows on rocky mountain slopes, favouring richer clay soils, from the Cape Peninsula to tropical Africa and on mountains throughout our area where it is the only representative of this family.

ANGIOSPERMAE – The flowering plants

APONOGETONACEAE – The water hawthorn family

Aponogeton distachyos
wateruintjie, waterblommetjie

A tuberous-rooted aquatic perennial with floating oval, blunt-tipped leaves 6-20 long x 2-7cm wide, borne on stalks arising from the crown of the plant, which is rooted in the mud. It has an edible, sweetly scented, many-flowered, forked flowerhead, used to make the local stew "waterblommetjie bredie". Each flower has one tepal. It is found in dense colonies in ponds, ditches and deep sluggish streams from Nieuwoudtville to Knysna. (July - Dec).

♣ Of the 43 species occurring in Africa Asia, Madagascar and Australia, 6 in are in southern Africa, but only one more species is found in our area: *A. angustifolius*, a more delicate plant whose slender, pointed leaves are half as wide, and whose white flowers have two tepals each, occurs in ditches in the northern parts of our area from Worcester, Malmesbury to Paarl and Stellenbosch.

Podocarpus elongatus   *Berries*

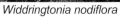

Widdringtonia nodiflora   *Aponogeton distachyos*

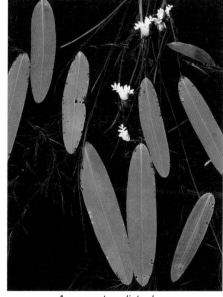

TYPHACEAE – The reed-mace, cat tail or bulrush family

Typha capensis papkuil, bulrush

Upright leafy stems with narrow 2-ranked leaves and a terminal flowering axis are produced by horizontal runners in the mud. The dense cylindrical, thicker lower portion of the flowerhead consists of female flowers, the upper, more loosely packed slenderer portion are male. The flowers themselves, lacking tepals, are reduced to 1 carpel or 2-5 stamens, packed together with hairs. It occurs along streambanks, and in standing water and marshes throughout southern and tropical Africa. (Dec-Jan).

POACEAE – The grass family

Ehrharta erecta

This insignificant sprawling and tufted annual becomes perennial when conditions permit, and even puts out roots where the stems are in contact with damp earth. In the illustration it is shown growing up along and between sheltering rocks. The broad flat leaves have a wavy edge. The smooth flowering shoot is branched with the awnless flowering units or spikelets quite tightly pressed to the stem.

It has a wide distribution from the Cape Peninsula to East Africa in shade, and may become weedy in moister gardens in the Cape. This and buffalo grass, are two of the food plants of the caterpillar of the Table Mountain Beauty butterfly, which is the unique pollinator of red-flowered summer blooming high mountain plants such as *Disa uniflora, Crassula coccinea*, some watsonias and many other species. To guarantee the survival of this swathe of red blooms we must ensure that the caterpillar's food plants are also protected in the same area.

♣ C. 17 more species of *Ehrharta* occur in our area, including the 1.5m high pypgras, *E. villosa*, which colonises coastal dunes.

Hyparrhenia hirta dektamboekiegras, thatching grass

A tufted perennial grass to 1.2m high with a typically ruddy tinted flowering stems. The leaves are narrow, 1-2mm wide, and the hairy flowers have bent awns. It is a food plant for the Table Mountain Beauty butterfly, and is widespread in disturbed areas, road-sides and on richer mountain soils. (Nov-May).

♣ C. 53 species occur in Africa and the Mediterranean, but only this and the introduced *H. anamesa* with leaves twice as broad occurs here.

Pentaschistis curvifolia

A tufted perennial to c. 50cm whose rigid, straight, sometimes rolled leaves arise from the ground, with shiny, white, persistent leaf sheaths and pale, dense, awned flowering heads. It can be found on shallow sandstone slopes and along paths from the Bokkeveld to Grahamstown. (Oct-Nov).

♣ 65 species occur in cooler parts, tropical Africa, and Madagascar. With c. 21 species in our area, it is the largest grass genus we have. Several have conspicuous stalked glands.

Pentameris macrocalycina

A tufted, branching perennial to 1m with stiff threadlike leaves, round in cross-section, and hairy ligules. The spikelets are twinned and 16-24mm long. It occurs on upper sandstone slopes from the northern Cedarberg to Uitenhage. (Sept-Dec).

♣ 4 more species occur here. 2 are similar: *P. hirtiglumis* of Hottentots Holland shale bands has leaves rolled and curved, and hairy sheaths and spikelets; the 1.5m *P. longiglumis* of Kogelberg.

Typha capensis

Ehrharta erecta   Tony Verboom

Pentameris macrocalycina   Peter Linder

Tony Verboom

Hyparrhenia hirta

Peter Linder

Pentaschistis curvifolia

69

Merxmuellera cincta   olifantsgras

A common reedlike, perennial, tufted grass to 2m tall with non-woolly leafsheath but with the ligule a band of tufts of white hairs 5-12mm long. It occurs sometimes in extensive stands in wetlands and alongside streams in the uplands from the Olifants River mountains to the Eastern Cape and is most conspicuous after fire. (Oct-Apr).

♣ C. 4 more species of *Merxmuellera* are recorded in our area out of a total of 14 species in Southern Africa and Madagascar. 3 have densely woolly leaf sheaths.

Phragmites australis   common reed, fluitjiesriet

A tall, reedy, almost woody cosmopolitan perennial to 4m+ with stems bearing broad lance-shaped leaves along their length, a long tapering fringed membranous ligule, and a conspicuous plumelike flowerhead at the tip. It occurs in fresh but not in brack water. It forms dense reedbeds which are vitally important for many water birds and weavers. (Feb-May).

♣ A sturdy, taller, look-alike invasive alien, the Spanish reed, *Arundo donax* is spreading in wet places in the Cape. It has distinctive flaring ear-like pockets at the base of the blade of the leaf, rather more tapering flower plumes, and a ligule which is a short fringed membrane: it should be removed.

Pseudopentameris brachyphylla

A perennial grass forming stout tufts to 1m tall with cylindrical, hollow, densely-leafy stems. The ligule is a hairy fringe. The wind-pollinated flowers with freely projecting stigmas and stamens are grouped into purple and pale yellow spikelets. Occasional on mountain slopes from the Hottentots Holland to the Klein River mountains. (Sept-Oct).

♣ There are four species confined to the South Western Cape and all occur in our area.

CYPERACEAE - The sedges

Tetraria brachyphylla

A densely tufted perennial to 60cm with reddish, hard, shining spikelets. It is recorded on lower slopes and coastal dunes from the Cape Peninsula to Plettenberg Bay. Most obvious after fire when it can be more easily seen, but also found in mature veld. (Aug).

♣ It is very similar to *T. compar* which flowers in winter and has brown sticky bracts.

Tetraria thermalis   bergpalmiet

An exceptionally coarse, tufted yellowish-green plant to 2.5m high, with flat, swordlike leaves, 30mm broad at the base, having a sharp cutting edge. The 3-sided solid flowering stems are longer than the leaves. The flowers are clustered within large dusky-brown overlapping bracts. Widespread on flats and mountain slopes from the Peninsula to Riversdale, it is one of the first plants to resprout after fire and baboons are said to relish the new growths. (June-Oct).

♣ There are c. 40 species in Africa and Australia, of which c. 14 occur in this area. The similar 1.5m *T. bromoides* throughout our area has longer rush-like leaves 3mm broad at the base. *T. involucrata* with similar thin leaves but a looser and more pendulous flowerheads grows in moist habitats in the Hottentots Holland and Jonkershoek. Another tall to 2m sedge of wet areas is the rigid and robust *Neesenbeckia punctoria* with sheath-like leaves with no blades, and some long cylindrical blades similar to the stem, and an erect flowerhead.

Merxmuellera cincta

Phragmites australis

Pseudopentameris brachyphylla

Tetraria brachyphylla

Tetraria thermalis

71

Carpha glomerata

vleibiesie, vleiriet

A robust tufted perennial to 2m with golden-brown spikelets and nutlet seeds each with 6 bristles. It is easily confused with *Prionium*, especially out of flower, but is distinguished from this species by non-serrated deeply w-shaped leaves It grows in scattered clumps on marshy flats and in watercourses from Citrusdal to KwaZulu-Natal and throughout our area. (Aug-Jan).

Ficinia radiata (=*Sickmannia radiata*)

stergras

A distinctive, low-growing tufted perennial 5-25cm tall, varying quite considerably in its dimensions; this specimen is unusually robust. The flowering heads are surrounded by a halo of broad bright golden, eye-catching bracts. It is most conspicuous after wild fires on flats and slopes from Ceres to Stilbaai. (Sept-Nov).

♣ The similar *F. pallens* has a smaller flower head on a stem as long to longer than the leaves.

Cyperus thunbergii

A robust tufted perennial to 1m tall with a stiff 3-sided solid stem and basal leaves slightly shorter than the stem. The stalks of the flower spikes are of unequal length and the flower clusters are surrounded by a number of bristly, leafy bracts. It occurs in damp places or forest verges along the coastal belt from Clanwilliam to KwaZulu-Natal. (June-Dec).

♣ There are about 200 species world-wide in warm moist areas, of which about 4 occur in the Cape.

RESTIONACEAE – The Restio family

Anthochortus crinalis

orgy grass

A soft, yielding, bright green tangled perennial to 80cm, with culms much-branched and with a minutely rough-pimply surface. The sexes are similar in appearance and the flowers are very small, with hairlike spathes and bracts. The ovary is 1-chambered with 2 styles. Forming yielding, dense, billowing tussocks a metre across or more, it recruits only from seed, and occurs, sometimes in extensive stands, on damp slopes and seeps from the Cape Peninsula to Worcester and Riversdale. (May).

♣ One other species is recorded from this area.

Cannomois virgata

besemriet

Plants forming tussocks 1-3m tall, with branched stems and persistent sheaths. The flowerhead is up to 30cm long and consists of large numbers of many- flowered brown spikelets, each 5-10mm long. The female plants with 1-chambered fruits and 2 long styles usually have solitary spikelets which are spindle-shaped and 2-5cm long, and release huge tick-like seeds which are buried by ants. It is frequent along streams and in wet seepages where it can form dense patches.

♣ There are 7 species, largely confined to the fynbos areas of the Cape, with two more recorded from this area, all with simple unbranched stems and none more than 1m tall.

Carpha glomerata

Ficinia radiata

Cyperus thunbergii

Cannomois virgata (Male)

Anthochortus crinalis

Ceratocaryum argenteum

Plants forming large tussocks, to 2,5m tall, with unbranched stems about 6mm in diameter and persistent sheaths. The female flowerhead consists of 3-8 densely packed spikelets within a shiny brown bony spathe 4-6cm long. Each spikelet has only a single flower with one chamber and 2 styles, enclosed by numerous slender pale brown papery bracts about 20mm long. The fruit is a nut. Similar in size to the female plant the male has a flowerhead with spathes which soon drop off, exposing very large numbers of 5mm long papery flowers laden with pollen. It is found in clumps in damp places. (Feb-Apr).

♣ Five more species have been recorded in the fynbos of the Cape, with 1 more in this area.

Chondropetalum ebracteatum

A tufted plant from 30-100cm whose unbranched stems soon lose their sheaths. Knobbly sharp-pointed dark, shiny male and c.3.5mm female flowers spiral up to the tips, the females producing 3-chambered dry fruits. It is common especially on lower sandstone slopes where it can be locally dominant, from the Cape Peninsula to the Langeberg mountains and throughout our area. (Oct-Dec).

♣ Of the 10 species 8 occur in our area. With unbranched stems: *E. decipens* has similar size flowers and is found only in Hermanus; Flowers smaller than 3mm, all of coastal sands are: *C. rectum*; *C. nudum* and the tall thatching reed *C. tectorum*; *C. microcarpum* has branching stems. The only species with persistent sheaths is *C. deustum*.

Chondropetalum mucronatum   rocket restio

Coarse sturdy erect unbranched stems grow crowded together with large pointed sheaths which drop off leaving conspicuous rings. The large brushlike heads of male flowers are interspersed with large tawny deciduous sheaths. The female flowers, with 3 styles and a 3-chambered fruit, hide within long, wide sheaths. It forms large stands within the cloud zone of the mountains in seeps on sandstone. Its common name refers to the exploding nature of the flower head when burnt. (Oct-Nov).

Hypodiscus aristatus

A tufted, resprouting perennial to 80cm with smooth unbranched stems, persistent sheaths wrapped tightly around the stems, and separate male and female plants with one to many similar, bristly spindle-shaped, 10-20mm spikelets grouped at the end of the stem. Each spikelet is subtended by a large brown, white edged spathe, the female of each produces a flower with 2 fluffy red styles and a one-chambered ovary with only one smooth, shiny nutlet, 8mm long, sitting on a pale green elaiosome which attracts ants to bury it. It is widespread from Clanwilliam to the Baviaanskloof in well-drained sand on rocky mountainsides. (May).

♣ 15 species are recorded, with c. 5 from this area. All have nutlet fruit buried by ants. Also with red styles: *H. alternans* confined to the Kogelberg area has a warty nutlet topped with ridges; *H. argenteus* has a silvery flowerhead and striped sheaths. With white styles: *H. albo-aristatus* has a single sheath per stem and *H. willdenowia* has a flattened striped stem.

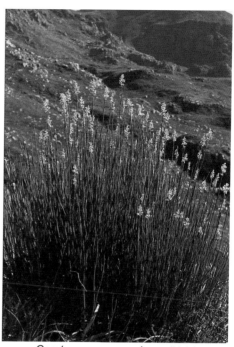

Ceratocaryum argenteum (Female)

Ceratocaryum argenteum (Male)

Chondropetalum
ebracteatum (Male & Female)

Chondropetalum
mucronatum (Female)

Hypodiscus aristatus
(Male)

75

Elegia capensis

Plants forming large tussocks, to 2,5m tall with whorls of numerous slender sterile branches at the nodes of the main stems. Male and female flowerheads are similar, with spathes which soon drop off. It is common along streams and wet seepages and it may form large dense stands, from Clanwilliam to Port Elizabeth.

♣ C.18 more species of *Elegia* have been recorded from this area. The only other *Elegia* species with dense clusters of sterile branches at the nodes, *E. equisetacea* of the Langeberg mountains, can be distinguished by having spathes which do not drop off.

Elegia filacea

Plants forming small tussocks, less than 50cm tall. The stems are slender, unbranched, and lose their sheathing leaves early. The male flowerhead is about 20mm long, with spathes 10mm long. The female is rather similar to the male, but with the flowers more or less obscured by the spathes. The flowers have 2 styles and one chamber per fruit. It is very common in conspicuous wheat-like fields on sandy flats at most altitudes from the Cedarberg to Port Elizabeth. (Feb).

♣ *E. stipularis* is similar but has branching stems and spathes tinged pink at flowering. 2 others with branching stems are *E. neesii* of mountainous areas with 30-60mm sheaths and *E. prominens* of coastal lowlands with sheaths no longer than 15mm.

Elegia persistens

The plants form loose tussocks about 50cm tall. The flowering stems are unbranched but may have occasional weaker, branched sterile stems. The leaf-sheaths fall off early. Conspicuous spreading brown papery spathes expose large clusters of male flowers. Two female cylindrical inflorescences, completely hidden within pale brown overlapping spathes, 2-3mm long with turned back tips, may be seen on the extreme left of the slide. The female flowers have 2 styles and a 1-chambered fruit. It is frequent, especially in the first years after fire, in gravelly soils on mid or lower slopes from Houwhoek to Bredasdorp. (Jan-Feb).

♣ Other unbranched species include: the widespread coarse *E. fistulosa* of wetlands which is almost unique in having hollow cylindrical stems; the to 1.5m *E. grandispicata* has 50-90mm sheaths; *E. spathacea* has a square tower-like flowerhead; *E. racemosa* has spathes with pale golden margins.

Mastersiella digitata

A tufted perennial with floppy branching stems rising to 30cm high, whose persistent sheaths are tipped with a point. The male flowerheads, grouped a few together, resemble small wheat heads but without the bristles, while the single female flowers, scarcely larger than the enclosing spathe, with 2 styles and one chamber containing one black nutlet harvested by ants. It is locally common on dry sandy, rocky slopes below 400m from the Cape Peninsula to Potberg. It forms a dense ground cover on heavier soils. (Mar-Sept).

♣ There are 3 species, but only this one in our area.

Nevillea obtusissima

A perennial with dull green unbranched erect stems forming clumps a metre or more across, whose persistent sheaths narrow abruptly to a strong tapering point, the male bearing knobbly clubshaped flowerheads, 2-3 at a time, and very contrasting female spikes, with 2-chambered fruits. It occurs on marshy slopes between 300-1000m on the mountains from Elgin and Kleinmond to Hermanus. (Mar).

♣ One more species occurs on the Riviersonderend mountains.

Elegia capensis (Male)

Elegia filacea (Male & Female)

Elegia persistens (Male & Female)

Mastersiella digitata (Male)

Nevillea obtusissima (Male)

77

Restio bifarius

A tufted perennial to 80cm with sparsely branched stems. The female flowers are grouped 1-3 at the tips of erect stems, each flower with 1-2 ovary chambers; the males are borne in abruptly pendulous clusters. It occurs quite commonly on dry mountain slopes between Jonkershoek and Hottentots Holland. In the Kogelberg valley it forms dense (rust-coloured) fields (Apr-May).

♣ *Restio* is the largest genus in the family with 90 species of which c.34 occur in our area, mostly less than 1m tall, mostly tufted, many tangled and many with rough, tubercled, branched stems. *R. bifidus* is similar but occurs in wet seepage areas and the male flowerhead is erect.

Restio dispar

A tufted reed to 2m, with sparsely-branched, slightly warty stems and persistent leafsheaths tightly wrapped around the stems. The slender female flowerheads are enclosed by distinctive long red spathes (right background), each flower with 3 fluffy white styles giving rise to a 1-chambered ovary, while the more arching males are shorter, paler and grouped along the ends of the stems (left foreground). It occurs along streams and among rocks on mountain slopes from the Cape Peninsula and Bain's Kloof to Bredasdorp. (Mar-Apr).

♣ *R. purpurascens* is similarly tall, lanky and from wet areas but has a rough bumpy stem and sheaths. Two are most distinctive with their strong 1-2m tall 4-sided square stems: the taller *R. quadratus* living in seeps and on streambanks; and *R. tetragonus* preferring wet sandy and clayey foothills of the coastal mountains.

Restio egregius

A rather open sparsely-branched, tufted but rather tangled perennial with slightly wavy, coarse stems and persistent sheaths. The male flowers are pendulous groups with pointed bracts. The upright single female heads have firm tapering bracts longer than the flowers, and flowers with 3 styles and a 2-chambered ovary bearing 1 or 2 seeds. It occurs usually below 1000m on mountain slopes from the Cape Peninsula to Villiersdorp and Bredasdorp. (Mar). Male and female are illustrated separately.

Restio perplexus

A fairly common tangled perennial with slender much-branched usually warty stems rising or spreading to 60cm, and tipped with extremely small flowering heads. Often interwoven into surrounding vegetation, as often trailing as erect and then sometimes rooting, it forms shapeless, soft green mats. Growing on rocky mountain slopes often under taller plants in damp places in some shade, it is very common in the Mossel River valley, Hermanus, where it is used as a filler at wild flower shows. It is widespread from the Cold Bokkeveld and Cape Peninsula to the Langeberg. (Aug).

♣ Another tangled plant *R. stokoei* of Stellenbosch to Swellendam flowers in autumn.

Restio bifarius (Male)

Restio dispar (Male & Female)

Restio bifarius (Female)

Restio egregius (Male)

Restio egregius (Female)

Restio perplexus   Anne Bean

ARACEAE – The arum Lily family

Zantedeschia aethiopica
arum lily, pig lily, varkoor

A deciduous stemless soft herb usually to less than 1m tall with swollen rhizomes and large stalked heart shaped leaves with a slimy sap. It has the capacity to remain evergreen as long as the soil remains damp and if growing in enriched water (such as that from a French drain) and especially in the shade, can become extremely tall, to 2m+, with huge flowerheads. The male flowers are arranged on the upper part and the female flowers on the lower half of the yellow spadix, the spathe being snowy white, handsome and long-lasting, the berries turning orange when ripe. The rhizomes are relished by the"iron pig" or porcupine. It is distributed throughout South Africa, favouring seasonally damp places. (June-Dec).

♣ There are 8 species confined more or less to southern Africa, but only this one in our area.

COMMELINACEAE – The spiderwort family

Commelina africana
wandering Jew, wandelende jood

A weak prostrate perennial with well-defined nodes and leaves 3-5cm long by 10-15mm wide, and yellow flowers. It is common on lower slopes or near streams from the Cape Peninsula eastward to KwaZulu-Natal, and throughout the tropics of the Old World. (Nov-June).

♣ There are about 230 species worldwide, of which 12 occur in South Africa, but only this occurs wild in our area. The pretty blue *C. benghalensis* of suburban gardens is an introduced weed of cultivation.

PRIONIACEAE – The palmiet family

Prionium serratum
palmiet

Feast your eyes on this magnificent sight of the Louw's river in the Kogelberg with its pristine palmiet bed. The plants are robust blueish-green shrubs to 2m or more, with sharply serrated leaves resembling giant pineapple tops, crowded at the tops of black netting-covered water-absorbent stems. Rooted into streambeds they mass into extensive stands with interlinked open pools. In the past they quite prevented the scouring and destabilization of river valleys in times of flood, but now are more often found as sad relict individual plants perched high and dry above the water line (and marking the position of the old water table) due to burning and other destruction wrought by man in his misguided attempts to channel floodwater away in the quickest manner. Left undamaged, the plant allows the water to flow through its mass, or even entirely to submerge the palmiet beds while leaving the ecosystem pristine. It was once widely distributed from the Gifberg to S. KwaZulu-Natal along the coastal mountains and rivers, but now sadly diminished. (Sept-Feb).

A detail of the plant with flowering heads displays the masses of small brown florets carried on strong stems raised above the leaves.

80

Commelina africana

Zantedeschia aethiopica

Prionium serratum

81

COLCHICACEAE

Androcymbium eucomoides patrysblom, men-in-a-boat

Stemless geophytes with long-lived corms, and lance-shaped tapering spreading 6-40cm long leaves. Oval whitish or greenish bracts incurve to conceal the 2-7 sour-smelling flowers which are 12-18mm long and produce nectar. The pollination agent is still not known, but could be mice. It grows on clay flats from Namaqualand to the Eastern Cape. (July-Aug).

♣ There are c.40 species One other here, *A. capensis*, has large white bracts sometimes with green stripes.

Baeometra uniflora beetle lily

A cormous geophyte to 25cm with 5-8 lance-shaped leaves attached along the stem, and sessile or short-stalked flowers facing upwards in a group of 1-5. The unscented flowers are cupped, the 15-28mm long tepals yellow-orange within with a black eye, the reverse reddish, 6 stamens, a three-chambered superior ovary and three short hooklike styles. The pollinators are monkey beetles which eat pollen and not nectar; the flowers being without nectaries. It grows on rocky sandstone or granite slopes from Malmesbury to Riversdale. (Aug-Oct).

♣ This is the only species in the genus.

Onixotis punctata water phlox, hanekammetjie

A cormous, usually 3-leaved geophyte with flat leaves 6-10cm long and 4-6mm wide, 2 at ground level and 1 raised up on the stem. It bears 5-20 white or maroon flowers, with or without pink spots, on a stem up to 30cm tall. It is recorded on flats and slopes from Ceres to Swellendam, in greatest abundance after veld-fires. (July-Sept).

♣ There are 2 species, the other being the marsh-loving pink *O. stricta* (= *triquetra*) with 3-sided leaves.

Wurmbea spicata spike lily, peper-en-sout blommetjie

A cormous geophyte with 3-channelled, basal leaves up to 20cm long. The unbranched, 5-20cm long flowering stem bears a spike of almost stalkless flowers, with the tepals joined into a tube below. It has a 3-forked style, and 6 stamens attached high up on the tepals in association with raised, fleshy, nectar glands. The corm is said to be poisonous, and the flowers are wonderfully scented in the evening. It occurs from the Gifberg and Nieuwoudtville to the Cape Peninsula and on to Swellendam. (Aug-Nov).

♣ There are about 37 species in Africa and Australia of which some 7 occur in this area. Two are foul smelling: *W. variabilis* has cream-coloured flowers and oval leaves; *W. marginata* on heavier soils has sombrely dark-coloured, crowded flowers. *W. recurva* of Somerset West also has red-purple-brownish tepals but they are bent backwards. Three are variously pale, *W. capensis* is cream and brown with long narrow leaves and hooked styles; two have dark-edged tepals: *W. monopetala* has flowers rather far apart and thin leaves; *W. inusta* is fragrant, with broad sheathing leaves and a dark band of colour across the middle of the tepals.

Androcymbium eucomoides

Baeometra uniflora   John Manning

Onixotis punctata

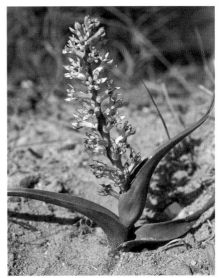

Wurmbea spicata

83

ASPHODELACEAE – The Aloe family

Aloe perfoliata *(=A. mitriformis)* — mitre aloe, kransaalwyn

A coarse, sprawling, branching succulent shrub with dark green compact coarsely-toothed leaves of which only the terminal ones face upwards. The flowering stalk is up to 5-branched, each branch ending in a dense usually rounded head of long, narrow tubular flowers varying from dull to bright red. It is most at home on flat rock sheets from Nieuwoudtville to Kleinmond, but is mostly flound in the northern part of our area. (Dec-Feb).

♣ There are about 500 species of *Aloe* widespread in Africa, the Middle East, Socotra and Madagascar and naturalized widely elsewhere, about 130 in Southern Africa but only four in the area of this book.

Aloe plicatilis — fan aloe, bergaalwyn

A coarse branching shrub or tree up to 5m with the terminal clusters of broad, blunt grey-green fleshy leaves arranged in a fan. The glossy scarlet flowers are borne on a raceme of c. 30 per leaf cluster. It is local in rocky sandstone on high mountains from Elandskloof to Jonkershoek. (Aug-Oct).

♣ It has no relatives among the aloes, although the dwarf *A. haemanthifolia*, which also grows on high mountain peaks in the Jonkershoek area, has similar leaves at ground level, and a rounded head of orange-red flowers. (Sept-Dec.).

Aloe succotrina — bergaalwyn

A succulent, branching shrub to 1m+, forming large clumps, whose stiff dull grey-green leaves have a white, prickly edge. The usually unbranched flowerstalk. up to 1m long, bears bright red tubular flowers up to 4cm long, the buds at first erect, but hanging when open. It is restricted to rocky sandstone slopes between the Cape Peninsula, Hangklip and Hermanus. (Jul-Aug).

Bulbine lagopus — kopieva

A tufted geophyte to 40cm with wiry roots and a tuft of narrow, basal leaves. The yellow flowers, each lasting only one day, are crowded in a long raceme on an un-branched flowering stalk. Each has 6 free spreading tepals, 6 hairy stamens, and the 3-chambered superior ovary gives rise to an upright globose dry capsule. It grows on rocky slopes from the Gifberg to the Cape and on to Lesotho. (Jul-Dec).

♣ Of the 50 species in Africa, four more occur here. All have salmon or yellow flowers. 2 bloom and leaf together in the latter half of the year: the annual *B. annua* of sandy coastal area with crowded cylindrical leaves and crowded flowers, and *B. praemorsa* of rocky slopes, with spaced flowers and thick, fleshy, channelled leaves. Two bloom in autumn with dry leaves, the scented *B. favosa* of sandy and limy flats, with spaced flowers; and *B. cepacea* of stony flats with unscented, crowded flowers.

Bulbinella nutans — katstert

Geophytes to 1m tall with 5-13 bright green leaves, the peripheral ones up to 25mm wide, the inner ones narrower. The flowers are white or yellow, unscented and long-lasting, so many are open simultaneously. Each flower has 6 free tepals, 6 unbearded stamens and a superior 3-chambered ovary. It favours damp, peaty soil from Namaqualand to Swellendam. (Jul-Oct).

♣ About 19 species occur in South Africa and New Zealand, of which 4 more are recorded in our area. The yellow-flowered *B. divaginata* of clay soils, without leaves and the white flowered *B. trinervis* bloom in autumn; and the spring-blooming white, pink tinged *B. caudafelis* and the bright yellow flowered, *B. triquetra* of damp places.

Aloe perfoliata

Bulbine lagopus

Aloe plicatilis

Aloe succotrina   Christine Wakfer

Bulbinella nutans

85

Kniphofia uvaria   red hot poker

A fleshy-rooted rhizomatous clumped perennial, 50-120cm tall, with strap-shaped, fibrous-textured leaves, V-shaped in cross-section. Long leafless stems are tipped with oval racemes of crowded, tubular, orange to greenish yellow, slightly pendant flowers. It is common in wet places on sandstone slopes from Namaqualand to the Karoo. (Oct-Dec).

♣ 65 species occur in Africa and the Middle East, but only two grow in our area. Both flower most abundantly after a veld fire.

Kniphofia tabularis   red hot poker

A fleshy-rooted rhizomatous clumped perennial 60-120cm tall with slightly fleshy strap-shaped leaves, V-shaped in cross-section. Long leafless stems terminate in elongated racemes of black-tipped red to orange tubular flowers, less crowded than those of the previous species. It is local from Tulbagh to the Hottentots' Holland mountains on wet cliffs and kloofs. (Dec-Jan).

 There are about 50 species of ***Trachyandra*** in Africa, of which 46 occur in South Africa and c. 10 in this area. All have short-lived white flowers on a stalk with an inconspicuous joint just under the flower. As the flower withers, the six tepals and anthers detach at this joint, leaving the ovary exposed.

Trachyandra hirsuta

A perennial with a fan of stiff, hairy, flat leaves 7-40cm long and 5-20mm wide, and a branched flowering stem to 60cm. The hairless flowers with free tepals are 10-12mm long. It occurs on lower mountain slopes or flats usually in renosterveld, sometimes in marshes, from Piketberg to the Cape Peninsula and Caledon. (Sept-Oct).

♣ Two more species have sparingly branched stems: *T. tabularis* of sandy flats with flowers on an ascending raceme and 9mm long fruits; and the edible trailing usually hairy *T. ciliata*[1] on damp sandy flats, with soft, spongy, straggling channelled leaves, conspicuous bracts and pods on down-turned stalks. A further two species are well-branched and wide-spreading: *T. divaricata* of coastal dunes and flats, with smooth fleshy leaves; and *T. revoluta* with linear, rough-textured leaves.

Trachyandra hirsutiflora   starlily

 A harshly hairy perennial with narrow leaves up to 60cm long and 2mm wide has an unbranched flowering stem shorter than the leaves. The densely hairy, 12mm long flowers with 6 free tepals are followed by very hairy, oval, erect pods. It occurs on sandy or rocky flats and slopes from Clanwilliam to Caledon. (June-Dec).

♣ In our area four further species with unbranched stems have been recorded: *T. hispida* with a few lance-shaped leaves; *T. filiformis* with few, narrow leaves sometimes mottled near the base; *T. sabulosa* with many narrow leaves which, with the stems, are roughly hairy, and knobbly long-stalked fruits; *T. esterhuyseniae* of sandstone seeps above 600m (Dec-Feb) has 1-2 stiff, narrow leaves, round in cross-section.

Kniphofia uvaria

Kniphofia tabularis

Trachyandra hirsuta

Trachyandra hirsutiflora

ANTHERICACEAE – The grass lily family

Caesia contorta   sokkiesblom, blue grass lily

A rhizomatous geophyte up to 30cm tall with untidy sprawling stems and strap-shaped leaves. The small nodding blue flowers with rough filaments striped blue and white are carried in open racemes, the tepals twisting as they fade. It occurs on flats and slopes up to high parts from Namaqualand to the Eastern Cape. (Nov-Mar).

♣ Two more species occur in the Cape but not in our area.

Chlorophytum undulatum   grass lily

A geophyte to 50cm whose stiff roots sometimes bear short tubers. The lance-shaped leaves have hairy edges, and the flowering stalk is usually unbranched. White flowers with red mid-region have stalks jointed in the middle and produce a three-winged capsule. It occurs on stony flats and slopes from Namaqualand to Somerset West. (Jul-Oct).

1

♣ There are about 90 species, mainly in tropical Africa and Asia, of which 1 other, the gifkool, *C. rigidum*[1] occurring in the west of our area, is distinguished by short stiff hairless leaves and flowerstalks jointed near the base.

ERIOSPERMACEAE – The cotton seed family

Eriospermum cernuum[1]

The inconspicuous flowering stem, up to c. 35cm high, appears without leaves straight out of the dry earth in the hot months. The flowers comprise a raceme of cup-shaped white flowers with erect stamens. Later a single leaf, erect lance- to heart-shaped, sometimes red-edged, arises directly from the ground. The common name for the family refers to the cotton-like long white hairs covering the seed. The tubers are important for identification. Found in damp, sandy places from Clanwilliam to Bredasdorp. (Feb-Apr).

♣ The erect lancelike leaf of *E. dielsianum*[2] differs in being hairy. The blueish erect leaf of *E. lanceifolium*[4] is up to 40mm tall, sword-shaped and leathery with wavy, sometimes hairy edges; *E. nanum*[5] has a spreading heart-shaped leaf; the renosterveld species, *E. pubescens*[6] has a heart-shaped leaf flat on the ground, with straight hairs pressed to its surface; the leaf of the dwarf *E. spirale* of the False Bay coast is a narrow cylinder; *E. schlechteri*[3] of Kogelberg to Shaw's mountain has an erect, elliptic, ribbed leaf and bright yellow flowers; *E. capense* of clay soils has a spreading heart-shaped leaf often with red ridges and a hairy edge.

ALLIACEAE – The onion family

Tulbaghia alliacea   wild garlic

This clump-forming, rhizomatous geophyte to 30cm high has brownish to green tepals 8-10mm long united into a tube more than half way, the mouth ornamented by a fleshy cylindrical slightly irregular orange corona, the stalked flowers being borne on a long flowerhead stalk rather ahead of the emerging linear leaves. At night the flowers are honey-coconut scented. It occurs throughout southern Africa, and is widespread on clayey or gravelly soil. (Mar-May).

♣ In the similar *T. capensis* of rocky slopes the corona has 6 lobes.

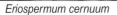

Caesia contorta
John Manning

Chlorophytum undulatum

Eriospermum cernuum

Tulbaghia alliacea
John Manning

HYACINTHACEAE – The Hyacinth family

Drimia filifolia

A bulbous geophyte with one to several erect quill-like leathery leaves present at flowering time and about the same length as the flowering stalk. They emerge from a conspicuously striped sheath. The cupped flowers are white, sometimes flushed purple, with all parts in three's and a superior ovary. It occurs on usually moist sandy slopes and flats from Namaqualand to Swellendam.

♣ Two more have leaves present at flowering time: the leaves of the 1m tall fragrant widespread *D. exuviata* equal the raceme in height and are grey and leathery; the tepals of the lightly scented 30cm tall *D. hesperantha* bend backwards and open at night.

*Drimia media (*incl. *Tenicroa, Urginea)* jeukbol

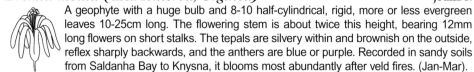

A geophyte with a huge bulb and 8-10 half-cylindrical, rigid, more or less evergreen leaves 10-25cm long. The flowering stem is about twice this height, bearing 12mm long flowers on short stalks. The tepals are silvery within and brownish on the outside, reflex sharply backwards, and the anthers are blue or purple. Recorded in sandy soils from Saldanha Bay to Knysna, it blooms most abundantly after veld fires. (Jan-Mar).

♣ There are about 60 species in South Africa of which 7 occur in this area. Three are more or less leafless at flowering time: *D. elata*, 50-90cm tall, has lance-shaped leaves that are often hairy on the margins and white, green or purple flowers 15mm long on stalks only a little shorter than the flowers and similar anthers; the 30cm tall *D. dregei* with one leaf dry at flowering time, whose crowded flowers with reflexed tepals open in the morning; and the 25cm *D. salteri* whose short-stalked flowers open at night and close at mid-morning.

Lachenalia montana

A bulbous geophyte to 33cm high, with two thin straight unspotted leaves folded upwards quite tightly together. The slightly pendant, cream and green bell-shaped flowers are crowded densely together on pinkish stalks, the inner tepals rather longer than the outer and the anthers protruding. Occurring from Franschhoek to Hermanus on sandy mountain slopes it normally blooms in masses only after fire. (Oct.-Dec.).

♣ There are 85 species distributed throughout the Cape Province, the southern Orange Free State and Namibia, of which 14 occur in our vicinity.

Lachenalia orchioides wild hyacinth, greenviooltjie

A bulbous geophyte 12-25cm tall, the usually spotted stem bearing 2 erect leaves up to 25mm wide. The cream to yellow-green or blue-purple, sessile flowers are sweetly-scented and borne in a crowded head, the tepals concealing the stamens and style. It occurs in slightly shaded places on a variety of soils from the Cedarberg to the Cape Peninsula and on to the Gourits River. (June-Sept).

♣ The sessile flowers of the similarly coloured heavily scented *L. fistulosa* are bell-shaped and face outwards, while *L. contaminata* with similar flowers is distinguished by its many grasslike leaves.

Drimia filifolia

Drimia media

Lachenalia orchioides

Lachenalia montana   Graham Duncan

91

Lachenalia peersii bekkies

A bulbous geophyte, to 35cm tall, with 1 or 2 leaves up to 20mm wide and often tinged maroon below. The carnation-scented bell-shaped 7-10mm long flowers are white with pink tips fading deeper pink. The outer tepals are slightly shorter than the inner ones and often green-tipped. It is common on rocky flats and slopes from Cape Hangklip to Hermanus. (Oct-Nov).

♣ It may be confused with variable blue to rose pink *L. rosea* which has 1 strap-shaped leaf and stamens visible at the mouth of the flower.

Lachenalia rubida bergnaeltjie, sandkalossie

A bulbous geophyte, 6-25cm tall, clasped at the base by 1 or 2, 150mm by 25mm leaves, sometimes spotted green or purple and often broadest in the upper half, but tapering abruptly into a V-shaped tip. The flowers, short-stalked, cylindrical, slightly drooping, 22-30mm long, coral to red, and grouped 6-20 together, usually appear a little ahead of the leaves. The outer tepals are only $3/4$ the length of the inner ones, and are tipped with yellowish-green or pinkish swellings; the inner are spotted or purple-tipped with white markings. The style eventually projects. It occurs on sandy soils from Lamberts Bay to the Cape Peninsula and east to George. (Mar-Sept).

♣ The very similar but more robust *L. bulbifera* has similar spotted to unspotted leaves, blooms from April on, its outer tepals equal the inner or are only very slightly shorter and have dark red or brown swellings while the inner are green-tipped, flanked by two purple zones.

Ornithogalum dubium yellow chincherinchee

A bulbous geophyte 10-50cm high with 3-8 hairy-edged, 5-20cm by 5-30mm leaves which appear before the flowers but often wither as they unfurl. The 10-20 flowers may be yellow, orange or white, and are 10-20mm long with a dark-coloured, very short style. It is a variable, widespread, and locally common plant of rocky slopes, stony clay, or sandy flats from Clanwilliam to Paarl, and Caledon to Port Elizabeth and the eastern Cape. (Aug-Dec).

♣ There are about 120 species in Africa and Eurasia, of which 8 occur in this area. *O. graminifolium*, on moist, stony mountain slopes, with dull white flowers in our area, (yellow or pink elsewhere), has 2-5 grasslike leaves up to 25cm long, and forming a brittle thin neck; the montane, white-flowered rough chink *O. hispidum*, has wiry, bristly-edged leaves; in both these species the leaves are dry at flowering time.

Ornithogalum thyrsoides chincherinchee, tjienkerientjee

A bulbous geophyte with up to 7 basal leaves 15-30cm long usually present but sometimes drying at flowering time. The flowering stems grow to about 50cm, and bear a variable number of white flowers, 3-6cm across, with or without a dark eye, and subtended by broad papery bracts. This species is commercially valuable in the export cut-flower trade because of its long-lasting qualities, but is extremely poisonous to livestock. It is recorded on lower slopes and sand flats from Namaqualand to Caledon, sometimes in large colonies.

♣ There are 4 other white-flowered species having leaves contemporary with the flowers. The straggling small *O. schlechterianum* of upper damp rock ledges has 3-10 soft spreading leaves. The rest are erect plants. They are the broad-leafed *O. esterhuyseniae* of high altitudes in the Hottentots Holland mountains; the widespread faintly honey-scented *O. juncifolium* has smaller flowers in a dense spike and has, like *O. dregeanum*, erect, strongly ribbed leaves, the latter being distinguished by orange-spotted sheaths on the neck of the bulb.

Lachenalia peersii

Lachenalia rubida

Ornithogalum thyrsoides

Ornithogalum dubium

93

Albuca flaccida (*=canadensis*)   soldier-in-a-box, geldbeursie

A bulbous geophyte 40-100cm high with 3-6 broad, channelled, soft leaves 20-60cm long by 1-3cm broad, clasping towards the base and withering at flowering-time. The flowering stem bears lightly fragrant, pendant yellow flowers, sometimes with green keels, 20-25mm long. The 3 spreading outer lobes and the 3 erect inner lobes with their hinged flaps at the top enclose the 3 fertile and 3 sterile stamens: the "soldiers"; the ovary is 3-chambered. It occurs most commonly in coastal sands on flats and lower slopes from Namaqualand to the Hermanus area. (Aug-Oct).

♣ There are about 60 species from Africa to Arabia and c.28 in southern Africa, of which 5 occur in our area. All here have yellow and green drooping flowers. The 1m tall *A. fragrans* has a faintly sweet scent and is the only one here with 6 fertile stamens; *A. cooperi*, yellow with green keels, has the old leaves forming a fibrous wrapping around the neck of the bulb, *A. juncifolia* has 4-10 stiff quill-like leaves and *A. echinosperma* resembles *A. flaccida* but is delicate with 1-3 leaves and warty seeds.

ASPARAGACEAE - The Asparagus family

Asparagus aethiopicus   haakdoring

A variable plant which may be a woody climber to 7m, or an erect shrub to 1m. It has narrow flat leaves in groups of 4-6, each leaf 1-4cm by 1-2mm. Hooked spines are present on all nodes, except sometimes on the flowering stems. The very sweetly scented flowers, some 7mm across, are borne in 3-5cm long racemes and give rise to red berries. It occurs in coastal forest and dryish bush from Namaqualand to the Transkei. (Jan-June).

Asparagus rubicundus   wild asparagus, wag-'n-bietjie

A fibrous-rooted, hairless shrub with smooth, glossy dark stems which can grow to 1.5m in height, especially in shade. Sharp slightly curving spines to 6mm long occur on all but the flowering branches. The 6mm long flowers, 1-2 in the axils of the bundle of 10, 3-20mm long needlelike leaves, give rise to red berries. It is widespread on sandy or granite slopes from Clanwilliam to Uitenhage. (Jan-June).

♣ Three other tall species in this area have similarly arranged flowers and needle-like leaves, *A. exuvialis* with minute spines, a white, membranous bark and flowers in groups of 2-6; the 3m scrambling *A. retrofractus* with spreading spines and grey stems, ribbed when young; the spiny climber *A. africanus*, to 3m, preferring moist places, with spreading brown spines and up to 6 flowers in a cluster.

Asparagus scandens   asparagus 'fern'

A soft scrambling non-spiny shrublet to 2m with flattened cladodes, 3 arranged in one plane, two together and one opposing. The long-stalked flowers are borne 1-3 in the angles of the cladodes, and are followed by orange berries. It is widespread in shade in bush and forest from the Gifberg to the Tsitsikamma mountains. (Sept-Jan).

Albuca flaccida

Asparagus aethiopicus

Asparagus rubicundus

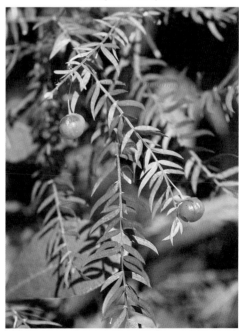

Asparagus scandens

HAEMODORACEAE – The bloodroot or kangaroo-paw family

Dilatris pillansii
rooiwortel

A perennial with bright red basal parts and a fan of stiff leaves up to 30cm long and 3-5mm broad. The softly-hairy pink flowers have round-tipped tepals up to 10mm long and about 6mm broad. The 3 stamens are well inside the tepals and the 3-chambered ovary is inferior. Recorded from the Cedarberg to Worcester and Bredasdorp, it blooms profusely after fires. (Aug-Jan).

♣ There are 4 species endemic to the South Western Cape, of which 3 occur in this area: the very similar *D. corymbosa* has pointed tepals, 2 of the stamens projecting beyond them.

Dilatris viscosa
A perennial to 60cm tall with reddish basal parts and a fan of hairless leaves, much shorter than the flowering stem. The sticky, hairy, orange flowers are arranged in a rounded head which can be 10cm wide, each flower being about 13mm long. It is recorded in swamps or high mountain slopes in the summer cloud belt from Ceres to Riversdale. (Aug-Dec).

Wachendorfia paniculata
rooikanol, spinnekopblom

A slender more or less hairy perennial, to 70cm high, with reddish, tuberous roots and a fan of pleated leaves up to 40cm long, as long as or shorter than the flowering stem. The yellow flowers are up to 25mm long and often have dark markings. Bracts are papery. One of the 3 stamens grows in a direction opposite from the off-centre style, which is possibly an arrangement to reduce self-pollination. The 3-chambered ovary has one seed per chamber. Flowering abundantly after fire. It is recorded in well-drained sands and coarse gravels from Clanwilliam to Port Elizabeth. (Sept-Oct).

♣ There are 4 species endemic to the fynbos, all occurring in our area: *W. multiflora* is half as tall with green bracts and leaves longer than the stem; *W. brachyandra* has stamens much shorter than the tepals and grows in moist places.

Wachendorfia thyrsiflora
A perennial with reddish tuberous roots, growing to well over 1m in height, with a fan of hairless, pleated leaves 60-90cm long and 5-9mm wide. The bright golden hairy flowers with 6 tepals and three equal-sized stamens are borne in crowded clusters on delicate side shoots of a thick hairy, unbranched stem. It is found in marshes and wet kloofs from the Cape Peninsula to Port Elizabeth, often in dense stands. (Sept-Dec).

LANARIACEAE – The Lanaria family

Lanaria lanata
cape edelweiss, perdekapokblom

A perennial to 80cm with a rosette of stiff, pleated, ribbed, narrow leaves from a fire-resistant, thick-rooted, black rootstock, and a densely woolly white head of flowers which are mauve within, with 6 tepals and stamens and a 3-chambered capsular fruit with one seed per chamber. Common and widespread on mountain slopes from the Hottentots Holland to Port Elizabeth, it is not conspicuous except after a veld-fire, when it blooms promptly and profusely looking like blobs of snow. (Nov-Jan).

Dilatris viscosa pillansii

Dilatris pillansii viscosa

Wachendorfia paniculata

Lanaria lanata

Wachendorfia thyrsiflora

AMARYLLIDACEAE – The Amaryllis or Daffodil family

Amaryllis belladonna
march lily, belladonna lily, maartblom

A bulbous geophyte with a leafless flowering stem 40-90cm long, bearing 2-10 trumpet-shaped, heavily-scented flowers in various shades of pink to near white. There are 6-10 strap-shaped floppy leaves 20-60cm long and 2-4cm wide, produced after the flowers. Occurring at lower altitudes on slopes of mountains and hills, it blooms as the vernacular name suggests, in autumn, not only but especially after veld fires, and is confined to the South Western Cape. (Feb-Apr).

♣ There is one more species recently discovered in the Richtersveld.

Brunsvigia orientalis
candelabra flower, koningskandelaar, perdespookbossie

A bulbous geophyte up to 50cm tall bearing a head of many asymmetrical flowers 5-6cm long with the lobes turning back in the upper half. They are followed by the familiar dry, detached fruiting heads, which scatter the seeds as they roll about in the wind, hence the common names. After flowering, about 4 tongue-shaped, closely-ribbed leaves 15-23cm long by 7-12cm wide emerge and spread out along the ground. It is locally common on sandy flats on the coastal plains between Saldanha Bay and Knysna. (Feb-Apr). Pollination is by sunbirds.

♣ There are c. 20 species confined to southern Africa, but only one in our area.

Cyrtanthus leucanthus
witbergpypie

A bulbous geophyte with a hollow flowering stem up to 25cm long, bearing up to 3 pale cream scented flowers, each 4cm long. The leaves are 2/3 as long as the stem and 1mm wide, appearing after the flowers are over. It seldom flowers except in the first season after a veld fire, and occurs on sandy and rocky flats in the Caledon district. (Jan-Mar).

♣ There are about 50 species in Africa, most of which occur in southern Africa and four in this area. This is the only cream-flowered species in the area and is probably pollinated by moths. Exceptionally in the family, black seeds are produced in this genus.

Cyrtanthus carneus
fire lily

The magnificent and robust geophyte with hollow flower stalks towering above the leaves and up to 1m tall, has 15-25 narrow, flaring large soft pink to crimson flowers up to 75mm long. Up to 10 suberect, 2-6cm wide strap-shaped slightly twisted leaves are usually green at flowering time. It occurs on coastal sands and sandy lower mountain slopes from our area to Mossel Bay and probably blooms only after a fire. (Dec-Feb). It might be sunbird pollinated.

Cyrtanthus ventricosus
fire lily

A bulbous perennial with leaves dry at flowering time, and 2-12 hanging, flaring tubular red flowers, 4-5cm long, sometimes with pink lobes, on a hollow 10-20cm stalk. It occurs on south-facing sandy slopes from the Cape Peninsula to the Baviaanskloof mountains. (Dec-May).

♣ The half-metre tall *C. angustifolius*, often with bulbs in clumps, has drooping 4-5cm long red flowers, yellow in the throat, and 2-4 strap-shaped 7-15mm wide suberect leaves dry or green at flowering time, grows in seasonal vleis and streams on mountain slopes from the Cedarberg to Port Elizabeth in the warmer months, especially after a fire. Both are probably pollinated by the butterfly *Aeropetes tulbaghia*.

Amaryllis belladonna

Brunsvigia orientalis

Cyrtanthus carneus

Cyrtanthus leucanthus

Cyrtanthus ventricosus

99

Strumaria spiralis wire lily

A diminutive geophyte 4-27cm high, with a wiry stem which is coiledbelow, and 4-6 threadlike shiny, sometimes spiral spreading leaves. The 1-4 flowers are short-lived, small, have a 3mm long funnel, face upwards, and are white or pink. It occurs on seasonally wet flats and in rock crevices from the Cape Peninsula to Heidelberg and Oudtshoorn. (May-Aug).

♣ There are 23 species, but only 2 in our area.

Strumaria tenella cape snowflake, tolbol

A bulbous geophyte c. 15cm high with 3-6 smooth narrow leaves which are green at flowering time. The 2-14 starlike white to pink, scented flowers, 6-12mm across, have 6 wide-spreading tepals and a style with a swollen base. In the illustration, the few, typically fat, fast-developing seeds can be seen within the distended ovary. As with others in this family, these must be planted as soon as they are ripe, as they cannot be stored. It occurs on seasonally damp, loamy flats from the Bokkeveld to the Peninsula and Montagu, and the Free State. (Apr-Jul).

Haemanthus canaliculatus

A very local, brilliant red to pink species with 6-20mm wide spathe bracts tapering upwards. The leaves, appearing after flowering, are smooth, usually upstanding, less than 3cm wide, 17-40cm long, and deeply channelled above. It is confined to marshes from Rooi Els to Betty's Bay and flowers only after a veld fire. (Flowers Feb-Mar, leaves May-Dec).

Haemanthus coccineus [1] april fool, blood flower, bergajuin

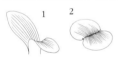

A bulbous geophyte with a speckled and barred flowering stem 6-20cm long. At the apex, a crowded group of red flowers is cupped by matching, overlapping, upstanding spathe bracts, 15-48mm broad. After flowering is over, 2 leathery, smooth, broad tongue-shaped leaves 2-21cm wide appear, curving out and downwards, following the fruiting stem to the ground with its contained mucilaginous round seeds. It occurs in forest, scrub and open veld from sea level on the beach to the lower mountain slopes from Namaqualand to the eastern Cape. (flowers Feb-Apr, leaves April-Oct).

♣ There are about 22 species endemic to southern Africa, of which 4 occur in this area. *H sanguineus* [2] *(=H. rotundifolius)* has rough-textured, unspeckled stems, crowded pink or red flowerheads, and leaves pressed flat to the ground, usually broader than long, appearing after flowering is over. The slender, bright red to pale-pink flowered *H. pumilio* can be found in the Stellenbosch district in seasonally waterlogged clay flats after a veld fire. Pollinators are not certainly known, with bees, butterflies and even ants visiting the flowers.

Hessea monticola

A bulbous geophyte to 25cm high with 2 strap-shaped leaves 1.5-3mm wide, which are dry at flowering time. Each flowering stalk supports 10-30 unpleasantly scented white to pink flowers with pink stripes down the throat. Each tepal is c.10-25mm long with a frilly edge. It occurs in seasonally wet rocky slopes or valleys from Cedarberg and Piketberg to the Riviersonderend mountains and flowers especially well after veld fires. (Mar-May).

♣ There are 14 species confined to southern Africa, but only this species in our area.

Strumaria spiralis

Haemanthus canaliculatus

Strumaria tenella

Haemanthus coccineus

Hessea monticola

101

Nerine sarniensis Guernsey lily, berglelie

A bulbous geophyte, with about 6 strap-shaped leaves 25-45cm long and 12-28mm broad, produced after the flowers. The flowers are bright scarlet (occasionally pink) and gold-dusted, about 4cm long, and borne on slightly flattened stalks. The colour of the bracts matches that of the flowers. It occurs on rocky mountain slopes from Clanwilliam to Caledon. (Mar-May).

♣ There are about 30 species widespread in South Africa, with innumerable garden hybrids, but there is only one other species in this area: *N. humilis*, whose pink or rosy flowers have green bracts, the stamens and style curving to one side, and leaves contemporary with the flowers.

AGAPANTHACEAE – The Agapanthus family

Agapanthus africanus bloulelie

An evergreen perennial 25-70cm tall with numerous thick strap-shaped leaves 10-25cm long and 9-12mm broad with mucilaginous sap. The flowers, 12-30, trumpet-shaped 25-40mm long and outward-facing are borne in a large head at the end of an unbranched stem. Common, especially in rocky places on mountains, it occurs from the Cape Peninsula to Swellendam and blooms especially profusely after veld fires. (Dec-Apr).

♣ There are two species in our area.

Agapanthus walshii bloulelie

An evergreen perennial to 70cm high with fleshy rhizomatous roots and rather short erect mucilaginous leaves. The many flowers hanging bell-like from the inflorescence stalk are narrow with slightly flaring mouths, up to 55mm long and vary in colour from pale to deep blue, occasionally white. It is rare on rocky sandstone parts of the Steenbras mountains and flowers profusely only after fire. (Jan-Feb).

HYPOXIDACEAE – The star flower family

Spiloxene capensis peacock flower, poublommetjie, sterretjie

A very variable cormous geophyte whose 4-12 leaves are Y-shaped in cross-section in the upper half. The solitary yellow, pink or white flowers on hollow stalks are enormously variable in size from 15-100mm across, sometimes with an iridescent dark centre, as shown here. There are 6 tepals and stamens and usually 3 chambers in the inferior ovary. It occurs in many kinds of habitat from Clanwilliam to Humansdorp. (Aug-Oct).

♣ There are about 30 species in the fynbos and Namaqualand regions of South Africa, of which 7 occur in this area. Two others bloom in the latter half of the year: *S. aquatica* of vleis and marshes with 2-7 white flowers per stem; and *S. flaccida* on rocky damp flats and slopes, with 1-3 yellow flowers on a solid stem. Three bloom from late summer into autumn: *S. curculigoides* with single lemon yellow flowers with a green reverse and 3-5 erect narrow leaves grow in seasonally damp places and among rocks; *S. monophylla* of Kogelberg to Elim with single narrow spreading leaf and single yellow flowers with pale green reverse, at ground level after fires; and the clump-forming *S. alba*, in damp places from Ceres to Hermanus, with 2 usually white but occasionally cream flowers per stalk, whose 2-5 erect succulent leaves elongate after flowering time. (Apr-June). Lastly, *S. schlechteri* of marshy flats with firm upright almost reedlike leaves and leaflike sheathing bracts and 1-2 yellow flowers with green or reddish reverse, borne on a 6-9cm long stalk. (Jun-Aug).

Nerine sarniensis

Agapanthus africanus

Spiloxene capensis
Spiloxene capensis
yellow

Agapanthus walshii

103

IRIDACEAE – The Iris family

The fibrous-rooted, evergreen slightly woody genus **Aristea**, blousuurkol, has crowded, smooth, firm, narrow, flattened or cylindrical leaves arranged like a fan. Blue (occasionally white), regular flowers, are borne in clusters up a branched or unbranched stem, each flower lasting only one day but several appearing successively over time from enclosing sheaths (spathes), the flower twisting on fading. The majority are pollinated by pollen-collecting bees, open early and are over by about midday. There are 50 species in sub-Saharan Africa and Madagascar, 33 of which occur in the Cape and 17 in this area.

Aristea africana
A low-growing clumped perennial 10-15cm high with narrow leaves 2-4mm wide. The stems are flattened and either unbranched or dichotomously branched, bearing diverging heads of typical blue flowers. These emerge from most distinctive green spathes and bracts whose edges are translucent and deeply curly-fringed. The flower has 3+3 tepals, 3 stamens and a 3-chambered inferior ovary. The stigma is 3-lobed and fringed. It grows on sandy flats and slopes from the Gifberg to Bredasdorp and Riversdale. (Oct-Jan).

♣ The slightly taller *A. recisa* has short rusty coloured fringed bracts and spathes, and soft sword-shaped leaves. Other short species with stems flattened in the lower parts and dichotomously branched are the cushion-forming *A. dichotoma* with narrow blue-green leaves; the diffusely growing *A. glauca* with strongly flattened stems which are winged below the flowers; and *A. oligocephala* with stems dichotomously branched and slightly flattened (elliptical in cross-section), narrow stiffly erect leaves, strikingly silvery translucent bracts, and spathes with broad green keels folded in the midline.

Aristea biflora
An evergreen tufted perennial to 40cm high whose unbranched stems bear flower clusters along their length, and narrow flat leaves. The lilac or purple flowers are flat and c. 60mm across, the inner with translucent bronze windows, and 3-lobed stigmas. It occurs in loamy clay in renosterveld in the Caledon district. (Aug-Oct).

♣ Another with large flowers, *A. lugens* of the Stellenbosch area, has mauve and white flowers with outer tepals dark blue-black.

Aristea juncifolia
A fairly slender plant with 6-11 cylindrical, tough, rush-like leaves up to 30cm long, stems round in cross-section and usually unbranched. The stalkless dark blue flowers are borne in few-flowered clusters along the stem and emerge from rusty-brown bracts/spathes prominently keeled above and folded along the midline below. It occurs in sandy mountain soils from Paarl to George. (Oct-Jan).

♣ Three other species in this area have cylindrical leaves: *A. racemosa* with dry-membranous bracts; and *A. zeyheri*, 2-3 leaves, green bracts and mostly terminal flower clusters. The tufted 50cm tall, pale blue *A. simplex* of Stellenbosch clay flats with stems oval in cross-section has flattened leaves, green spathes, and grows in renosterveld.

Aristea spiralis
Basal scimitar-shaped leaves up to 30cm long form clumps with flattened, 2-winged, usually unbranched flowering stems up to 50cm long, bearing the exceptionally large flowers, up to 30mm long greenish-white to pale blue, lilac, or deep blue along the upper parts. These emerge from wide brown or green papery-edged bracts and are particularly conspicuous at dusk, and after veld fires. It is the only *Aristea* to produce nectar and is pollinated by a long-tongued horsefly. It occurs in sandy places on mountain slopes from the Cape Peninsula to Willowmore. (Sept-Jan).

♣ A shorter clumped perennial, *A. cantharophila*, has narrow leaves, unbranched stems 20-40cm high, and lilac to cream-coloured flowers with a dark centre which are open all day. It is one of a few species pollinated by monkey beetles and occurs on clay or granite soils from Kuils River, Sir Lowry's Pass, Greyton, Elgin to Bot River.

Aristea africana John Manning

Aristea biflora

Aristea juncifolia John Manning

Aristea spiralis

105

Aristea capitata (= Aristea major)   maagbossie

The tallest in the genus, it makes a stout and stiff-stemmed plant up to 1,5m high with firm flat leaves up to 20mm wide. The brilliant blue flowers are 12-16mm long and emerge from translucent-papery bracts, tapering to a long thin point, with a central brown keel. They are crowded in lateral groups on columnar spikes up to 30cm long and give rise to 3-winged stubby pods. It is common on steep lower mountain slopes in sun or part shade from Piketberg to Caledon. (Oct-Dec).

♣ Two more blue flowered species are a metre or more tall: the branched *A. latifolia* of shady kloofs from Bain's Kloof to the Hottentots Holland with broad soft leaves and rounded, gently lobed pods; and the 1.5m tall short-branched *A. rigidifolia* of sandy flats with firm leaves, elliptical in cross-section and 3-winged pods.

Aristea bakeri (= A. macrocarpa, A. confusa)

A rhizomatous tufted perennial to 1m or more whose stems are round to slightly flattened and much-branched with tough sword-shaped leaves. The uncrowded sessile flowers have rounded dry-rusty spathes with transparent edges. The pods are oblong and three-winged. It is recorded flowering mostly after fire on stony sandstone slopes from 200-1500m. throughout our area and from Piketberg to the Swartberg and the Eastern Cape. (Oct.Dec).

This geophyte genus **Babiana**, bobbejaantjies, has extremely deep-seated corms clothed with previous seasons' fibres, and hairy, pleated, 2-ranked leaves. Each long-lasting, sessile flower has a bract and 2 green more or less joined bracteoles, and 3 short style-branches. There are about 68 species and 9 in our area. Baboons like to eat the corms, hence the vernacular name.

Babiana ambigua

The 3-6 hairy leaves are longer than the flowering stem, 4-8cm in length and 3-10mm wide. The fragrant blue-mauve flowers are borne on stems which curve close to the ground. They have cream or white markings, a tube 1-2cm long, unequal tepal lobes up to 4cm long, and purple anthers. The bracts are smooth or slightly hairy. It is common on sandy flats and lower mountain slopes from Vanrhynsdorp to Riversdale. (July-Sept).

♣ Other species whose leaves overtop the flowering spike are *B. patersoniae* of the Hermanus area whose fragrant flowers on erect stems are white to pale blue with yellow markings; the dwarf *B. villosula* of Hottentots Holland and Somerset West, whose lightly scented flowers are pale blue with a white eye, and tube 18-30mm long; and the 5-15cm tall, fragrant *B. sambucina* whose mauve to purple flowers have white and sometimes red markings; the leaves of the diminutive *B. montana* only slightly overtop the flowering stems: the mauve flowers have pale and purple markings, large shaggy bracts and large orbicular stigmas.

Babiana angustifolia

This species has slanting stems up to 20cm long, and lance-shaped leaves only half as long. The dark blue to violet flowers have black or red markings on half the tepals and a tube 11-17mm long. It occurs on damp clay flats and slopes from Piketberg to Kogelberg. (Aug-Sept).

♣ Another species with stems overtopping the leaves is the purple, blue, white or yellow unscented or violet-scented 10-20cm *B. stricta* with 10-16mm tube and centrally placed dark anthers.

Babiana purpurea

A slender geophyte to 15cm high with leaves shorter than the flowering stems. The fragrant pink to purple flowers with pale blotches have an 18-28mm tube and dark arching anthers. It occurs on clay flats and slopes from Robertson to Bredasdorp. (Aug-Sept).

Aristea capitata

Babiana ambigua

Babiana angustifolia

Aristea bakeri

Babiana purpurea

The rhizomatous genus **Bobartia**, the rush lily, has long flattened or cylindrical similar-looking rushlike leaves and stems. The flowers are enclosed in densely packed bract-wrapped bundles towards the end of the branches. Each flower lasts only one day, but several emerge successively from the same bundle. There are 15 species, of which 4, all yellow-flowered, occur in this area.

Bobartia longicyma
grootbiesie

The cylindrical leaves and stems, equal in length and up to 1,8m long, form large, coarse tufts when mature. The flowerheads are slightly flattened and consist of 2-20 flower bundles up to 45mm long and 7mm wide. It is recorded in the sandy lowlands from the Palmiet River to Napier. (Aug-Nov).

♣ The trailing cylindrical leaves of the 1m tall *B. indica* are longer than the flowering stems and there are 4-40 bundles of flowers per stem.

Bobartia filiformis
biesroei

The stems and leaves are thin and slightly flattened and more delicate than the last, the stems being up to 50cm long but the leaves a little shorter. The flowerheads have 1-3 bundles of flowers each. The flowers are unusual in that they open in dull weather and at twilight, closing in bright sunlight, so this species is less noticed than the others. It is nevertheless common on sandy lower and midslopes of the mountains from the Cape Peninsula to Riversdale and Elim. (Sept-Dec).

Bobartia gladiata

The 20-80cm *B.gladiata* has flat stems, narrow leaves, elliptic in cross-section, and 3-12 flower bundles per flowerhead. It occurs on mountain slopes and coastal flats in fynbos from the Cape Peninsula to Bain's Kloof to Hermanus. (Sept-Dec).

Lapeirousia corymbosa
koringblommetjie

 A cormous geophyte 5-30cm high with a single basal leaf much longer than the stem and a few smaller leaves on the stem. The stalkless, regular flowers with 4-7mm-long tube, blue with a white star, but sometimes cream or white, with a 6-branched style, are borne in large clusters on a much-branched flowering stalk. It grows in sand, less often in clay, from the Cape Peninsula to Tulbagh and Elim. (Sept-Nov).

♣ 35 species occur in southern Africa and 4 in this area. All have a 6-branched style. A fire-dependent species is the very fragrant cream and red small-flowered regular *L. micrantha*, tube 8-10mm, tepals 3-5mm, borne in groups high above the curved, crisped leaves. The cream or pink irregular *L. anceps* with red markings on the lower tepals, has a tube 2 - 8cm long, tepals only 10-12mm long. The much larger rare, irregular white or blue *L. neglecta* sometimes with markings on the lower tepals grows 28-55mm high with 3-6 swordlike leaves, has a 10-14mm tube and appears only after a fire.

Tritonia cooperi

A geophyte with 4-6 leaves arising from ground level and 1 or 2 smaller stem leaves which may be flattened or, in drier areas, rounded. The irregular, sessile flowers are borne in clusters on unbranched or branched stems 40-60cm tall and emerge from a pair of brown, blunt-tipped bracts. The 4-8cm long flowers are white, cream or pale pink with red markings, darkening with age. The 3 stamens arch in one direction under the upper lobes inside the long tube and there are three style-branches. It is pollinated by long-tongued flies and occurs on sandy mountain slopes from Worcester to Caledon and Riversdale. (Nov-Dec).

♣ There are 3 in this area: all have similar colouring & long tubes. The small *T. flabellifolia* has long tapering bracts and evenly spaced stamens. *T. crispa* has leaves with ruffled edges.

Bobartia filiformis

Bobartia longicyma

Bobartia gladiata

Lapeirousia corymbosa

Tritonia cooperi

Ixia dubia kalossies

A cormous geophyte with thin wiry usually unbranched stems, 20-75cm tall, with 5-7 leaves sword-shaped to linear and 10-50cm long by 1.5-8mm wide. The flowers are deep gold to orange, often with a dark eye, usually reddish on the reverse, and borne in crowded groups of 4-10. The short tubes are threadlike in diameter and blocked by the 3 free filaments. It is fairly common on sandy flats and slopes from Piketberg to Caledon. (Oct-Dec).

♣ 3 other cream, yellow or orange species are the branched *I. paniculata* with its most easterly range at Kleinmond, cream to biscuit coloured with a 4-7cm flower tube and 6-12 flowers per spike; the yellow *I. esterhuyseniae* of Jonkershoek with lily scent; and cream or yellow *I. odorata* with sweet fragrance and flower tube trumpet shaped with the filaments fastened to its walls within.

Ixia micrandra pink ixia, kalossie

A cormous geophyte with thin wiry stems 20-60cm tall with 2-3 more or less cylindrical leaves 12-30cm long. The flowers, 13-25mm long, are white to pink with projecting anthers. It occurs on mountain slopes and hills in the Caledon and Bredasdorp areas. (July-Sept).

♣ Of the 50 species, all in S.A., 12 occur in our area. All the other white, pink, mauve or blue-coloured ixias in this area have broad leaves except *I. flexuosa*, whose faintly-scented flowers are carried on a flower stem angled between the flowers, and *I. cochlearis* of Jonkershoek with rose or salmon flowers. The broad-leaved species *I. trinervata* of the Elgin area has bright to deep pink flowers; the white, pink and pale mauve *I. polystachya* prefers wet shaded places; *I. scillaris* has crowded, out-facing pink flowers with bright yellow projecting anthers; the white or purple *I. versicolor*, with a dark eye, has leaves loosely twisted above; the leaves of the pink *I. stricta* are dry and twisted at flowering.

Sparaxis grandiflora ssp. violacea fluweelblom, botterblom

A cormous geophyte 10-25cm tall, branching, if at all, only below ground and bearing only a few cormlets in the lowest joints of the stems after flowering. There are 6-10 sometimes prostrate out-curving leaves 4-13mm wide and shorter than the stem. The 1-5 long-lasting flowers are 35-45mm long and in our area may be cream, red-purple, violet or yellow with a yellow, purple or black eye, with or without dark markings. The style is 3-forked. The flowers in this genus emerge from quite distinctive large papery bracts which become torn at the tips. It occurs on damp clay flats from Clanwilliam to Caledon. (Aug-Sept).

♣ There are 14 species confined to the fynbos, of which only 2 others occur in this area, the taller but otherwise similar *S. bulbifera* which branches above ground with plentiful bulbils at the stem joints after flowering; and the yellow to buff, sour-scented *S. fragrans* with narrower leaves, found between Bot River and Napier.

Hesperantha falcata aandblom

A geophyte 6-30cm tall with 3-5 narrow curved or straight leaves which are only half as long as the flowering stems. The 1-8 long-tubed flowers arise singly from soft green or perhaps red-flushed bracts. The style forks into 3 long branches at the mouth of the flower. The flowers are white or yellow, the reverse flushed red, pink or brown, the white forms opening and becoming sweetly-scented at dusk; the yellow forms being without scent and opening during the day. Widespread from Nieuwoudtville to the Cape Peninsula, east to Port Elizabeth. (July-Oct).

♣ About 55 species occur south of the Sahara, of which 36 are found in the Cape and 4 in this area. *H. radiata*, opening after sunset, has similar colouring but the many sweet-scented nodding flowers have slightly recurved tepals. The flowers of *H. montigena* of high altitude Jonkershoek with oblong often prostrate leaves, are also white with red reverse. *H. pilosa* has hairy leaf margins and veins and is white and sweet-scented at night, or blue, opening in the daytime and unscented.

Ixia dubia

Ixia micrandra

Sparaxis grandiflora ssp. violacea

John Manning

Hesperantha falcata

111

The cormous geophytic genus **Geissorhiza**, the wine cups and satin flowers, are small plants whose flowering stems often nod in bud, with soft bracts, green at least in the lower half, from which the stalkless, long-lasting, unscented, usually cup-shaped flowers in every colour but orange, open in the daytime, emerging singly. The tepals are joined at the base to form a tube from which the long style forks into 3 only near the tip. All 84 species occur in the Cape Province, of which c. 17 are recorded in this area, several being very rare and local and many flowering most profusely after fire. The untreated species, c. 9 in number, have mostly white or yellow flowers.

Geissorhiza ovata   pink satin flower, pienk satynblom

A geophyte 6-15cm high, with sparsely branched or unbranched flowering stems bearing 2-4 flowers each. The 2 lowest leaves are broad, oval, rounded at the tip and pressed to the ground. The flowers have a tube up to 27mm long and the tepals are pink or white with a deeper pink reverse. It occurs in sand on mountain slopes or coastal flats from Clanwilliam to Riversdale. (Aug-Oct).

♣ *G. tenella* of seasonally wet sandy flats and dunes has sticky, winged leaves and white to pale pink flowers, darkening with age.

Geissorhiza nubigena

A 15-30cm tall geophyte whose 2-3 linear, 2-3mm wide leaves have two grooves on each surface, and are often sticky below. The unbranched spike bears 2-5 rose pink flowers, 27-40mm long with the tube well beyond the green, often red-tipped bracts. It occurs on the upper slopes of the Hottentots Holland and Kogelberg mountains in well-drained sand. (Dec-Jan).

♣ The 20cm high *G. schinzii* of Houwhoek-Shaw's Pass has leaves sticky, with sand adhering, and large flowers pink with deeper pink veins.

Geissorhiza aspera

A slender geophyte to 35cm whose sword-shaped leaves with thickened edges and midrib are shorter than the flowering stems. The stems are characteristically rough to the touch. The flowers, arranged in a 3-7-flowered spike, are glossy blue to violet or occasionally white, and may have a dark eye. It sometimes makes sheets of colour on sandy flats and slopes from the Gifberg to Bredasdorp. (Aug-Sept).

Geissorhiza ramosa

A blue-flowered species with small flowers on a branching stem. The leaves are narrow with slightly thickened edges and midrib, 1-2.5mm wide. The flowers are blue to purple, 5-10 per spike, with a 2-3mm long tube, and tepals spreading to 7-13mm across. One filament is shorter than the other two. It occurs on stony mountain slopes from Tulbagh to Swellendam. (Oct-Dec).

♣ There are 4 more blue to purple flowered species in our area: the summer-flowering *G. hesperanthoides* of marshy higher slopes throughout our area has narrow leaves with 2 grooves on each side; the pale blue *G. cataractarum* trails from cliffs alongside waterfalls from Betty's Bay to Hermanus; the purple tepals of the fire-responsive *G. burchellii* of upper elevations from Bain's Kloof to Hottentots Holland spread or curve backwards; the violet *G. lithicola* of Kogel Bay to Rooiels lower slopes has a 1-4-flowered spike and rounded leaves.

Geissorhiza ovata

Geissorhiza nubigena

Geissorhiza aspera   John Manning

Geissorhiza ramosa

113

The cormous geophyte genus **Gladiolus** has long-lasting sessile flowers arranged in a spike, each arising between 2 green bracts. The style forks into three branches just beyond the mouth of the flower and the anthers of the 3 stamens are usually grouped to one side. One or more basal leaves arise from soil level and may be present with the flowers or appear afterwards, but other smaller leaves are also present as sheaths round the flowering stem. All members of the genus have winged seeds. There are about 150 species in Africa and Eurasia, of which 105 occur in southern Africa and 21 in this area.

Gladiolus brevitubus
A delicate herb 12-40cm high with usually two sheathing leaves on the kinked stem. The nearly regular very short-tubed orange or pale red flowers with a slight sweet scent, borne 2-8 on a spike, are reminiscent of *Ixia* and very atypical of *Gladiolus*. No nectar is produced, but bees collect the yellow pollen. Occurring between 200-1500m in sand on rocky mountain slopes from the Hottentots Holland to the Riviersonderend and Klein River mountains it blooms well after fires but can be found even in unburnt short growth veld. (Oct-Dec).

Gladiolus blommesteinii
The stem and single smooth basal leaf are 30-70cm high, with 3 shorter stem leaves. The 1-4 pink to mauve-blue flowers arise from clearly-veined bracts, and have distinctive lemon-throated red streaked lower lobes. It is common on the lower and middle mountain slopes from Worcester and the Hottentots Holland mountains to Bredasdorp, but has not been recorded in the Hermanus area. (Aug-Oct).

♣ The similar, pink *G. ornatus* of wet sites in Jonkershoek, has lemon markings outlined in red.

Gladiolus bullatus   Caledon bluebell
Varying from 45-100cm high, and often taller than the adjacent veld, it produces 3-4 narrow leaves, even the lowest and longest only about half the height of the spike, and all sheathing the stem for much of their length. The 1-2 flowers emerge from conspicuous purple-brown ridged bracts. They are short-tubed, bell-like, c. 4cm long, unscented, pale within, variously spotted with purple, streaked with yellow, and with shades of blue on the reverse. It is quite common from Houwhoek through Kogelberg and the Klein River mountains to Potberg in stony sandstone, clay or limestone soils; the pollinator is presumed to be a long-tongued bee. (Aug-Sept).

Gladiolus carmineus   Hermanus cliff gladiolus
Usually about 30cm tall, the unbranched flowering stem of this unscented intense pink species bears 2-3 (occasionally up to 6) funnel-shaped flowers 6-10cm long, only 1 of which is usually open at a time. Its pollinator is presumed to be the Table Mountain Beauty butterfly. It produces its 3-5 flat trailing leaves in winter, in years alternating with the flowers. Recorded from Hangklip to Potberg on sandstone cliffs to within metres of the shore. (Feb-Apr).

Gladiolus cunonius (=Anomalesia cunonia)   rooipypie, suikerkannetjie
A sturdy geophyte 20-45cm tall with several soft sword-shaped leaves. The long-lasting flowers are 38-44mm long, including the extraordinarily long upper tepal. It occurs on the lower slopes of mountains near the sea among rocks and on coastal dunes from the Cape Peninsula to Knysna and is pollinated by sunbirds. (Sept-Oct) See pollination p. 32.

Gladiolus brevitubus

Gladiolus carmineus

Gladiolus blommesteinii

Gladiolus bullatus

Gladiolus cunonius   John Manning

115

Gladiolus brevifolius   pypie

This delicate plant is small-flowered and only occasionally scented. It becomes 15-85cm tall, and is usually leafless when in flower, except for the sheathing leaves on the stem, the lowest of which is rust-tipped. It bears 8-16 flowers 3-5cm long whose colour varies from pale to deep pink and (rarely) white or mauve, the lower lobes usually blotched with yellow or pink, and yellow pollen. The single, usually hairy leaf is produced only after flowering is over. It is very common on lower sandy flats from Piketberg to Agulhas. (Feb-Apr).

♣ Other similar species which are leafless when in flower in autumn are the delicate blue or grey flowered some-times fragrant *G. vaginatus* of coastal sands, with yellow, red-spotted throat and pale mauve pollen, and the almost identical *G. subcaeruleus* of clayey soils usually further inland; and the usually fragrant blue, grey, pink or lilac *G. martleyi* (incl. *G. pillansii*). All are pollinated by bees. These species are only reliably distinguished on leaf and corm characters which are not accessible to the casual observer.

Gladiolus debilis   painted lady

A geophyte 25-50cm high with one basal leaf longer than the spike and 1-2mm wide. The flowers, unscented, white or pink, grouped 1-3 together, have red markings on the lower tepals and long straight tubes. It is pollinated by long-tongued flies and blooms most abundantly in the early years after a veld fire. It occurs on rocky sandstone slopes from Bain's Kloof to Bredasdorp. (Sept-Oct).

♣ The large painted lady, *G. carneus* with a fan of 4-5, 2-19mm wide leaves and a slanting, often branched spike of 3-11 white to deep pink flowers has similar markings.

Gladiolus hirsutus (= G. punctulatus)   pypie

This non-fragrant, occasionally lightly scented pale to deep pink or mauve 'pypie' grows 25-90cm tall, with a single basal hairy leaf 2-6mm broad and usually shorter than the stem. The spike carries 3-8 short-tubed flowers. The pollinators are mostly long-tongued bees. It occurs on the flats and lower mountain slopes from the Koue Bokkeveld to the Langeberg and is common throughout our area. (June-Oct).

♣ The usually fragrant *G. gracilis* with an even more irregular flower in grey-blue, mauve or pink with pale side tepals, dark-marked and streaked, has one harsh-textured basal leaf that is H-shaped in cross section and 2 stem leaves: it favours heavier soils.

Gladiolus liliaceus   large brown afrikander, aandpypie

This large-flowered *Gladiolus* grows 30-80cm high with 2 flat, narrow basal leaves often equalling or exceeding the spike in height. The spike consists of 1-6 flowers. By day, (shown here), cryptic and unremarkable, unscented and not fully expanded, the tepals are translucent rusty brown, red or cream. Occurring most abundantly in heavier soils from sea level to mountain slopes, it is common and extremely widespread from the Cedarberg to Port Elizabeth over a range of altitudes. Dusk effects an astonishing and unique transformation in this flower, as the tepals expand, become translucent lilac, and exude a powerful, delicious carnation scent and copious sweet nectar for visiting moths. Held in a refrigerator after the colour change, it can be maintained in its night time apparel for photography in daylight next day. (Aug-Dec).

♣ Another brown afrikander, *G. maculatus*, of heavier soils, is constantly dull yellow to lilac, brown-spotted and streaked, leafless at flowering time, and strongly perfumed day and night (Apr-June).

Gladiolus brevifolius

Gladiolus debilis

Gladiolus liliaceus

John Manning

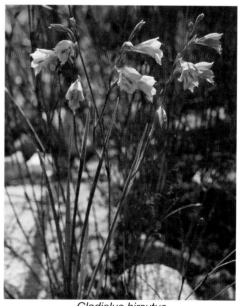

Gladiolus hirsutus

117

Gladiolus nerineoides

A geophyte 35-60cm high whose unbranched flowering stem, bent towards the horizontal, is sheathed by 2, (-1) short green leaves. (3-)5-10 open-faced, gold-dusted, bright red flowers with a tube 25-31mm long open simultaneously into a conspicuous false head atypical of *Gladiolus*. The foliage leaf is produced in the previous wet season, and is withered by flowering time. It is pollinated by the Table Mountain Beauty butterfly which also pollinates a range of other summer flowering bright red flowers. It is a narrow endemic of the mountains from Bain's Kloof to Hottentots Holland near Somerset West on rocky outcrops from 500m-1500m. (Dec-Jan).

Gladiolus priorii   rooipypie

A geophyte 30-70cm high with ca. 4 leaves reaching up to the base of the unbranched spike. Up to 5 unscented scarlet 3-5cm long-tubed flowers arch outwards from the rather wavy stem. Occurring on sandstone and granite slopes from Saldanha to Hermanus it is one of the first winter flowering species. The red colour, absence of scent and copious nectar indicate a bird pollinator. (Apr-Jul).

♣ The salmon-red-flowered, sunbird-pollinated *G. miniatus* of limestone outcrops from Bot river eastwards has six broad short leaves and a simple or branched spike of 9cm long red-striped blooms. The once extremely common scented kalkoentjie, *G. alatus*, with three broad, brilliant orange-red upper tepals and three long, narrow lime-green tepals tipped with red occurs at lower altitudes. The very rare, unscented *G. overbergensis*, with up to 5, 7-9cm long scarlet flowers per spike, rounded tepals, the lower sometimes tending orange or yellow, and 4 minutely prickly-sandpapery leaves, appears after fires from Hermanus to Bredasdorp in sandy-loamy soil.

Gladiolus tristis   vlei aandblom, trompetters, marsh afrikanders

A common geophyte 17-120cm high with three leaves, two basal and perhaps equalling the spike in length, grooved and 2-4mm in diameter. The spike is mostly vertical, bearing (1-2-4(-11) large cream flowers sometimes with darker midlines and reverse. Faintly scented in the day, they become strongly carnation-scented and fully expanded in the early evening and are most likely pollinated by sphinx moths. Usually associated with seasonal wetlands where it may form large colonies, it occurs from Nieuwoudtville to Port Elizabeth with flowering peaks at different times throughout the range. (Aug-Jan).

♣ Another very fragrant species with pale flowers, the rare greenish-yellow *G. acuminatus* of stony shale from Onrus eastwards, has 5 or more leaves at flowering time. The 20-100cm high, large-flowered *G. carinatus*, of deep sandy lower slopes in the north of our area, intensely freesia scented, greenish and yellow with three stem leaves, has a distinctively purple stem base mottled with white. Lastly, a white or yellow *Gladiolus*, *G. trichonemifolius* with three narrow leaves, round and 4-grooved, tepals sub-equal, 1-3(4) flowers per spike, and with a star-shaped blackish mark in the throat also likes seasonal wetlands. Some populations are freesia-scented. Once widespread and common, it is becoming rare due to development of wetland habitats.

Gladiolus undulatus   large white afrikander

A geophyte 25-150cm high, with at least two flat-faced basal leaves, 5-12mm wide and reaching up to the middle of the 3-12-flowered, sometimes branched spike. The most noteworthy feature of these long-tubed pale flowers in pinkish cream, green or lilac, is their remarkably wavy tepal lobes, with red or purple lines or spear-shaped markings and blotches in the throat, (not visible in our specimen). Occurring from Kogelberg to the Kamiesberg favouring marshes or permanent stream valleys in coarse sand, it is pollinated by very long-tongued flies. (Nov-Dec).

Gladiolus nerineoides

Gladiolus priorii

Gladiolus tristis

John Manning

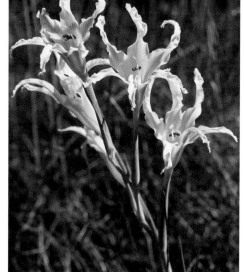

Gladiolus undulatus

119

Chasmanthe aethiopica
suurkanol, cobra lily

An unbranched sturdy cormous geophyte to 60cm with several fairly firm sword-shaped ribbed leaves in a fan, present at flowering time. The flower spike has many 22mm long, stalkless orange flowers arranged in a flat plane. The uppermost tepal extends strikingly further than the others to about 3x length of the lower tepals, the tube being conspicuously constricted below a pouch where it disappears into its set of green bracts. The style is longer than the perianth tube and forks briefly into three. Pollinated by sunbirds, the bright orange seeds have a juicy covering and are eaten and hence dispersed, by birds. It occurs mostly on coastal hills and flats from Darling to the Eastern Cape, often in bush or forest margins. (Apr-July).

♣ One more species out of a total of 3 occurs in our area. *C. floribunda* is very similar but is branched and often grows taller than 1m; the floral tube gradually widens upwards.

Romulea flava
A low-growing geophyte 10-50mm, the flowering stem in shade occasionally up to 10cm tall. The basal leaf is threadlike, ascending or spreading, the 2-3 stem leaves shorter and broader. The regular flowers, 1-4 or more, and usually 20-40mm long, are variable in colour, bright to pale yellow or white, (occasionally blue, rarely pink) with a yellow eye (often streaked with 3-5 dark lines in the throat) usually with a greenish-brown reverse. The outer floral bract is green, the inner membranous and brown-streaked; the style is 6-branched. It occurs on slopes and flats throughout our area and from the Bokkeveld to Humansdorp in sandy and clayey places. (June-Sept).

♣ There are about 88 species from the Mediterranean region southwards through Africa, of which 77 occur in South Africa and 14 in this area. Two others in our area are golden, *R. setifolia* of sandy places in the Hottentots Holland has 3-6 leaves; *R. triflora* of moist sandy sites in Stellenbosch, Jonkershoek and Hermanus has 2-6 leaves. Flower colour is however, too variable to be a reliable discriminant of the other species, these are only certainly based on characters of the corm and bracts which are obscure to the amateur.

Romulea rosea
froetang knikkertjies

A stemless geophyte with 3-6 threadlike, rather stiff hairless leaves up to 36cm long. The flower stalks are 3-8cm long and the pale lilac-pink or sometimes white flowers with a dark zone above a yellowish cup, are up to 25mm long. The tepal lobes are yellowish-green and dark-striped on the reverse. It is common on sandy flats especially in disturbed places from Nieuwoudtville to Port Elizabeth. (July-Nov). It is a proclaimed weed in Australia, and is naturalised in Tristan da Cunha and St Helena.

♣ 7 more species have this colour range.

Romulea tabularis
A geophyte nestling in *oxalis,* varying from 10-35(-60)cm, usually extending up to half of this length aboveground, with one or two threadlike to compressed cylindrical basal leaves and shorter stem leaves. The 2-4 or more flowers are 15-35mm long and emerge from bracts the inner of which is reddish or greenish with a brown-dotted membranous edge. The cup is golden or orange, the upper half of the flower blue-violet or lavender, sometimes white or cream, the reverse of the outer three irregularly green, brown or purplish. It occurs in moist sandy or clayey flats at low altitude from Clanwilliam to Bredasdorp. (July-Oct).

♣ Two more have flowers palish lavender-blue: the very similar tall *R. gigantea* of the rocky coastline, is uncertainly distinguished by flowers 15-22mm long and stem usually branching above ground. The widespread *R. minutiflora* has flowers 7-15mm long, several leaves and almost no above-ground stem.

Chasmanthe aethiopica   John Manning

Romulea flava

Romulea rosea

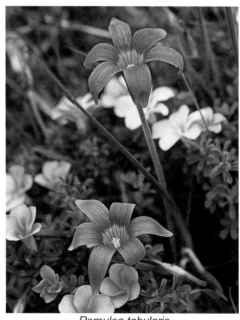

Romulea tabularis

The cormous geophyte **Moraea** has long, usually narrow leaves which may be attached anywhere along the flowering stem from ground level to just below the flowers. The flowers, clustered within sheathing bracts, appear one at a time. They are usually short-lived, symmetrical and iris-like and have 6 (sometimes 3) tepals. The centre of the flower is occupied by 3 stamens grouped around or secluded beneath 3 forked, more or less frilly or crested, petal-like style-branches. The genus now includes *Hexaglottis, Homeria, Gynandriris* and *Galaxia* and totals 195 species in sub-Saharan Africa, of which 123 occur in the Cape Province; 44 are known in this area to date and 35 treated in the text.

Moraea angusta

This large-flowered species grows up to 40cm high with an unbranched stem which is often sticky at the joints. A single cylindrical hairless leaf is attached near the ground. The non-scented, pale yellow (occasionally grey-blue) 3-5cm long flower, is veined purplish below and has clear yellow nectar guides. The pollen is usually orange-red, sometimes yellow. It occurs on lower mountain slopes in sandy or rocky soil from the Cedarberg to Knysna, and is seen most often after fires. (Aug-Nov).

♣ *M. neglecta* with similar stem, nodes and leaf but brighter yellow, scented flowers and black-dotted nectar guides occurs on deep sands; other similar cream to yellow species are the unscented *M. anomala* which, however, is never sticky and favours clay ground; the branched, non-sticky unscented *M. vallisavium* has one leaf, a brown-dotted nectar guide, dark-speckled claw and occurs in damp places on the Klein River and Kogelberg mountains; the non-sticky, hairy dwarf *M. papilionacea*, with 3-4 basal leaves has nectar-guides outlined in green or red.

Moraea fugax

A sturdy geophyte usually up to 50cm tall, it has 1 narrow trailing leaf (occasionally 2), much longer than the stem, and attached just below the flowers. The yellow, blue or white flowers are about 24-40mm long with 6 spreading tepals, the outer broader, with yellow honey-guides, well-developed erect style crests and a strong sweet scent. It is found mainly in sandy coastal areas from Namaqualand to Mossel Bay. (Aug-Dec).

Moraea gawleri

A slender, branched geophyte to 45cm with usually 2-3 leaves, shorter than the stem, sometimes coiled. The flowers, here blandly yellow, may be cream, brick red, often with dark veins, some-times bi-coloured, with erect style-branches and 6 more or less equal tepals sometimes bent downwards. It occurs from Namaqualand, throughout the fynbos to Humansdorp, more often on clay soils but also in sand. (Jul-Oct).

♣ The much-branched *M. inconspicua* with sticky stems and small dull yellow to brown drooping tepals occupies much the same habitat.

Moraea tripetala

A usually unbranched slender plant to 50cm tall. it has 1 narrow leaf longer than the stem. The flowers are most commonly pale mauve to deep violet, but occasionally pale pink or yellow, and have 3 large outer tepals, bearded within. The other 3 tepals are minute. It is widespread and common on flats and slopes from Nieuwoudtville to George. (Aug-Dec).

♣ *M. cooperi* is a yellow species similar to *M. tripetala*, but has distinctive purple veining and a tepal tube below the cup.

Moraea angusta

Moraea fugax

Moraea gawleri

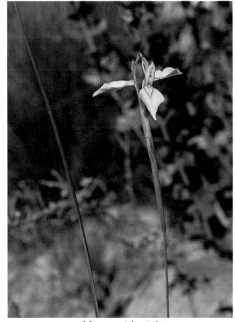

Moraea tripetala

Moraea tricuspidata

Usually 25-60cm tall and branched with 1 narrow, flattened, hairless leaf attached at ground level. The white or cream unscented flowers emerging from soft green bracts with threadlike tips, are speckled and slightly hairy within; they have 3 horizontal outer tepals up to 30mm long. The 3 inner tepals are very small with a whiplash coiled tip and the style crests do not emerge much beyond the cup.

Occurring most often on lower mountain slopes on heavy clay soils from the Cape Peninsula to Grahamstown, it blooms after veld fires. (Sept-Nov).

♣ The following all have whiplash inner tepals: The similar but sweet-scented pallid *M. viscaria* resembles the white form of *M. tricuspidata*, but has a purple-flushed flower, sticky stems and 2 leaves; *M. unguiculata* has reflexing outer tepals in white, cream, blue and brown, boldly upstanding coiled inner tepals and style crests; the 1m tall non-sticky, hairless, sturdy *M. bellendenii*, of sandy places, well branched above, has long-lasting bright yellow flowers and one basal trailing leaf. The small purple *M. debilis*, fading to pale mauve, a single often hairy trailing leaf, non-sticky, unscented, with a white nectar guide, occurs on shale and clay in the Kogelberg and Houwhoek and flowers October– November.

Moraea lugubris   kersblakertjie

A geophyte up to 16cm tall but often less, with 2 or more non-hairy, dissimilar leaves. The lower is narrow and attached at ground level, the upper, much shorter and broad-based, is attached just beneath the flowers. The bright blue flowers are up to 18mm long with red pollen. The feathery styles are unique in the genus. Local from Nieuwoudtville to Bredasdorp, and throughout this area, it occurs from sea level to mid-altitudes, most often on damp sandy soils, but also on decomposed granite. (Aug-Nov).

♣ There are also 2 stemless species; the unscented *M. tricolor*, mauve, yellow or red, has 3 short leaves; the sweet-scented *M. ciliata* may be blue, white, yellow or pale green, with 2-6 hairy leaves in a fan.

Moraea lurida   aasuintjie

This small geophyte grows to 30cm high with a single long narrow, channelled, trailing leaf. The stems carry only a few flowers, whose colour range of unusual sombre maroon, violet or cream with contrasting cream or orange edges is reminiscent of carrion flowers, and with a similar quite awful scent. There are 3 large outer tepals, 3 half the size or less, and 3 almost erect style branches. It appears in dense populations on rocky sandstone or granite slopes the first season after a wild fire between Sir Lowry's Pass, Kogelberg and Bredasdorp. (Aug-Oct). 3 colour forms are shown.

Moraea ramosissima

A sturdy geophyte to 120cm high with several shiny leaves arranged in a fan. Many large, bright yellow unscented flowers, c. 8cm across, are carried on a much-branched stem, the 3 outer broad and 3 inner slightly narrower tepals forming a shallow cup before curving out and down away from the upstanding style crests. Large groups flower in damp sandy or stony flats in response to a wild fire but seldom in later years, and the root system is remarkably spiny to deter moles, see p. 35. It is recorded between the Gifberg and the Eastern Cape. (Oct-Dec).

♣ Another branched unscented yellow with 6 almost equal tepals, the sticky *M. bituminosa* differs in its 2 thin flat leaves.

Morea tricuspidata John Manning

Moraea lugubris

Moraea ramosissima John Manning

Morea lurida
Anne Bean

125

Moraea villosa
uiltjie, peacock moraea

A geophyte 15-40cm high with a single leaf usually longer than the hairy 1-2-branched stem. The outer tepals of the gorgeous pink, lilac or purple flower c.6cm across, have yellow nectar guides accompanied by iridescent blotches of deep green or blue sometimes haloed by orange or yellow. The inner tepals are speckled whiplashes with a broad base. Once common on heavier soils of mountain slopes in the Western Cape, its habitat has been sadly diminished by agriculture, but in our area it still occurs on the stony granite and clay west slopes of the Hottentots Holland above Gordon's Bay. (Aug-Sept).

Moraea (=Hexaglottis) lewisiae

A geophyte up to 90cm tall with 2-3 trailing, channelled, flat or twisted leaves. The fragrant yellow flowers are borne in lateral flower clusters with 6 more or less equal tepals up to 24mm long and an exceptional style divided uniquely for the genus into 6 threadlike branches. It occurs on dry sandstone and clay slopes from Namaqualand to Humansdorp and flowers quite late in the season. (Oct-Dec).

Moraea (=Galaxia) fugacissima
clock flower

A tufted, stemless geophyte 3-6cm high, with several narrow cylindrical, erect, channelled leaves arising, as do the many fragrant yellow flowers, directly from the ground. The 6 tepals are almost identical in size and shape, and form a cup 11-19mm across. The 3 stamens join to form a column around the projecting style with its fringed tip. Widespread from Namaqualand to Humansdorp, it grows in wet sand and clay flats. (Jul-Sept).

♣ The very similar *M. angulata* of Malmesbury to Gordons Bay differs in the leaves being scimitar-shaped and lacking a channel below, and the flowers being without perfume. The style of the similar white, yellow-eyed *M. albiflora* of St Helena Bay to Gordons Bay is shorter than the stamens.

Moraea (=Galaxia) versicolor
galaxia

A 2-5cm tall stemless geophyte whose oval to lance-shaped leaves, close to the ground, usually have wavy edges. The pink to purple flowers arising from ground level, usually have a yellow eye, in this case zoned in black, and the stamens are clearly shorter than the lobed stigma. It grows on lowland granite and clay flats and slopes from Tulbagh and the Cape Peninsula to Houwhoek. (Aug-Sept).

♣ Two galaxias have purplish flowers with black eye: in *M. barnardiella* the style is shorter than the anthers; the style of *M. melanops* of Shaw's Pass is longer than the anthers.

Moraea (=Homeria) ochroleuca
apricot tulp

A sturdy cormous geophyte 35-75cm tall, with one, occasionally two, channelled leaves which arch out and trail downwards. The cupped flowers have 6 more or less equal tepals, with a central column of stamens but inconspicuous style crests. They are yellow or orange (as in this slide) or bicolored, 3-4cm long, fairly substantial for a tulp, and with a strong, foul scent. They flower almost exclusively only after a fire and grow on rocky sandstone slopes from Citrusdal to Caledon and throughout our area. (Oct-Dec).

♣ 9 more tulps occur in our area. *M. elsiae* with yellow flowers has sticky stems; the filament column of *M. miniata* of the north-west of our area is swollen and hairy towards the base; cormlets are produced at each node of *M. bulbillifera* of coastal areas; *M. comptonii* of the west part of our area is heavily sweet-scented; the pale-cream-flowered *M. pyrophila* has one spine-tipped rigid leaf inserted high up on the stem.

Moraea villosa

Moraea versicolor

Moraea ochroleuca

Moraea lewisiae   John Manning

Moraea fugacissima

127

Ferraria crispa
spinnekopblom, uiltjie

This 20-80cm tall cormous geophyte with a chain of old corms lacking fibrous covers, has slightly fleshy, broad, overlapping leaves partly concealing the branched, straight or slightly twisted stem. Each flower, about 35mm across, lasts for only one day and is carrion-scented. It has petal-like style-branches as in *Moraea*. It is recorded in sandy and loamy places from Clanwilliam to Willowmore and along the coast from Kleinmond to Mossel Bay. (July-Oct).

♣ There are 10 species from the Cape to tropical Africa but only one in this region.

Tritoniopsis antholyza (=Anapalina nervosa)
An unbranched sturdy cormous geophyte to 90cm with a fan of 3-6-veined leathery flattened leaves up to 7cm long. The crowded more or less 2-ranked flowers may be dull pink, pale or bright red or salmon, and are 4-7cm long, with a much-elongated upper tepal, dark-streaked lower tepals and anthers 32-40mm long. It is common on stony sandstone mountain slopes and upland flats from Van Rhynsdorp to Port Elizabeth. (Nov-Apr).

♣ The rosy *T. pulchra*, of the Hottentots Holland to Agulhas area with 2-3-veined leaves, lacks the elongated upper tepal. (Feb-June).There are 22 species endemic to the Cape mountains, c.13 occur in this area.

Tritoniopsis lata
A 15-30cm high geophyte with 1-3 long narrow 1-3 veined leaves emerging from a neck of wiry fibres at ground level, and 3-5 smaller stem leaves. The irregular 29-44mm long pink flowers are borne in a sparse short spike at the tip of a sturdy, usually unbranched stem, and arise singly from dry brownish bracts. It occurs in sandy and rocky places on the mountains from Tulbagh to Caledon. (Feb-May).

♣ Other pink-flowered species include: *T. ramosa* with smaller flowers on branched stems, the upper tepals of the former being clearly broader than the lower; the unbranched *T. dodii*, a dull pink with dark markings. 2 are yellow with mauve or brown markings, *T. parviflora* and a more robust species *T. flava. T. caledonensis* and *T. unguicularis* have cream coloured flowers with mauve markings. All are commonest after fire.

Tritoniopsis triticea (=Anapalina triticea)
An unbranched geophyte which produces a sturdy leafy stem, to about 90cm. The lowest leaves are narrowest at the base, widening but still narrow above with 3 veins, becoming brown at flowering time. The long-lasting scarlet flowers, 25-30cm long with stamens 20-23mm long and a 3-branched style, are borne in a dense spike, and pollinated by *Aeropetes tulbaghia*, the Table Mountain Beauty butterfly. It occurs on rocky mountain slopes from Stellenbosch to Mossel Bay. (Jan-Apr).

♣ Other intensely red species are *T. burchellii*, with similar (3-veined) leaves, size, flowers and flowering season, but larger flowers and stamens 30-37mm long; the 1.3m tall *T. williamsiana* of the Klein River Mountain has 2-4 veined leaves, a slightly more open flowering head and blooms earlier. (Dec-Jan).

Micranthus alopecuroides
combflower

A geophyte 25-45cm high with flat sword-shaped leaves. The 8mm long pale to dark blue flowers, the smallest in the family, are arranged tightly packed in two rows up the stems, hence the vernacular name. Although the individual flowers are small and the plants not very tall, the display of brilliant blue in summer at a time when most other spring bulbs are over is very eye-catching. It occurs often in large populations in sandy soils from Bain's Kloof to Elgin. (Oct-Dec).

♣ The other species in our area, the widespread *M. junceus*, with hollow cylindrical leaves, blooms a little later.

Ferraria crispa

Tritoniopsis antholyza

Tritoniopsis lata

Micranthus alopecuroides

Tritoniopsis triticea

129

Pillansia templemannii

A cormous evergreen geophyte to 1.2m with a few erect hairless, sword-shaped leaves, 10mm broad, with a distinct spiral twist, and lacking a midrib. The loose cluster of 10mm long short-tubed, regular, long-lasting, stalkless bright orange flowers with 6-branched styles is borne on a branched stem. It is pollinated by bees and monkey beetles. It occurs on the lower stony slopes and flats from False Bay to Hermanus where it forms large colonies. It seldom blooms except after fire, when it may be seen in spectacular sheets of colour. (Oct-Nov).

♣ There is only 1 species.

The cormous genus **Watsonia** includes species which are among the tallest and stoutest members of the family. They have sword-like leaves and spikes of sessile, long-lasting flowers, arranged in two ranks, and a 6-branched stigma. The tepals form a narrow tube which curves to face outwards, widening to 6 more or less equal lobes, and anthers lying either along the floor of the flower, or arching over it. Flowering in most species is particularly profuse after veld fires. Many species can occur in massed populations, and many species have winged seeds. There are about 50 species confined to South Africa, of which 12 occur in this area. All but one are treated below.

Watsonia angusta

A geophyte 1-2m high with several lance-shaped leaves, 12-20mm wide and half as high as the branched stems. The loosely packed scarlet flowers with a tube 35-44mm long have narrow tepals, one at the top slightly hooded, those at the bottom quite recurving, the purple-black anthers arched beneath the top tepal, below the stigma. Distributed over the whole winter rainfall region, from Piquetberg to the Transkei in permanent wetlands, it is sunbird pollinated and has a winged seed. ((Nov-Feb).

♣ Another widespread red *Watsonia* (also pink, purple or occasionally yellow), is the 50-200cm tall, branching *W. meriana* often with bulbils in the angles of the lower leaves. It has very large flowers, tube and tepal lobes being 60-76mm long, violet anthers on reclining stamens and a liking for sandy, seasonally damp localities. The bright orange-flowered, dainty *W. stenosiphon* of rocky coastal Kleinmond to Cape Infanta has rather soft leaves with inconspicuous veins, unbranched flowering stems bearing flowers with a 35mm long slender tube, (hence the name) and stamens arching below the top tepal.

Watsonia schlechteri

Sturdy plants, growing singly, 30-90cm tall with leaves 32-36cm long and 6-9mm broad, whose edges are as strikingly thickened as the midrib. The unbranched flowering stems bear numerous 4-5cm long flowers arising out of 25mm long bracts which do not clasp the stem. The cylindrical, outcurving tube of the bright red (occasionally deep pink) flowers bears narrow lobes half as long as the tube, and overarching violet stamens. They occur as solitary plants scattered on rocky, well-drained mountain slopes from Bain's Kloof to Swellendam and the Klein Swartberg. (Nov-Feb).

♣ Another red, *W. coccinea* in the west of our area, has long-branched stigmas often entangled in the anthers. It also occurs in seeps and seasonal marshes; and almost never flowers in veld more than two years after a fire.

Watsonia zeyheri

A geophyte to 80cm with simple or sparsely-branched stems and c.4 lance-shaped leaves half the length of the spike, with thick midvein and edges. The bright salmon-orange flowers have 3-4cm long tepals with a dark central line, and the violet stamens arch under the upper one. It grows in damp places and seeps, and on riverbanks on the coastal plain from the Cape Peninsula to Cape Infanta and inland to Franschhoek. (Sept-Dec).

Pillansia templemannii

Watsonia angusta   John Manning

Watsonia schlechteri

Watsonia zeyheri   John Manning

131

Watsonia borbonica   suurkanol

A common clump-forming plant to 2m with firm glossy leaves 50-70cm long and 2-4cm wide. The faintly scented pink or purple 50-76mm long flowers, borne on sturdy, much-branched stems, emerge from the bracts which are often sticky within but do not clasp the stem. The flower tube widens conspicuously to the throat and bears wide lobes equal in length to the tube or longer; the stamens, tipped with violet-coloured anthers, lie along the floor. Common on mountain slopes from Worcester and the Cape Peninsula to Bredasdorp, it blooms in late spring and is especially profuse after fires. (Oct-Dec).

♣ *W. rogersii* is very similar, but shorter-stemmed to 50cm, and smaller-flowered: 22-25mm long. Where the two grow in the same locality, *W. rogersii* occupies the lower slopes, *W. borbonica* the upper, up to 1500m.

Watsonia laccata

A geophyte 20-50(-60)cm high with leaves 1/3rd to 2/3rds the height of the unbranched flowering stem. The margins and midrib of the leaf are thickened and translucent, and the clasping floral bracts are 1/2 dry even in bud, becoming quite dry and torn post-flowering. The pink, purple to pale orange trumpet-shaped flowers have a tube 19-24mm long with the stamens lying along the floor and the pale yellow anthers at first facing upwards. It may be bee pollinated. It is found between Caledon and Knysna in seasonally wet, light soil on the coastal plain. (Aug-Nov).

♣ With yellow anthers: the narrow endemic in marshes from Franschhoek Pass to Kleinmond, 15-30cm high pink or purple *W. distans* with 17-24mm narrow tube weakly flared in the upper half and arching stamens, may bloom only after fires; another similar sized species is the red or purple *W. aletroides* whose almost tubular, 50mm long, usually somewhat hanging flowers have pale inner tepals It grows in hard dryish clays, often intermingled with *W. laccata* and sometimes hybridising with it and is presumed to be bird pollinated.

Watsonia marginata

A robust geophyte 50-200cm high whose broad, blue-green leaves, (2)-3-5cm wide, reach only 2/3rds as high as the spike, and whose translucent, thickened edges and midrib may become purple. The branching spike is many-flowered in pale purple-pink, the flowers emerging from firm, dry bracts which become torn. The flowers turn out sideways, with the anthers arranged, uniquely in the genus, symmetrically about the style and facing outwards. In the throat of the flower at the base of each tepal lobe is a callus of unknown function, which is also unique to this species. It occurs in sandy soils from near sea level to midslopes from the Bokkeveld to Hermanus.as scattered individuals. (Sept-Dec).

Thereianthus bracteolatus

A cormous geophyte to 30cm high with cylindrical, firm-textured leaves up to 15cm long, sometimes withering at flowering time. A sturdy, unbranched flowering stem with hard brown bracts carries 7-14 deep blue to purple, rarely white, flowers each about 7mm long, in a spirally arranged spike. The style is 6-branched. It occurs on well-drained soils at a wide range of altitudes, from Clanwilliam to Bredasdorp. (Sept-Nov).

♣ There are 7 species confined to the southwestern Cape, of which 3 occur in this area. *T. juncifolius* has leaves often overtopping the flowering stems the flowers have a white eye, and it prefers wet sites; *T. spicatus* has a dense spike of mauve flowers with darker markings on the three lower tepals.

Watsonia borbonica

Watsonia laccata

Watsonia marginata

Thereianthus bracteolatus   John Manning

133

Nivenia levynsiae

A delicate rhizomatous-rooted rounded shrublet to 25cm tall, from a thick underground base. It has fans of blue-green leaves each up to 40mm long and 1-2mm wide. Each flower is 18-20mm long, with a tube up to 15mm long. The heads of blue flowers are raised above the adjacent leaves. Found only on the mid to high slopes of the mountains from Kogelberg to Kleinmond, it inhabits dry rocky ridges. (Dec-Feb).

♣ A genus of 9 species restricted to the Cape fynbos, of which 3 occur here, the rounded 20cm high *N. concinna* of the Nuweberg and Groenland mountains, whose bright blue flowers with a tube 20mm long nestle among the leaves.

Nivenia stokoei   bush irid

A shrub with a fire-resistant woody underground rootstock, fibrous roots and woody stems 60-150cm high. The leaves form fan-shaped clusters, each leaf being up to 9cm long and 1,5-3mm broad. The large terminal brilliant gentian-blue flowers up to 6cm long with a tube 25-40mm long, are pollinated by long-tongued flies. It is a common but very local plant from the lower stony slopes above Betty's Bay and Kleinmond up to 800m at Highlands. (Jan-Mar). Larger specimens in the wild have been estimated to be over 150 years old.

Klattia stokoei   kwasbos

An evergreen shrub 50-120cm tall with irregularly branched woody stems and two-ranked smooth rigid leaves, the widest in the genus at (4-)7-14mm across. The crimson bracts and bright red flowers make it one of the most unmistakeable plants of the area. It produces copious nectar, and is known to be pollinated by the malachite sunbird. It is an endemic species and one of the glories of the Kogelberg Biosphere Reserve, occurring from near Sir Lowry's Pass to Kleinmond on damp upland south slopes in seeps and near stream banks in peaty sand. Such habitats are easily disrupted by human trampling, so keep away from the damp area, and do not walk up to the plants to photograph them: rather use a long lens. There is also always a danger of your boots carrying in *Phytophthora* soil-borne fungus disease. (Dec-Feb).

♣ There are two other species, *K. flava*, on the uplands of the Hottentots Holland and Groenland mountains; and the blackish-purple-flowered *K. partita* of the wet uplands of Kogelberg and Langeberg mountains. Be equally circumspect when approaching these species.

Witsenia maura   bokmakierie's tail

An evergreen resprouting shrub 1-2m tall with smooth 2-ranked leaves arising from the sparsely branched upright or spreading sturdy stems. The remarkable pairs of two-toned purple-black and yellow flowers have a c. 50mm long nectar-filled tube, the lobes of the tepals remaining always closed; Orange-breasted sunbirds have been observed visiting the flowers for nectar. Only a maximum of three quite large seeds can be produced by each flower. Growing in substantial colonies on hummocks probably raised by their own growth above the marshy ground, from Cape Point to the Langeberg mountains but mostly at low elevations, many of its original stands have been exterminated by human development and the draining of marshes, in Hermanus and elsewhere. (Apr-Sept).

♣ There is only one species.

Nivenia levynsiae

Nivenia stokoei

Klattia stokoei

Witsenia maura   Anne Bean

135

TECOPHILAEACEAE

Cyanella hyacinthoides
raaptol, lady's hand

A geophyte with annual above-ground parts 25-40cm high and an edible, deep-seated corm. The leaves, present at flowering, are basal, lance-shaped and hairless to delicately hairy. The stalked, violet-scented flowers, ca. 20mm across, in blue, mauve or white, are borne on a branched raceme. Six free, spreading tepals surround 6 stamens with joined filaments, of which the anther of the lowest is twice the size of the others. The anthers open by apical pores so the flower is buzz-pollinated by carpenter bees. It is most often found on clay or granite slopes in renosterveld from Namaqualand to Riversdale. (Aug-Nov).

♣ Only one more, similarly-scented, occurs in our area, the yellow-flowered *C. lutea*, of clay or limestone flats.

ORCHIDACEAE – The orchid family

Acrolophia bolusii
A robust evergreen perennial with leathery, erect, narrow, sharp-tipped leaves overlapping and enfolding one another, fanlike, up to 80cm tall. The branched flowerstalk bears loosely arranged rather drab flowers c.10mm across which are not resupinate. The face of the frilly, scoop-like lip at the top of the flower has many finger-like projections, and a small knoblike 1mm long spur is visible at the back. It grows on low-lying coastal sands from Hopefield to Bredasdorp and blooms well after a fire. (Oct-Dec).

♣ There are 4 more species, 3 are resupinate - having the lip with its projections at the bottom of the flower; *A. micrantha* has a dark liver-coloured flower except for a clear white lip; the green and maroon, *A. capensis* flowers from December and the similar larger flowered *A. lamellata* of coastal sands flowers in October.

Eulophia litoralis
An erect, rather slender plant to 65cm, with occasionally a single leaf, not always present, borne alongside. There are 6-27 resupinate flowers in a loose raceme, lacking pouches or spurs, each with a puff of yellow hairs on the bright yellow lip. It is found on coastal dunes in the Southern and South Western Cape. (Nov-Jan).

♣ Of about 200 species throughout the tropics and sub-tropics, 3 are from this area. The whitish coastal *E. aculeata*, and the lemon-yellow *E. tabularis* of sandy damp areas, have stiffly erect fan-folded leaves usually developing with the flowers.

Holothrix villosa
An unbranched erect inconspicuous geophyte 3-36cm tall with spreading hairs on a bractless flowering stem and rounded leaves pressed flat on the ground. Many single-spurred, yellow to creamy-green flowers borne close to the stem have 5 forward projecting fingerlike tepals with fleshy tips. It is a common and widespread orchid, recorded from the Richtersveld to the western and eastern Cape. (Aug-Dec).

♣ There are 55 species, 5 in our area. The water-storage cells in the leaf enable some species to endure the driest of orchid habitats. *H. cernua* with yellower flowers and stem hairs curved back and downwards blooms mainly after fires. The small (to 16cm) *H. mundii* has white flowers; *H. brevipetala* has drab pinkish flowers with scarcely opening mouth; the tan-coloured *H. schlechteriana* has many spidery floral lobes and short fine hairs.

Bartholina etheliae
spider orchid

This entrancing diminutive orchid with its single small platelike leaf pressed to the ground, and a single fringed, knob-tipped, short-spurred white and purple flower raised up on an elegant stalk to 28cm high, is usually sparsely scattered in burnt areas. It occurs throughout our area. (Aug-Oct).

♣ One other species, *B. burmanniana* lacks the knob tips.

136

Cyanella hyacinthoides

Acrolophia bolusii

Eulophia litoralis

Holothrix villosa

Bartholina etheliae

Disa atricapilla

Variably 5-30cm tall with several narrow leaves and a corymbose flowerhead of up to 20 close-packed flowers. The colour pattern is distinctive, imitating that of a female sphecid wasp, the large winglike side sepals 2-toned red and white with black tips, and the petals and lip more or less maroon and speckled. This bamboozles the male wasp into attempting copulation, which facilitates the transfer of the pollen mass to its body. This disa is widespread and sometimes abundant after fires, from sea-level to 2000m in the Western Cape. (Nov-Dec).

♣ There are about 162 species of *Disa* in Africa and Madagascar of which 131 occur in South Africa and c.51 in our area. A second species, equally profuse in the same circumstances and area is *D. bivalvata*. It imitates a female spider wasp, *Pompilidae*, in the altogether white lateral sepals. That the wasps are less than critical in their judgement is evidenced by hybrids between the two disas.

Disa (=Monadenia) comosa

A plant with a slightly twisted stem 8-60cm high bearing 2 or 3 semi-erect basal leaves and a number of smaller leaves close to the stem. It carries a cluster of 1-20 flowers, resupinate, lime-green, open-faced flowers, each with a single spur up to 24mm long. It occurs on half-shaded rock ledges or in damp crevices on mountains up to 2000m from Cedarberg to Uniondale. (Sept-Nov).

♣ 2 have fire-triggered green (with yellow) flowers: the flowers of the almost spurless *D. cylindrica*, are enfolded in long bracts; *D. sabulosa*, confined to sand at Hangklip has a 10-15mm long spur and notched petals. 4 others have a shallow top sepal and a thick lower lip: *D. bolusiana*, *D. atrorubens*, *D. ophrydea* and *D. rufescens*.

Disa ferruginea   cluster disa

A slender, grasslike plant to 45cm with narrow basal leaves which are dry at flowering time, and a crowded raceme of unmistakeable bright red to orange flowers carrying a 7-20mm long spur and a narrow 10-12mm long lip. It occurs on sandstone slopes between 750-1350m in dry to damp places from the Cape Peninsula to Albertinia. Mimicking *Tritoniopsis triticea*, it is playing a dangerous game, for it produces no reward for the visiting *Aeropetes* butterfly, relying on the gullibility of the butterfly to continue its visits. Recent studies have shown lessened seed set in these and other so-called "dry" flowers. Both plant species flower in late summer.

Disa (=Herschelianthe) graminifolia   blue disa

A slender-stemmed geophyte to 1m with 4-6 basal grasslike leaves, and some short stem leaves. The single-spurred, sweetly-scented flowers, c .3cm across, borne 2-6 on a stem, are blue with 2 green petals visible inside the hooded upper sepal; the tonguelike lip curves out and strongly down. It is found on dry sunny mountain slopes in dense vegetation between 300-1000m in the South Western Cape and is pollinated by carpenter bees. (Jan-Mar).

♣ 3 more with several blue flowers per stem include the very similar spring-blooming *D. purpurascens* of low altitude rocky areas, with irregularly edged upturned lip edges; *D. spathulata*, on damp or well-drained shale or sand, in colour purplish, greenish or reddish with a long thin, broad-tipped lip; the lip of *D. venusta* carries a strikingly copious white old-man's beard and *D. lugens*, liking restio tussocks on coastal flats and slopes, has a copious broad-bearded green and purple lip and a slender spur.

Disa cornuta

Each flower of this only other "blue" disa in our area, has a purple helmet, 12-18mm long, 2 strongly contrasting silvery-white lower lobes and a dark eye. The flowers of this very distinctive orchid are large and profuse on a strong leafy stem up to 1m tall. Found in wet places. (Nov-Dec).

Disa atricapilla   William Liltved

Disa comosa

Disa ferruginea   William Liltved

Disa graminifolia   William Liltved

Disa cornuta

139

Disa tenuifolia
yellow disa

Variably 5-30cm tall with numerous narrow basal leaves and some hugging the stem, and 1-3 flowers, bright yellow, open-faced and c. 30mm wide, per stem. They are pollinated by carder and leaf-cutter bees, without which they do not set seed. They are often quite abundant especially after fire in damp places from Porterville to Riversdale. (Nov-Jan).

♣ The diminutive *D. telipogonis*, with bright yellow, brown-striped flowers has long-whiskered tapering tepals.

Disa tenuicornis

This robust species 12-50cm tall has narrow tapering overlapping leaves grading into the floral bracts. Numerous small flowers, with hoods 8-10mm long, downward facing, with purple-green spur, arising from dry brown bracts, are white with red lines, spots and edges, and form a crowded spike. Large populations can be found locally after fire in damp peat above 700m.

♣ The similar pungent-scented *D. obtusa* differs in some brown or purple mottling.

Disa tripetaloides

Slender evergreen plants, 10-60cm tall, spreading by stolons to form groups, with narrow rounded basal leaves up to 14cm long, grading into stem leaves. Flowers, white to blotchy pink, resupinate, deeply helmeted, 14-33mm across and standing clear of the bracts, each with a spur 2-3mm long, are borne 7-10 on a flowerstalk. It occurs mostly along streams or in moss on damp mountain slopes, from sea level to 1000m from the south western to the Eastern Cape and KwaZulu-Natal. (Nov-Jan).

♣ *D. caulescens* is distinguished by maroon stripes on the petals. Two more pink disas have measurable spurs; both are small but red blotched and their top sepals do not form hoods so their flowers are open-faced: *D. vaginata* has a spur 5-6mm long, and *D. glandulosa* 2-3mm long. 5 species have no measurable spur including the spectacular spurless swamp-loving 1m tall *D. racemosa* with a lax spike of 2-12 substantial purple-veined pink, hooded flowers, pollinated by carpenter bees. 4 more are spurless including the white and pink-flushed *D. rosea*, and the rosy-pink yellow-barred *D. pillansii*.

Disa uniflora
red disa, rooi disa

This best known and most striking of all the Cape orchids is unmistakable when its large glowing, red, (occasionally pink or yellow) blooms are seen in the spray of a waterfall or beside a mountain stream. The evergreen plants grow up to 60cm tall with a number of stem leaves. The tiny petals are enclosed within the 2-6cm long hooded, spurred upper sepal. The short narrow lip at the front of the flower can clearly be seen in the illustration. It is still fairly widespread in the southwestern Cape in its often inaccessible habitat, although many populations have been eliminated in the past by flower pickers. It is pollinated by the large Pride of Table Mountain butterfly, *Aeropetes tulbaghia*. (Jan-Mar).

Bonatea speciosa
green wood-orchid, phantom orchid, oktoberlelie

A sturdy tuberous geophyte to 1m with a leafy stem. The soft, dark green, sharply pointed leaves measure up to 13cm by 4cm. The green and white flowers with a deeply 3-lobed lip, spur 25-47mm long and narrow petals, are carried in a fairly dense head. It is quite frequently seen in sandy soil in coastal scrub and forest margins from sea level to 1200m, from Malmesbury along the coastal belt and up into Zimbabwe. (June-Feb). As is hinted by the enormously long spur and pale colour, it is pollinated by long-tongued hawk-moths.

♣ Although there are about 20 species in Arabia and Africa, there are no others in this area.

Disa tenuifolia   Colin Paterson-Jones

Disa tripetaloides   William Liltved

Disa tenuicornis   William Liltved

Disa uniflora   William Liltved

Bonatea speciosa   William Liltved

141

Ceratandra atrata

An erect plant to 35cm with numerous narrow hairy leaves. The open flowerhead has numerous greenish-yellow flowers, c. 24mm long, with hornlike pegs projecting forward. It is common in damp places from sea level to 1500m flowering after fires. (Sept-Jan).

♣ Four more species occur in our area: the strongly sweet-scented *C. venosa* with white and pink flowers; the small, 20cm tall green and pale yellow *C. harveyana* in fynbos; the 40cm pinkish-green to purple *C. globosa* of wet places, with petals and lip white; and the green and yellow *C. bicolor* with a rather lax flowerstalk. Several produce oil and are visited by oil-collecting bees.

Disperis capensis   moederkappie

A slender plant to 43cm with 2 narrow leaves up to 9cm long. It usually has a single resupinate flower in which the petals are joined to the uppermost sepal, forming a hood. The lateral sepals are characteristically pouched with long, narrow, recurved tips. It fools carpenter bees into visiting by mimicking a *Polygala* flower, but actually produces no reward. It occurs in open well-drained fynbos from near sea level to 900m in the Western and Southern Cape. (June-Sept).

♣ There are about 84 species from Africa to New Guinea, of which 26 occur in South Africa and four more in our area.

Disperis paludosa

Growing 20-46cm tall with 3-5 stem leaves and flowerstalks, it carries 2-4 magenta and green flowers spotted purple within and c.24mm across. Each lower sepal has a substantial curving spur 2-3mm long, and the upper sepal forms a distinct hood with the joined side petals. It secretes oil to attract an oil-collecting bee. It is occasional in permanently damp sandstone habitats from the western to the Eastern Cape. (Oct-Jan) especially after fires.

♣ *D. circumflexa* is a ghostly pale pink or pale yellow, *D. cucullata* is pale green with greenish spots; and the tiny deeply hooded *D. villosa* is greenish-yellow, hairy in parts with a strong, sweet scent.

Evotella rubiginosa

This rare, slender leafy plant to 29cm has a dense spike of unpleasantly-scented, pink, maroon and green flowers c.15mm across, without spurs. It is pollinated by oil-bees and grows in marshes with restios between 450-1250m. (Oct-Jan).

♣ There is only one species.

Pterygodium acutifolium

Slender plants to 47cm with 3-4 large stem leaves, and flowering stems bearing 1-14 lime green and yellow, resupinate flowers, c. 17mm across, the top sepal joined to the 2 side petals to form a shallow pouched hood, the lateral sepals also pouched. It is common and widespread in wet places up to 1500m, notably after fires. (Sept-Dec).

♣ There are about 15 species found in South Africa, 7 of them in this area. All have yellowish to greenish-yellow flowers. The very similar, strongly scented moederkappie, *P. catholicum* becomes reddish as it ages; *P. volucris* has many strongly scented small lime-green-yellow flowers and inconspicuous bracts; the pale yellowish sinuous-stemmed montane *P. platypetalum* of rock shelves has 1-2 flowers, c.18mm across, with wide-flaring side sepals. Three more have very insignificant flowers; of these, *P. alatum* has a particularly strong sweet scent. *P. caffrum* has a sharp acrid odour.

Ceratandra atrata   William Liltved

Disperis capensis   John Manning

Evotella rubiginosa

Disperis paludosa   William Liltved

Pterygodium acutifolium   William Liltved

143

Satyrium rhynchanthum

This species is up to 40cm high with 2-6 stem leaves. The flowering stem is densely packed with up to 40 non-resupinate flowers standing clear of the bracts. The flowers, c.12mm across, are white to pale pink with purple spots within. A conspicuous column tipped with a unique single sticky gland is flanked by two rounded pollen masses and 2 conical 5-6mm long spurs arising from the relatively shallow hooded raised lip tapering to a pointed tip. It is locally common in the Western Cape in marshes, streamsides or moist slopes between 300-1000m. (Nov-Dec).

♣ Over 80 species are found in Africa and the east, about 17 occurring in this area. In this genus the lip is at the top of the hooded flower, whose twin spurs are the basis of the generic name.

Satyrium carneum   rooitrewwa

A vigorous sturdy plant to 80cm with 2 very broad leaves, up to 23cm long, pressed flat to the ground, and several more enfolding the stem. The unscented strongly hooded pale pink or rose-coloured flowers are 35mm across with a pair of 18-25mm long spurs. Local between on coastal dunes and fynbos near the sea. it is increasingly rare due to habitat destruction in the South Western Cape. It is visited by sunbirds. (Sept-Nov).

♣ Other deeply hooded species with down-curving bracts from the coastal area are: the white *S. candidum* with round leaves pressed to the ground and bracts with hairless edges; the liver-pink *S. lupulinum;* the pink smaller and erect-leafed *S. hallackii* ssp. hallackii in wet places of Bettys Bay; and the greenish yellow *S. odorum* from sea-level to 650m.

Satyrium coriifolium   ewwa-trewwa

A robust plant to 77cm with 2-4 thick, stiff leaves enfolding the stem. The conspicuous bright orange unscented deeply hooded flowers form a dense elongated spike. Each flower is about 26mm across with 2 spurs 9mm long. Once occurring abundantly on coastal sands and clayey mountain foothills from sea level to 750m, it is now becoming rare due to development and encroachment by alien weeds. It is recorded from the South Western Cape to the Eastern Cape. (Aug-Dec).

♣ *S. foliosum* with spurs 20-25mm long, half as high, and fading to an apricot tan, starts off pale yellow and is confined to black peaty soils in the cloud zone of the Hottentots Holland. The widespread pallid *S. ligulatum* has perianth lobe tips browning early. *S bicorne* has down-turned large bracts between the yellow-green flowers. *S. humile* has oval leaves raised from the ground. The cream-coloured *S. stenopetalum* has several stiff upstanding leaves, flowers nestling in upright wraparound bracts and spurs up to 30mm long.

Satyrium bicallosum

A drab ivory 5-33cm tall plant with 1-3 partly spreading oval leaves, a crowded flowerhead of 6-150 flowers c. 6mm across, and the mouth of the flower almost completely divided vertically into two entrances by the descending lip.

♣ *S. bracteatum* is sometimes a stout plant to 30cms with creamy yellow flowers overcast with reddish brown stripes nestling in large overtopping green bracts, lacks spurs, instead having only 2 pouches, and stinking of rotten meat, it is pollinated by carrion flies. Another straight to upcurved bract species *S. pumilum* is up to 3cm high, rosette-like, and has a similar smell.

Satyrium rhynchanthum

Satyrium carneum William Liltved

Satyrium coriifolium John Manning

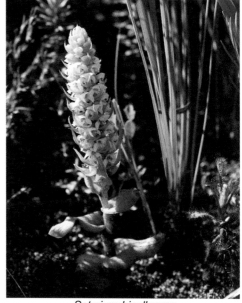

Satyrium bicallosum

145

Corycium carnosum   kapotjie

A sturdy, leafy geophyte to 55cm with narrow lanceshaped leaves and a crowded spike of pink flowers. The flowers are slightly fleshy (hence the specific name), c.18mm long with a pink hood and paler lip. It is locally common from the Cape Peninsula to the Eastern Cape from sea level to 1500m. (Oct-Jan).

♣ There are 14 species, of which another 5 are recorded in our area. The weedy and common *C. orobanchoides* has small green flowers edged with dark maroon, and a strong and unpleasant scent. The other species are rare.

PIPERACEAE – The pepper family

Peperomia retusa

Soft, sappy prostrate, creeping perennial herb, rooting at the nodes to form a carpet, with rounded, glossy simple leaves without stipules. Minute flowers with 1-10 stamens but lacking petals and sepals, are borne on delicate green spikes. It is probably present, but very inconspicuous, in many moist indigenous forest patches on mossy boulders and in humus on the forest floor in shade from the Cape Peninsula to Mpumalanga. (Jan-Mar). This is the only species here, out of 1000 mostly in the Americas.

MYRICACEAE – The waxberry family

Morella (=Myrica) serrata[1]   waterolier

Dioecious spreading tall shrub to 3m with narrowly elliptic, toothed, conspicuously net-veined leaves, the margins rolled under, and gold-spangled glands visible in bright light or when viewed with a magnifying glass. Nodules on the roots fix nitrogen. The wind-pollinated flowers are borne in catkins and give rise to drab, round, warty fruits, 3-4mm in diameter. It occurs on rocky streamsides from Bain's Kloof to Mpumalanga. (Aug-Dec).

♣ The treelike *M. integra*[2] of rocky streamsides in the west of our area, has narrow elliptic only rarely toothed leaves, and the 60cm tall *M. quercifolia*[3] of coastal flats and limestone with coarsely-scalloped leaves can be seen throughout the area; both produce 3-4mm diameter berries.

Morella cordifolia   glashout, waxberry

A dioecious shrub to 3m, with overlapping, stalkless heart-shaped, toothed leaves, 5-10mm across, and 5-8mm diameter warty greyish fruits borne on axillary spikes. The heavy coating of the berries was once a source of wax for making domestic candles and furniture polish. Common on flats especially near the sea shore, it is an important dune-stabiliser from Yzerfontein to the Eastern Cape. (May-Aug).

Corycium carnosum

Peperomia retusa

Morella serrata

Morella cordifolia

John Manning

PROTEACEAE – The Protea family

The genus **Brabejum** has only one species. It differs from all the other indigenous proteas in having its flowers in pairs and leaves in circles; all the rest have one flower in each floral bract and alternate leaves. This consigns it to the subfamily *Grevillioideae*, to which silky oak and *Hakea* belong. All the close relations of the wild almond are in Australasia; it is only rather remotely related to the rest of our *Protea* flora.

Brabejum stellatifolium   wild almond
It is a large shrub or sprawling tree to 8m, with elephantine sinuous branches and a low rounded canopy. The long lance-shaped toothed leaves are attached in whorls of 4-9 and the dense racemes of drab white flowers give rise to one-seeded, velvety, almond-shaped and -sized fruits in summer, visible as very young pink-flushed velvety ovals in the illustration. Because the buoyant fruits are dispersed by winter floods it grows in association with permanent streams and rivers throughout our area and from the Gifberg to Riversdale on sandstone. (Dec-Jan).

Diastella fraterna   Palmiet silkypuff
A single-stemmed shrublet to 70cm high and 1m across with oval leaves 8-14mm long and 1-4mm wide and twisted when young, and white to cream flowerheads up to 15mm across, later with papery involucral bracts. It occurs from Kogelberg to Kleinmond and the lower Palmiet River catchment from sea level to 450m and blooms throughout the year.

♣ The very local *D. thymelaeoides ssp. thymelaeoides* grows up to 1.5m tall with rounded overlapping scale-like leaves 8-14 x 4-9mm, and white, occasionally pink, posies 10-15mm across with inconspicuous bracts It occurs on the Hottentots Holland mountains, northern Kogelberg and around the Steenbras dam in isolated patches, flowering all year. The sweetly scented subspecies *D. thymelaeoides ssp. meridiana* with 12-22 x 4-9mm leaves and white or pink 20mm posies nestling in conspicuous pale involucral bracts occurs on coastal slopes from Rooiels to Cape Hangklip and Betty's Bay and is threatened by building development.

Diastella divaricata ssp. montana   mountain silkypuff
A low, single-stemmed sprawling, mat-forming shrublet covering an area 1-3m in diameter: this is our smallest, most delicate protea. The small well-spaced simple, oval leaves are clothed when young with long, black hairs. The pink posy-like flowerheads, up to 15mm across, are surrounded by silky involucral bracts. It occurs from 300-1200m in small scattered groups on sandstone mountain slopes throughout our area. (Jan-Dec).

Aulax umbellata   broad-leafed featherbush
This 2.5m tall, single-stemmed fairly open shrub with separate male and female plants bears simple leaves, 2-15mm wide, blunt-tipped and broadening upwards, becoming 2-11cm long. Yellow spikes of male flowers in the foreground and the posy-like heads of the female on a separate, but adjacent plant are both shown here. The mature fruits are retained on the parent plant until it is killed, for instance by a fire, after which they are released in masses. The plants often grow in large populations, the bright gold of their flowering phase transforming a landscape in late spring and summer. It occurs on sandstone from Kogelberg to Riversdale on coastal slopes and flats. (Nov-Feb).

♣ There are 2 other species, both occurring in this area: the many-stemmed needle-leaved *A. pallasia* which sprouts from a fire-resistant stump after veld fires, and the single-stemmed *A. cancellata* of the Hottentots Holland and other mountains, with narrow channelled needle-like to spoon-shaped 5-10cm long leaves.

Brabejum stellatifolium

Diastella fraterna

Diastella divaricata ssp. montana

Aulax umbellata

149

Sorocephalus clavigerus

needle-leaf clusterhead

A shrub on a single thick stem sparsely branched to 1m, densely clothed with overlapping channelled, simple, stiff and tough needle leaves 7-25mm long. A large terminal flowerhead consists of small headlets of 6-9 pale yellow flowers, each arising singly at a bract. It occurs in scattered clumps on stony or sandy well-drained slopes from 450-1200m on the Hottentots Holland to Klein River mountains. (Jul-Dec).

♣ *S. palustris* differs in being a mat-forming shrub from the Kogelberg, and *S. tenuifolius* of the Palmiet river valley, is a wispy upright shrublet whose leaves are not channelled and whose flowerheads are shaggy-woolly.

Spatalla, like Sorocephalus, is distinguished by having undivided leaves. Somewhat elongated flowerheads are mostly terminal on branches and flowers are grouped into one or three headlets, encircled below by small floral bracts and facing away from the center. Whether the headlets arise immediately above the foliage leaves, or above a length of leafless stalk, is the basic grouping of the species adopted in this text for the species in our region. There are 20 species in the fynbos, of which eight have been recorded from this area.

Spatalla curvifolia

white-stalked spoon

A rounded, woody, single-stemmed shrublet to 80cm with lax needlelike leaves, 25-50mm long, channelled above and usually curved. One to several rather loose flowerheads, 3-7cm long with stalks up to 7cm long, are composed of needlelike involucral bracts interspersed with stalked one-flowered headlets with densely hairy creamy white to yellow 7-9mm long flowers. These have fleshy red basal swellings and purple style-tips. It grows in groups on well-drained sandy or rocky slopes from sea level to 330m from Kogelberg, Babylonstoring and the Riviersonderend and along the coast from Steenbras to Bredasdorp. (Jan-Dec).

♣ Two more species with long-stalked flowerheads are *S. longifolia* of Fransch Hoek to Kleinmond, an erect rigid 1m tall shrub with similar leaves, floral bracts and heads, but the leaves blacken on drying and the flowerheads are grayish pink, lacking red swollen bases; and *S. propinqua*, an erect shrub with 3-flowered headlets in silvery-pink flowerheads on 10-30mm stalks, found from Slanghoek to the Hottentots Holland above Stellenbosch.

Spatalla racemosa

lax-stalked spoon

This small, slender, single-stemmed loosely branched shrublet grows to 50cm high. It has fine-pointed 15-35cm long needle leaves, and a loosely open 10-30mm long stalkless flowerhead of 1-flowered headlets with 4-5mm long stalks, and very short floral bracts. It is plentiful in drier places on stony sandy slopes from the Kogelberg to Klein River mountains. (Sept-March).

♣ *S. confusa* among summit rocks on the Hottentots Holland has almost stalkless flowerheads, 10-25mm long and three-flowered headlets on 1mm stalks.

Spatalla setacea

needle-leafed spoon

An erect well-branched rounded shrub on a single stem, up to 1m tall with curved 20-30mm long needle leaves exceeding the stalkless rounded 10-25mm diameter flowerhead. Each headlet consists of a single 10-12mm long shaggy silvery pink flower, inflated at the base. It occurs in scattered clumps from Slanghoek and Hottentots Holland to Kogelberg in peaty southern slopes between 900-1250m. (Oct-Dec).

♣ Five others with stalkless flowerheads occur in our area. Three grow in wet places: straggly *S. prolifera* of the Palmiet and Steenbras valleys has threadlike leaves also almost obscuring the 20mm rounded flowerheads. *S. parilis* of the northern Hottentots Holland has each headlet with a 2-3mm long stalk and 4-6mm long floral bracts; *S. mollis* of the Hottentots Holland to Kleinmond mountains has dense, cylindrical white flowerheads rising above the upper leaves.

Sorocephalus clavigerus

Spatalla curvifolia

Spatalla racemosa

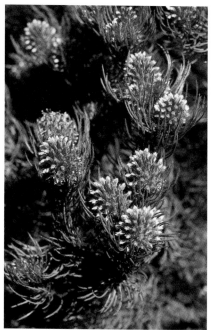

Spatalla setacea

151

Paranomus are shrubby mountain shrubs characterised by much-forked leaves which curve upwards, but some species have two kinds of leaves with the youngest flowering stems bearing simple leaves which are broadest near the apex. The flowers, clustered 4 together, arise from a leathery bract which becomes woody later, grouped into a spike-like flowerhead There are 18 species of woody shrubs in the Cape with 5 in our area.

Paranomus sceptrum-gustavianus   King Gustav's Sceptre
A coarse sturdy shrub to 2m with hairless leaves of 2 forms, simple ones up to 8cm long wedge-shaped below, broadest above; and dissected leaves up to 12cm long with rounded tips. The creamy, silvery flowerheads have a heavy sweet scent. It occurs on sandstone slopes from the Hottentots Holland to Bredasdorp and inland mountains as solitary plants or isolated groups or occasional larger groups, between 150-500m (Jul-Mar).

♣ *P. adiantifolius* also has leaves of two forms, the simple ones rounded, more squat and clasping the stem, the dissected leaves much longer and sparsely lobed, the flowers pink with glistening white hairs. Three more species are up to 1m tall and have only dissected leaves: *P. sp. nov.* of Palmiet valley shales with flower length 7-9mm is highly endangered; the faintly sweet-scented *P. spicatus* of Sir Lowry's Pass to Pringle Bay has flowers 14mm long; the similarly scented *P. bolusii* of Groenland to Klein River Mountains has flowers 10-12mm long.

Serruria is a group of c. 50 species distinguished from all other proteas except *Paranomus* by their dissected feathery leaves with cylindrical segments (see glossary), and from the latter (with its spikes of flowers), by the rounded loosely or tightly packed heads of headlets with or without bracts. These shrubs, seldom over 1m high, vary from prostrate to erect and single-stemmed to multistemmed resprouters and their flowers are either straight or curved in bud, a basic distinction used here to delimit the groups. 17 species occur in the area of this book.

Serruria adscendens   Kleinmond spiderhead
This attractive rounded shrub to 1m tall has a single main stem, numerous reddish branches and leaves each with 10-17 tips. Curved buds open into perfumed silvery pink mop-heads without bracts, just emerging from the leaves, comprising 5-25 headlets with 6-10 flowers each. It is wide-spread and social on flats and lower slopes from Betty's Bay to Bredasdorp and regenerates from seed after veld fires. (Aug-Dec).

♣ 3 with curving buds: the similar prostrate resprouter *S. rubricaulis* has red stems, vertical leaves with 12-18 rounded tips, no bracts and coarse pink mopheads. The smaller rounded shrub with curved buds and pink silky mopheads is the single-stemmed *S. nervosa* of the limy and acid sands of the lower slopes of the Klein river mountain to Elim. Each mophead has 1-3 headlets totalling 20-22 sweetly scented flowers. Lastly the erect *S. acrocarpa* of Hottentots Holland sandstone midslopes, a multistemmed resprouter with a 15-45-pointed leaf and single, sweetly scented yellow or pink heads supported below by oval bracts.

Serruria rostellaris   remote spiderhead
 A compact erect single-stemmed shrublet to 0.5m with 12-17-tipped leaves. Straight buds open into single white or pink stalkless posies which nestle into the upper leaves, encircled by lance-shaped bracts, purple below. It is very local in dense groups on damp sandstone slopes from 450-800m on Groenland, Babilonstoring and the Klein River mountains. (Sept-Nov).

Paranomus sceptrum-gustavianus

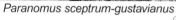
Giorgio Lombardi

Serruria adscendens

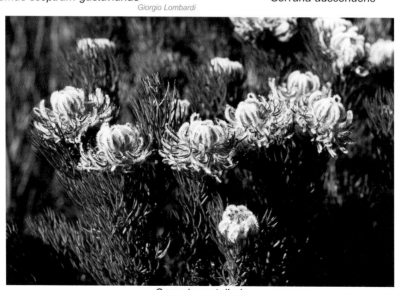

Serruria rostellaris

153

Serruria elongata   long-stalked spiderhead

An erect, single-stemmed shrub with hairless leaves in whorls close to the ground, each leaf divided into as many as 60-70 leaflets. Leafless flowerhead stalks up to 50cm long bear erect buds borne in bractless clusters which open into sweet-scented silver pink flowers: a yellow form occurs in the Steenbras catchment. It is widespread from Du Toit's Kloof and the Riviersonderend to the Bredasdorp mountain and throughout our area on sandy lower and midslopes. (Jul-Oct).

♣ The rare silvery pink flowered *S. altiscapa* of Villiersdorp and the slopes above Nuweberg is an exaggeratedly long-stemmed version of the preceding species, growing to 2m high.

Serruria kraussii   snowball spiderhead

This single-stemmed erect shrublet 0.3-1m tall by 0.5m across with erect, 20-29-tipped, hairless leaves. has spherical, unscented silvery white mopheads of 5-12 headlets up to 7cm across on short stalks, with straight buds and lance-shaped flowerhead bracts. It is very local up to 460m on granite and sands from Jonkershoek to Helderberg. (Aug-Nov).

♣ Two more single-stemmed straight-budded species are *S. fasciflora*, widespread on lower mountain slopes, faintly sweet-scented, often pink-flushed, with hairy 10-15-tipped leaves and headlets of 5-7 flowers each; the sprawling, tangled creamy-yellow-flowered *S. inconspicua* of Kogelberg and Groenland has very small heads of 1-5 bractless headlets with 3-8 flowers each, immersed in the 8-14-tipped leaves.

Serruria flagellifolia   Houwhoek spiderhead

A sparsely branched single-stemmed shrub, flat on the ground with vertical simple or few-pointed leaves. 6-12 straight pink buds make up each solitary sweetly scented flowerhead with a long stalk and conspicuous oval cream bracts. It is seldom noticed in the field, and is easily confused with the parasitic *Cassytha*. It occurs on Kogelberg, Groenland and Babilonstoring mountain on sandstone midslopes. (June-Nov).

♣ Two more straight-budded sprawlers are the single-stemmed equally sparsely branched *S. deluvialis* of the Palmiet Valley, with similar but more crowded leaves, and solitary, stalkless, flat-topped, sweetly-scented, silvery cream woolly flowerheads with narrow involucral bracts arising from 10-14 straight, shaggy buds. *S. gracilis* of the Hottentots Holland and northwards is a resprouter with straight, red buds 25-40 together opening into sweetly scented deep pink heads, 20mm across or more, enfolded within purple pink bracts.

Serruria phylicoides   bearded spiderhead

An erect, rounded, single-stemmed shrub to 60cm has 20-30 tips per hairless leaf, giving the plant a feathery look. Straight buds open into silver-bearded, deep pink to carmine flowers grouped into stoutly stalked, naked-necked shaggy posies 15mm in diameter clustered at the ends of the branches. Conspicuous cream to orange bracts up to 10mm long surround each head. It occurs from Du Toit's Kloof to Hottentots Holland and the Riviersonderend and Klein River mountains on sandy slopes and flats from 330-1800m. (Aug-Dec).

♣ The sweetly-scented, naked-necked usually single flowerheads of *S. heterophylla* of Kleinmond and Hermanus mountains look very similar, but its upper leaves have only 1-3 tips, but up to 8 lower down the stem. The naked-necked posies of the straight-budded *S. rosea*, with similar habit but broader rosy involucral bracts, are made even more conspicuous because they are grouped into clusters, the leaves having up to 60 points. It occurs in our area on the sandy midslopes of the Hottentots Holland.

Serruria elongata

Serruria kraussii

Serruria flagellifolia

Serruria phylicoides

155

Protea is an African genus of 114 species of which 29 occur in this area. Their bisexual flowers are crowded within goblet or crater shaped heads surrounded by colourful bracts. The upright species have terminal flowerheads, mostly without scent and pollinated by birds, others bear flowerheads close to the ground, are often musty or yeasty scented and are pollinated by rodents. Most are serotinous. When the bracts open a mass of plumed fruits is dumped into the landscape, to germinate at once in their thousands when autumnal cool soils and rain trigger them into growth. For as long as the fruits lie on the ground they are eaten by rodents and insects, so the earlier the fire (the longer before the autumn rains) the fewer fruits survive to replace the parents.

Protea cynaroides
giant protea, king protea, groot suikerroos

Our national flower and the protea depicted on our coinage, this 2m tall, coarse, sparsely branched shrub has a fire-resistant stump. The spoon-shaped leathery leaves are up to 30cm long, with conspicuous, long leafstalks. The enormous flowerheads measuring up to 30cm across and varying in colour from pale greenish cream to a soft deep pink, look like 'eyes' in the veld. It occurs on sandstone from sea level to 1500m from the Cedarberg to the Eastern Cape, wherever the annual rainfall exceeds 400mm. Blooms all year round.

Protea mundii
forest sugarbush

An upright shrub or occasionally a tree up to 12m which makes it the tallest tree-like protea, with a single trunk and stems without hairs at maturity. Bright green elliptic leaves tapering to the base only half conceal the neat modest-sized pink or pale green goblets, 6-8cm long, whose bracts are lightly fringed with pale hairs. The flowers scarcely project from the mouth. In our area it is found in stands fringing forests from 200-1300m in permanently moist situations in Kogelberg, Kleinmond and Hermanus mountains, but also between George and Uitenhage. (Jan-Sept).

♣ The very similar *P. lacticolor* of the Hottentots Holland from 600-1500m on moist shale and streambanks, differs in its blue-green leaves which are heart-shaped at the base.

Protea nitida
waboom

A somewhat gnarled tree up to 10m but usually less, usually single-stemmed, mostly fire-resistant and resprouting from buds protected by the thick corky bark but sometimes from a stump. Its blue-grey-green oblong leaves 8-18 x 1-6cm form a light canopy. Oblong buds open into cream to pink craterlike flowerheads with the flowers at all times projecting strongly from the disproportionately small bracts, the bracts spreading far apart at maturity around the 8-16cm wide floral mass. A characteristic plant throughout the fynbos often forming open woodland on drier, lower scree slopes from 0-1200m. (flowers all year).

♣ The squat, stunted *P. rupicola* with its 4-10cm diameter shallow heads of tightly packed pink flowers projecting well beyond the short bracts will only be encountered on summit rocks of the highest peaks of the Hottentots Holland Mountains but is widely distributed on other Cape mountains.

Protea coronata
green sugarbush

An erect shrub 2-5m tall with shaggy stems, becoming untidy with maturity. Hidden by a mass of lance-shaped leaves 6-9 x 1-3cm, the flowerheads are oblong goblets 9-10cm long with unique shiny apple-green bracts which curve inwards across the top of the head, while a mass of shaggy white-tipped flowers just project, giving a most distinctive appearance to this protea when cleared of its upper leaves. Occurring from the Cape Peninsula to George it forms dense stands on heavy clay soils in high rainfall areas between 200-750m. (Apr-Sept).

Protea cynaroides

Protea mundii

Protea nitida

Protea coronata

157

Protea compacta   Bot River protea, Botrivierprotea

This stiffly upright, single-stemmed shrub to 3.5m has its sparse branches largely concealed by overlapping oblong leaves. The flowerheads are 9-13cm long with velvety pink bracts overtopping and incurving over a cone of pink flowers. It occurs in dense stands from near the Palmiet River mouth eastwards to Struisbaai on coastal flats and foothills. (Apr-Sept).

♣ *P. repens* has cream or green or red hairless flowerhead bracts, gummy on the outside, and with the tips spreading. It is a copious source of nectar, which sometimes pours out. *P. burchellii* is very similar, except that the flowerheads are surrounded by cream or pink, shiny almost greasy-looking bracts, and which curve inwards over the much shorter, dark-bearded flowers within, fringed with brown, black, or occasionally white hairs. It occurs in the western part of our area.

Protea longifolia   long-leaf sugarbush

Single-stemmed erect to sprawling shrubs to about 1.5m high, with crowded narrow leaves, 9-20cm long. The flowerheads, 8-16cm long, have smooth translucent green, white or pink bracts and a long-pointed black beard of flowers protruding from within. It occurs in open stands between Sir Lowry's Pass and Cape Agulhas on low hills and mountain slopes to 150m, rarely higher, on sand or clayey ironstone gravel. (May-Sept).

Protea neriifolia   narrow-leaf sugarbush

An erect tree-like shrub to 3m, branching close to the ground from a single strong trunk. It has bright green oblong leaves 10-18mm long and 14-30mm wide with an unthickened edge, and flowerheads 10-13cm long and 6-8cm wide. The lower bracts are papery, eventually curving backwards like wood shavings; the upper are tipped with a white or black fringe and may be pure white, pale pink or deep rosy red, concealing pale flowers. Below the fringe are fine silver hairs, which distinguish it from the otherwise similar *P. lepidocarpodendron*. Found in large numbers from Tulbagh through to Port Elizabeth but it is absent from the Klein River mountains where the latter grows. (Feb-Nov).

Protea speciosa   brown-bearded sugarbush

A many-stemmed, resprouting, fire-resistant shrub to 1,2m with thick leathery leaves 9-16cm long and up to 6cm wide. Plants growing in the Hermanus area have very narrow leaves (10mm) and were previously thought to be a different species. The oval flowerheads 9-14cm long are surrounded by brownish, pink or cream bearded bracts which almost conceal the flowers. It occurs widely through this area and beyond as solitary, scattered plants on the mountains between sea level and 1300m. (June-Jan).

♣ The large flowerheads of the sprawling *P. magnifica*, with similar bearded bracts of green, cream, pink or carmine, open wide to reveal a projecting dense white, brown or black central cone of flowers.

Protea grandiceps   red sugarbush

A single-stemmed, rounded shrub up to 2m tall by 3m across bearing blue-green, almost stalkless oblong leaves, 10-21cm long by 3-6cm wide, with wavy red to yellow edges. The 9-14cm long cup-shaped flowerheads have incurving conspicuously fringed and bearded bracts concealing the woolly-bearded flowers. It can be erect to sprawling, the flowerheads green, cream, pink, coral or carmine, It forms dense stands near the snow line on fire-protected rocky refuges and steep slopes of the Kogelberg and the Hottentots Holland mountains in our area. (June-Jan).

♣ The exquisite rosy-pink *P. stokoei* of the high mountains from Jonkershoek to Betty's Bay, with dark-bearded incurved bracts, always has a single erect stem.

158

Protea compacta

Protea longifolia

Protea neriifolia

Protea speciosa

Protea grandiceps

159

Protea acaulos
aardroos

A prostrate shrublet with a few trailing stems resprouting from a subterranean branch system. The smooth, oval leaves, upstanding from the stem, are variable in size from 6-25cm long by 1-7cm wide and taper gradually to the base. The crater-shaped, 3-6cm wide flowerheads have green, hairless, slightly incurving pink-tipped outermost bracts, which later curve backwards to reveal the brownish tips of the flower cluster within. Widespread from the Cedarberg to Bredasdorp it favours deeper sandy or granite-derived soils from sea level to 1500m. (Jun-Nov).

♣ *P. scolopendriifolia*, another resprouter with prostrate stems and long-stalked slightly sandpapery tongue-shaped leaves up to 60cm long by 2-8cm wide, has dark brown basal flowerhead bracts, several rows of silvery-pink pointed upper (inner) bracts and a strong yeast scent - probably mouse-pollinated. *P. caespitosa* has rosy pink goblets filled by the slightly longer brown-tipped flowers. Another small-headed species, *P. scolymocephala*, is a neat, erect shrub on a single stem, and up to 1.5m tall with narrow leaves. Once growing in thousands on the sandy plains of the Cape, it is now reduced over much of its range due to human spread and development.

Protea lorea
thong-leaf sugarbush

A mat-forming resprouting shrublet with underground stems and only the needlelike leaves up to 45cm long emerging in tufts from the soil. A pale yellow goblet-shaped flowerhead, up to 12cm long and 8cm across nestling within the leaves, contains a woolly flat-topped white flower cluster and is surrounded by tapering, pointed bracts. Most conspicuous in the first years after a burn, it is scattered on the lower slopes from 450-650m from Wemmershoek to Kogelberg. (Jan-Feb).

♣ The needle-leaves of *P. angustata* are born on short branches, and the applegreen rounded bracts of the crater-shaped flowerheads surround chocolate-tipped yeasty scented flowers. *P. subulifolia* has needle leaves up erect stems. The strongly stalked axillary flowerheads are yeasty-scented and have tan-coloured to pink papery bracts.

Protea scabra
sandpaper leaf sugarbush

A clumped shrublet with subterranean stems, has entirely sandpapery channelled 10-30cm long leaves varying from needlelike to 25mm wide, in tufts at ground level. Creamy pink crater-shaped stalkless flowerheads 3-4cm long, with flowers only just as long, favours shale soils from the Hottentots Holland to Klein River mountains. Flowering in the second year after fire. (Apr-Oct).

♣ *P. aspera*, with sandpapery leaves very like *P. scabra*, differs in flowerheads 6-10cm long on short shoots, and grows in shale and sand from Shaw's mountain lowlands to Agulhas. Another low-growing, resprouting mat-former with reedlike leaves and cream (to pink) goblet flowers near the ground is *P. scorzonerifolia*. It differs in having branches produced above the ground, in having the flowers longer than the flowerhead bracts, and in having only the edges of the leaves sandpapery.

Protea cordata
heart-leaf sugarbush

This low-growing reseeding protea with erect unbranched smooth reddish stems bears its huge heart-shaped leaves well spaced out, 14 x 16cm but reducing markedly in size upwards. Each year a new crop of stems is produced with its conspicuous distinctive red-flushed leaves. Stalked rounded buds opening into crater shaped flowerheads 4-5cm across are clustered at ground level, with loose papery brown bracts protecting creamy flowers with bright red tips. Occurring from sea level up to 1200m in every kind of habitat, it is found from Du Toit's Kloof through to the Bredasdorp mountains. (June-July). Although having the character of a rodent pollinated species, it lacks the yeasty scent and its pollinators are at present uncertain.

♣ The only other ground protea with broad leaves arranged in this manner is *P. amplexicaulis* with its single, branched, prostrate stem bearing craterlike purple-black yeasty scented flowers. It occurs only in the Hottentots Holland part of our area.

Protea acaulos

Protea lorea

striped   mouse

Protea scabra

Protea cordata

The genus **Leucadendron**, the "sunshine proteas", conebushes or "tolbosse", consists of about 80 species of large simple-leaved shrubs with male and female flowers in cones on separate plants, the males often having smaller leaves or smaller and clustered flowerheads (See glossary p. 309). It is confined mainly to the fynbos areas of the Cape but extends into KwaZulu-Natal. Approximately nineteen species have been recorded in our area. The character of the fruits can be discovered only by allowing a cone to dry and open up. In some species cones are dropped annually and may be found under the parent plant; in others, the cones are held intact until the mother plant dies. The name "sunshine protea" refers to the delightful golden yellow leaf colour of many species when in flower, often transfusing whole mountainsides with a yellow wash visible a long way off.

Leucadendron elimense ssp. vyeboomense — Vyeboom conebush
A sparsely branched shrub to 1.5m with narrow hairless leaves ca 43mm x 11mm in both sexes. The spicy-scented male flowerheads are up to 46mm across, (foreground) the females half as wide, but often grouped up to four at a time, (background); the structure and cone behaviour is as for L. tinctum. It occurs only on Bokkeveld shale soils in the vicinity of Vyeboom near Grabouw. (Sept-Oct).

♣This rare species has three subspecies, all confined to shale soil, all threatened with extinction due to agriculture and invasive alien plants. L. elimense ssp.salteri with rather broader leaves, may just still survive on gravel soil in the Hemel en Aarde valley and Shaw's Pass behind Hermanus. A third variant occurs on the Elim flats. All grow fast, make seeds soon and die in c.10 years after a fire.

Leucadendron gandogeri — broad-leaved conebush
A sturdy rounded shrub to 1.6m with a single stem and large oval leaves up to 11cm long by 3cm wide in females, 8 by 2cm in males, hairless when mature. The involucral leaves, yellow but often tinged with orange or red, form an open cup around the flowerheads: (females top, males below). Brown, recurved, fringed involucral bracts form a scalloped eggcup at the base of the hairless cones whose female flowers appear up its flanks. The cones are retained on the bush until fire opens them. It is found in dense stands on stony sandstone slopes from Stellenbosch to Bredasdorp from sea-level to 1350m. (Aug-Sept). The similar **L. microcephalum** with large involucral bracts, staining oily-brown and forming a halo around the flowerheads are distinctive; the outermost bracts being recurved at the tips (see closeup of the male).

♣ The flowerheads of the very similar June-flowering L. laureolum are entirely concealed by the overarching involucral leaves. The cones have a rippled surface.

Leucadendron linifolium — line-leaf conebush
A dense, single-stemmed shrub to 2m tall, with narrow, slightly flattened and twisted leaves, tapering towards the base, 7-27-35mm long and 1-3mm wide. The male flowerheads (upper left) are borne above the leaves on leafless stalks, the rounded females (lower right) nestle in the uppermost leaves with a collar of small broad-based, pointed, browning involucral bracts. The flowers emerge all over the surface of the cone. The mottled dusky nutlets are retained within the cone until the death of the parent plant. It occurs from the Strand, Bot River, Hermanus, Bredasdorp to Riversdale on level seasonally waterlogged sands over clay. (Sept-Oct).

♣Two more have small narrow leaves. Both are really almost outside our area: the needle-leaved very rare L. laxum, occurring from Stanford to Bredasdorp on moist flats, with flowers constricted to a cluster at the top of the flowerhead, the cones becoming cherry red later before shedding nutlets in late summer; and L.teretifolium, found on clay soils from Bot River, Stanford to Riversdale with long thickish, non-tapering cylindrical leaves, green, pointed cones whose flowers emerge along the flanks, with involucral bracts long and pointed.

Leucadendron elimense ssp. vyeboomense
(Male and female)

Leucadendron gandogeri
(Male and female)

Leucadendron linifolium
(Male and female)

Leucadendron microcephalum
(Male)

163

Leucadendron platyspermum plateseed conebush

A conspicuous light green shrub, with clusters of branches arising just below last year's flower-head. The leaves of the 1.3m tall male are up to 4cm long and 5mm wide, and flowerheads (in the upper part of the illustration) 13 x 12mm; those of the 1.7m tall, sparingly branched females up to 7 x 1.3cm, flowerheads (below in the illustration) encircled by 28mm long leaves maturing into a huge 5 x 4cm cone. The floral bracts, each 15mm long by 32mm wide, are joined tightly into a continuous spiral enclosing the largest fruits in the genus, thin and flat with huge lateral wings, which cleave tightly to the roof of their cells. (See ecology p. 37). The dense stands seen in our area are planted orchards for harvesting; natural populations as at Bot River are less dense. It is a Red Data vulnerable species and occurs in the wild from Groenland to Elim in hard gravelly or sandy or shaly soils. (Sept).

Leucadendron spissifolium common spear-leaved conebush

This resprouter is represented in our area by the ssp. spissifolium, up to 1.3m tall with many hairless stems. The hairless, shiny red-tipped leaves, 25-63 x 1.5-6.4mm in the males, 27-81 x 3-17mm in the females, are slightly twisted along the axis. The male cones are up to 18mm (r. and behind) and the female (l. foreground) up to 15mm diameter, with a faint lemon scent, and are haloed by ivory-coloured pointed involucral leaves. Female flowers emerge up the flanks of the cone, and the cones are retained until the parent plants are destroyed by fire. It grows on damp sandy slopes from sea level to 1500m, and as is typical of resprouting plants, tends to be not in dense populations but widely scattered. The species has the most extensive distribution in the genus, from the Gifberg to Cape Peninsula, Kogelberg, Elim and the Langeberg, the other subspecies discontinuously through the Southern Cape mountains to near Port Elizabeth and Port Shepstone.

♣ Two other c. 1.5m tall resprouting narrow-leaved tolbosse are *L. lanigerum* on clays of the Cape flats to the Strand, distinguished by its gritty, rough-surfaced leaves from the next resprouter: *L. salignum* with smooth leaves, which is widespread dotted along all mountain firebreaks in the fynbos.

Leucadendron tinctum spicy conebush

Spreading, single-stemmed shrubs to 1.3m. The oblong, blue-green leaves are up to 11cm long by 5cm broad in the female and less in the male. They become larger and more crowded towards the tips of the branches forming an opulent, loose yellow, reddening cup of involucral leaves around the flower heads, the colour intensifying at flowering time. The pepper or spice-scented flowers are constricted by an encircling collar of oily, yellow, tightly recurved involucral bracts, to emerge as a cluster on the summit of the cone.[1] The nut-like fruits are held in yellow, reddening cones until they are released in late summer. Occurring in fairly dense stands on stony, acid sands in the Caledon and Bredasdorp districts, it has been recorded throughout this area. (July-Aug).

♣ Other broadish-leaved species with similar flowerheads, involucral leaves, bracts and non-persistent cones are the endangered *L. globosum* of south-sloping loam soils in the Elgin valley which has rather smaller leaves; *L. sessile*, confined to moist granite soils from Hottentots Holland to Kogelberg, with narrower leaves, never becoming pale before turning red, and there is a conspicuous high collar of notably erect, brittle, brown bracts; the involucral leaves of the very similar *L. daphnoides* on the Panorama trail at Jonkershoek become very pale cream before turning red.

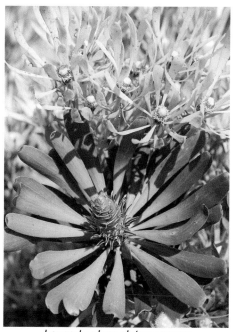

Leucadendron platyspermum
(Male and Female)

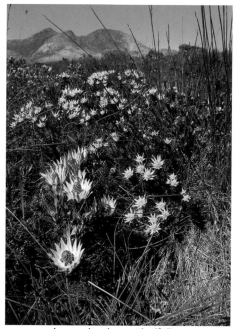

Leucadendron spissifolium
(Male and Female)

Leucadendron tinctum (Female)

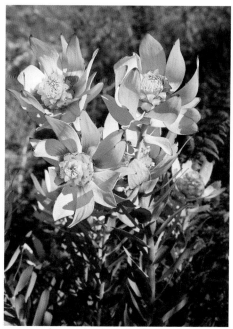

Leucadendron tinctum (Male)

Leucadendron xanthoconus   sickle-leaved conebush

A dense shrub to 2m with a single main stem. (Male yellow, visible to the left, female, greenish, to the right of the slide). The narrow leaves, twisted at the base, about 6mm wide and 65mm long, are slightly sickle-shaped and silver-hairy when young. Rather longer yellow involucral leaves splay out round the flowerheads and the pointed, erect, brown involucral bracts envelop only the base. Female flowers emerge all the way up the flanks of the hairy cone. Mature cones containing their narrow-winged dusky fruits are retained until the death of the parent plant. It occurs in large stands from the Cape Peninsula to Riviersonderend and from the Groenland mountain to Potberg including Kogelberg and the Klein River mountains on sandy lower slopes and flats. (Aug).

♣ Two other narrow-leafed, reseeding, single-stemmed species occur in our area. In both the female flowers emerge up the flanks of the flowerhead, all retain cones until the death of the parent and the fruits are winged: *L. salicifolium* the social, 3m tall species of damp sand throughout our area has yellow involucral bracts forming a conspicuous cup subtending the cone, and copious pollen shed in clouds when in flower in the spring. The treelike 4m tall *L. coniferum* growing on wind-blown coastal sands from Kogelberg to Bredasdorp has only about four oval point-tipped involucral bracts.

The genus **Leucospermum**, the pincushions, consists of 46 species of treelike to shrubby or prostrate woody shrubs, occurring mainly in the fynbos regions of the Cape Province; one occurs in Zimbabwe. Thirteen are recorded in this area. The simple toothed leaves have characteristic glandular swellings on the edge which secrete a sugary liquid. These are called extra-floral nectaries, but their function is still only speculative. A striking feature is the long sturdy styles, the 'pins' which give the genus the name of pincushion proteas. The visibility of the flowerheads is unaccentuated by either involucral leaves (as in *Leucadendron*) or bracts (as in *Protea* itself), but relies on the flowers alone. It has a nutlike seed. (See ecology p. 37).

Leucospermum bolusii   Gordon's Bay pincushion

An erect rounded shrub to 1.5m tall, with a single main trunk and oval leaves tipped with a single gland. Clusters of up to 8, short-stalked, sweetly-scented, creamy-white, rounded flowerheads up to 2cm across, with straight styles, are borne at the branch tips. It occurs in large numbers on steep slopes between Gordon's Bay and Kogelbay from sea level to 150m and is easily seen from the coastal road. (Sept-Dec).

♣ The more slender *L. truncatulum*, throughout our area, with crowded grey leaves lacking a gland has similar but yellowish flowerheads 2cm across, which turn crimson with age. The sweet-scented, white-flowered *L. calligerum* of Houw Hoek mountain in our area has longer inward-curving styles.

Leucospermum cordifolium   the pincushion

This best-known pincushion and dependable garden plant is up to 1.5m high and 2m across with one main stem and spreading drooping branches bearing heart-shaped 2-8 x 2-4.5cm hairy leaves, becoming hairless, and with up to 6 glandular teeth. The leaves vary much in size and shape. 1-3 short-stalked terminal flowerheads 10-12cm across and yellow, orange or crimson have particularly conspicuous pins. It occurs from Arieskraal and Houwhoek to Kleinmond and Bredasdorp. Originally present in Hermanus, it was nearly eliminated but re-introduced, and has naturalised and is spreading fast on the lower slopes. (Aug-Jan).

♣ The delicate prostrate *L. cordatum* on yellow-brown scree slopes slopes near Rooiels has heart-shaped leaves with a single glandular tooth.

Leucadendron xanthoconus
(Male and Female)

Leucospermum bolusii

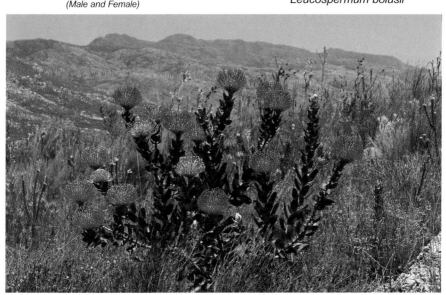

Leucospermum cordifolium

167

Leucospermum conocarpodendron ssp. viridum green tree pincushion

The tallest and widest pincushion protea, it is a sturdy dense-crowned tree 3-5m tall on a single thick trunk, with woolly branches and corky bark. The stalkless leaves are deep green, 6-12 x 2-5cm with 3-10 glandular teeth. Terminal rounded flowerheads 7-9cm across and bright yellow, are grouped 1-3 together. It usually occurs in stands on the lowlands from the Cape Peninsula, Hottentots Holland and Kogelberg to Stanford. (Aug-Dec).

♣ A second tree-like species, the limestone loving *L. patersonii* whose orange to crimson flowers have bold orange styles and broad leaves with 3-8 teeth survives in Kleinmond.

Leucospermum gracile Hermanus pincushion

A mat-forming shrub to 1.5m across with a single main stem and leaves 20-45mm by 2-5mm with 0 or 3 glandular teeth. The top-shaped, yellow flowerheads, 25-30mm across, become greenish with age. It is still abundant on the mountains from Onrus and Hermanus to Bredasdorp. It prefers south-facing aspects or higher northern slopes from 100-330m but may occur up to 1200m in well-drained sands. (July-Dec).

Leucospermum gueinzii kloof fountain pincushion

A coarse hairy shrub to 3m with a single main stem and smooth bright green leaves up to 10 x 3cm. The deep orange flowerheads, up to 14cm across and with the styles twisted outwards, occur in groups of 1-3 and become bright crimson with age. It occurs in moist sheltered kloofs near streams on heavy clay soils from 300-1000m on the Hottentots Holland mountains from Jonkershoek to Sir Lowry's Pass; and also recorded from Houw Hoek. (Aug-Dec).

Leucospermum lineare needle-leaf pincushion

Two forms of this plant occur, the more usual having a sprawling habit and golden yellow flowers. A local, more erect form with deep orange flowers is found at Franschhoek. The plants have narrow leaves 4-10cm long and only 2-7mm wide, 1-3 glandular teeth, and flowerheads up to 9cm across, usually solitary but sometimes in groups of 2-3. It occurs on granite-derived clay and gravelly soils between 300-1000m in the mountains from Bain's Kloof to Jonkershoek but is nowhere common. (July-Jan).

Leucospermum prostratum yellow trailing pincushion

A trailing perennial with numerous slender unbranched stems up to 2m long. The vertical olive-green leaves are up to 40mm long by 2-6mm broad with no glandular teeth. Clusters of up to 3 spherical, sweetly-scented flowerheads, 20-25mm in diameter, open bright yellow and become orange with age. It occurs mainly on sandy coastal flats from Kogelberg eastwards to Bredasdorp. (July-Dec).

♣ Another mat-forming *Leucospermum*, the sweetly-scented *L. hypophyllocarpodendron* with bright yellow inflorescences and narrow erect leaves with 2-4 red glandular teeth, occurs at Stellenbosch in our area.

Leucospermum conocarpodendron ssp viridum

Leucospermum gracile

Leucospermum lineare

Leucospermum gueinzii

Leucospermum prostratum

169

Leucospermum oleifolium
Overberg pincushion

An erect, single-stemmed rounded shrub growing to 1m, with lance-shaped leaves up to 6 x 2.5cm with 0-2-5 glandular teeth. The flowerheads, each 25-40mm across, are grouped in clusters of from 2-5. The flowers open bright yellow and turn crimson with age, each cluster usually containing a range of different shades, and remaining colourful for up to two months. Occurring in a variety of habitats from sea level to 1000m, often in dense stands, it has been recorded from Bain's Kloof to Hangklip but not at Hermanus. (Aug-Jan).

Mimetes argenteus
silver pagoda

An erect single-stemmed, sparsely-branched shrub to 3.5m with oval, spreading, silvery-hairy leaves 40-65 x 18-36mm with 1-3 teeth. The terminal flowerheads, 10-12cm across and 8-15cm long, have deep carmine to mauve leaves separating the clusters of 6-9 flowers. It is rare on moist southern midslopes on the Hottentots Holland to Riviersonderend mountains but does not occur at Hermanus. (Mar-June).

♣ There are 13 species of which 8 have been recorded in our area. Three more, all in the Kogelberg Biosphere Reserve, are silvery-leafed, rare and vulnerable and occupy marsh habitats easily damaged if walked into: two are the 2-6m tall *M. arboreus* with salmon pink flowerheads; the 1-3m tall *M. hottentoticus* with cream tepals and bold, erect red styles tipped with conspicuous black knobs.

Mimetes hirtus
marsh pagoda

A single-stemmed well-branched shrub to 2.5m with lance-shaped green leaves 25-45 x 5-18mm becoming hairless. The flowerheads have a crown of smaller pink leaves, and the flowers, grouped 9-14 between inconspicuous green leaves, are enfolded by yellow, red-tipped bracts. It occurs from the Cape Peninsula, throughout our area and on to Elim. It is vulnerable because it prefers lowland marshes and stream-banks which are becoming damaged by development. It has been exterminated in the municipal area of Hermanus but is still locally abundant in Betty's Bay. (May-Nov).

♣ *M.capitulatus*, in high places throughout our area, has reddish flowerheads. The inconspicuous *M. palustris* of the Klein River mountains, with clasping leaves, has skimpy pale yellow flowerheads.

Mimetes cucullatus
common pagoda, stompies

A sturdy shrub to 2m with many stiff stems arising from an underground rootstock called a lignotuber. The oblong hairless leaves are up to 55mm long. The flowerhead is up to 10cm long topped by a crown of smaller, red leaves, and comprises bundles of 4-7 flowers held together from above by an orange-red clasping leaf; colour varies from red and orange to yellow, cream or greenish. It is widespread from the Koue Bokkeveld to the Cape Peninsula, throughout the Kogelberg to Betty's Bay coastal plain, to Hermanus, Elim and on as far as the Kouga Mountains on sandstone slopes in sparse clumps and extensive stands, varying in height and dimensions. (all year).

Leucospermum oleifolium

Mimetes argenteus

Mimetes hirtus

Mimetes cucullatus

171

VISCACEAE – The mistletoe family

Viscum capense
mistletoe, voëlent

A small parasitic shrub up to 50cm in spread with leaves reduced to scales and male and female flowers on separate plants (but still possibly on the same host plant). The unstalked berries are translucent white and smooth. It may be found parasitising the branches of *Chrysanthemoides, Euclea, Maytenus* and *Pterocelastrus* from Namibia to Caledon. (Jul-Oct).

♣ There are c.100 species mainly tropical with 3 in our area. The leafy *V. pauciflorum* has smooth stalked orange berries, parasitises *Rhus, Euclea* and *Maytenus* and occurs from the Bokkeveld plateau to Hangklip.

SANTALACEAE – The sandalwood family

Osyris speciosa

A woody shrub with an extensive lignotuber from which it resprouts copiously after fire with short very twiggy and leafy branchlets, and abundant small flowers with 4 sepals and no petals. The 4 anthers are fastened to the sepals by hairs. The inferior ovary matures into a brilliant astringent red to purple berry. The huge crop lights up as red patches in the burnt landscape. As fruiting comes to an end, buds from low on these branchlets grow into sturdy strong perennial leafy branch systems to about 80cm high, but no further flowers are produced until a fire initiates the cycle once more. It occurs on lower sandstone slopes and flats from the Hottentots Holland to Bredasdorp in fynbos. (Sept-May).

♣ There are 9 species, 1 more here: the widespread *O. compressa*, a 5m green-blue shrub or tree in scrub and forest margin throughout the Cape to tropical Africa produces its purple fruits most of the year.

Thesium carinatum

A yellowish-green, root-parasitic shrublet to 70cm with narrow leaves 10mm long and triangular in cross-section. Clusters of short-stalked cloyingly scented flowers 2-3mm long with 5 bearded sepals and stamens, and an almost stalkless stigma, are immersed among leaflike bracts. Occurring on mountain slopes from Clanwilliam to the Cape Peninsula. It may bloom at any time of the year.

♣ There are c. 300 species, of which c. 32 species have been recorded in our area, differing in technical details of the flowers and leaves.

Thesium euphorbioides

A distinctive, slender, single-stemmed root-parasitic shrub to 2m, with a few short branches near the top, usually rising well above the surrounding plants. The broad, oval, leathery, blue-green leaves enfold the upper stems. The tiny white flowers are borne in clusters among the large bracts at the end of the branches. It occurs on rocky slopes from Tulbagh and Worcester to Stellenbosch, and Caledon to Uitenhage. (Aug-Jan).

Thesidium fragile

A brittle, often yellowish root-parasitic shrublet to 50cm with scale-like leaves and bracts, smaller than the flowers, male and female flowers with 4 sepals and stamens on separate plants. The fruit (seen here) is white, with an orange calyx. The lower leaves (not visible here) are sometimes longer and spreading. It occurs on sandy flats and slopes from Saldanha to the Eastern Cape. (all year).

♣ There are 5 species, of which two more occur in our area: the leaves and bracts of the very small *T. hirtum* are larger, overlapping and rough-hairy; the females of the 40cm tall *T. fruticulosum* have greenish fruits and large, overlapping leaves longer than the flowers.

Viscum capense

Osyris speciosa

Thesium euphorbioides

Thesium carinatum

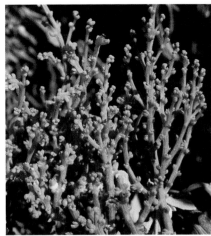

Thesidium fragile

173

AIZOACEAE – The mesemb or vygie family

Acrodon subulatus

A compact tufted fleshy perennial succulent to 10cm high, with leaves triangular in cross-section and bearing a few flexible teeth at the tip. Solitary white to pink flowers having "petals" with a dark edge and midrib, and stamens gathered into a central cone, give rise to 5-chambered woody capsules, more than 20mm long, which open when wetted, closing again each time on drying, and having a large woody knob in the mouth of each chamber. The seeds are dispersed by heavy drops of rain. It grows on lower slopes in renosterveld and coastal fynbos in our area. (Nov-Apr).

♣ There are 5 species but only one more, the prostrate white or pink perennial with visible internodes, *A. parvifolius,* occurs in clay streambeds on the Hermanus coast.

Acrosanthes teretifolia   spekvygie

A cryptic sprawling plant to 80cm with smooth, stubby fleshy leaves in pairs. The single, white, stalked flowers arise in the axils of leaves or in the forks between branches, and comprise 5 sepals joined into a tube, no petals, many stamens fastened near the mouth of the tube, and a 2-chambered, superior ovary with 2 styles.

♣ There are 5 species, all in the Cape, but only this one in our area.

Carpobrotus acinaciformis   sour fig, khoi fig

The prostrate stems are up to 1,5m long with heavy triangular leaves up to 9cm long and 15-20mm thick. The brilliant magenta flowers are 12cm across. It favours loose sand and is found throughout this area at low altitudes. (Aug-Oct).

♣ A third species, the pink to purple-flowered *C. mellei, (=C. pillansii)*, with flowers 5-8cm across, occurs at high altitudes throughout this area. All produce fleshy fruits.

Carpobrotus edulis   sour fig, suurvy

A coarse mat-forming, creeping perennial, rooting at the nodes, with prostrate stems up to 2m long. The dull green fleshy leaves are triangular in cross-section and 4-8cm long. The yellow flowers fade to pinkish and are followed by fleshy edible fruits used to make a sweet, uniquely Cape jam/preserve. It is usually found in loose sand and is used as an important stabiliser of road verges in the Cape and elsewhere in the world. (Aug-Oct).

♣ There are about 13 species, mainly South African, but others are found in Chile and Australia. Three occur in this area.

Erepsia anceps   altydvygie

A slender woody hairless shrublet to 50cm with distant pairs of tapering leaves triangular in cross-section and less than 5mm diameter with an outcurving point. The narrow-petalled pink or magenta flowers are about 30mm across, borne well spaced at the ends of the branches, and give rise to a 5-chambered capsule. It is frequent throughout this area and as far east as Danger Point and flowers most abundantly after fires. (Dec-Apr).

♣ There are about 20 species occurring in the fynbos region, of which only c. 6 have been recorded in this area. All have pink, magenta or purple flowers, tuck their pollen and anthers under in the interior of the flower, and most remain open day and night.

Acrodon subulatus

Acrosanthes teretifolia

Carpobrotus ~~edulis~~ acinaciformis

Carpobrotus ~~acinaciformis~~ edulis

Erepsia anceps

Christine Wakfer

175

Aizoon sarmentosum

A sprawling non-fleshy many-stemmed perennial with stems up to 50cm long, bearing pairs of cylindrical leaves up to 45mm long. The hairy flowers, about 10mm across, have a superior ovary of 5 chambers with many seeds in each, which give rise to woody top-shaped fruits which persist on the older stems. It occurs on sandy flats and lower slopes from Namaqualand to Swellendam. (June-Oct).

♣ There are about 20 species in the Mediterranean area, Africa and Australia, of which 15 occur in South Africa, but only 1 here.

Lampranthus furvus   vygie

A neat rounded non-hairy shrublet to 25cm tall with blue-green leaves 10-15mm long. The pink to purple flowers are up to 3cm across, close at night and are followed by 5-chambered capsules which are open at the throat. (compare *Ruschia*) It occurs among rocks on mountain slopes from Clanwilliam and Worcester to the Cape Peninsula and eastwards to Caledon. (Nov-Jan).

♣ There are about 80 species in southern Africa, of which c. 9 occur in this area. Other pink species are the shrubby estuarine *L. calcaratus,* the mat-forming *L. wordsworthiae,* and the rosy-flowered creeping, node-rooting *L. filicaulis.*

Lampranthus bicolor   vygie

An erect or spreading shrublet, woody at the base, to 50cm, with brilliant yellow flowers with a coppery reverse (not visible on the slide), which gives the plant a striking two-tone effect. Common in sand from Tulbagh to the Cape Peninsula and Bredasdorp. (Oct-Dec)

♣ Other yellow-flowered species are the pure yellow shrubby *L. glaucus;* and the creeping *L. explanatus* and mat-forming *L. reptans* with long-stalked yellow or white flowers.

Ruschia macowanii   vygie

An open, sprawling shrub to 20cm high, spreading to 50cm across or more, but not rooting at the nodes. The hard, fleshy leaves 20-35mm long by 4mm thick are joined to form a slight sleeve around the stem. The outer petals have a central dark stripe and the paler inner petals and stamens form a cone in the centre. The 5-chambered fruits open when wetted, when a distinctive bony lump, called the 'closing body' can be seen in the throat of each chamber. It occurs from Velddrif to Bredasdorp, commonly near the sea. (July-Oct).

♣ There are upwards of 220 species in South Africa, mostly in the drier parts and c. 7 here, only one, *R .rigida*, a small rounded shrublet having white flowers 10mm in diameter. The rest have rosy to purple flowers, often with a dark stripe, and often with a central cone of stamens.

Tetragonia decumbens   kinkelbos

A sprawling perennial with branches to 1m long bearing fleshy oblong leaves, broadest towards the tip, whose surface cells swollen with sap glisten in the sun: one of many so-called ice-plants in this family. The yellow flowers have sepals free to the base, no petals, a more or less inferior ovary with one seed per chamber and stamens more than double the sepal number. The fruit is a nut with rigid wings. It is common on coastal dunes from Namibia to the Eastern Cape. (mainly Aug-Nov).

♣ Some 7 species occur here. 2 have stamens equal in number to the sepals and greenish flowers: *T. caesia* has flowers solitary in the leaf axils, and barrel-shaped fruits, whereas *T. echinata* has flowers 2-4 together and round, spiny fruits with horns. 4 have many stamens and yellow to orange flowers: the broadly rounded leaves of *T. nigrescens* and *T. herbacea* are often red below and the thin-stalked flowers, often purple on the reverse, are in axillary umbels; 2 have narrow leaves with recurved edges; *T. fruticosa* is erect or sprawling with long trailing stems and most of the flowers in terminal racemes; *T. namaquensis* is a small shrub with ascending branches to 30cm.

Aizoon sarmentosum

Lampranthus bicolor

Lampranthus furvus

Tetragonia decumbens

Ruschia macowanii

177

GRUBBIACEAE – The grubbia family

Grubbia tomentosa

A woody, many-stemmed, branching shrub to 2m with a fire-resistant stump. The pairs of narrow, open-backed leaves, tapering to both ends, are attached to knobs on the stems. The short-hairy pinkish insignificant flowers, borne in conelike clusters about 5mm across, give rise to red-purple berries. This is one of the few fynbos plants with a fleshy fruit. It occurs scattered on the drier, rocky mountain slopes from Ceres to George. (Dec-Jan).

♣ The 3 species of *Grubbia* which constitute this family all occur in our area. *G. rourkei* of the Kogelberg resembles *G. tomentosa*, but it is single-stemmed with narrower, more spreading leaves. *G. rosmarinifolia* of swamps and stream-sides throughout this area has very narrow leaves, woolly clusters of white flowers, and hairy wind-dispersed fruits.

BALANOPHORACEAE.

Mystropetalon thomii (incl. M. polemannii)   aardroos

A soft, leafless, tuberous perennial plant, wholly parasitic on the roots of members of the Protea family, mostly *Leucadendron* and *Protea*, with annual above-ground stems to 25cm. These consist of a dense spike of red unisexual flowers, the females on the lower and males on the upper part. The male flowers have spoon-shaped bracts. The seeds are dispersed by ants. It is recorded infrequently from the Malmesbury and Caledon areas, but when it does occur it is found in crowded groups. (Nov-May).

RANUNCULACEAE – The ranunculus or buttercup family

Anemone tenuifolia   wild anemone, syblom

A tufted perennial with stems to 60cm, and a number of divided, rather hard, dark green leaves 10-20cm long, with 3-toothed segments. The handsome, hairy, pink or white flowers are 8-10cm across. The closeup shows many yellow stamens surrounding a cone of brownish styles each representing one free carpel. It occurs on moist slopes from the Hex River mountains and Piketberg to the Cape Peninsula and eastwards to Humansdorp, and blooms most profusely after veld fires. (June-Feb).

♣ Anemone is a cosmopolitan genus of c. 150 species, with 3 in South Africa but only 1 in this area.

Knowltonia vesicatoria   brandblaar, katjiedrieblaar

A tufted perennial to 1.2m with a horizontal rhizome producing leathery long-stalked compound leaves whose 3 or more oval leaflets have toothed edges. Creamy-green flowers clustered on flowerstalks not much longer than the leaves produce smooth berries at first green, ripening black. It occurs in scrub or woody kloofs from the Bokkeveld Mountains to the Eastern Cape. (Aug-Oct).

♣ There are 8 species, but only 2 more here. Both are silky-hairy with vertical rhizomes and flowerstalks much longer than the leaves: *K. anemonoides* flowers after fire, has pink-flushed cream flowers, leaves oval shaped with scores of teeth on the margins and hairy fruit; *K. cordata* of forest margins and rocky places has heart-shaped leaflets and hairless fruits. All are said to be poisonous.

Grubbia tomentosa

Anne Bean

Mystropetalon thomil

Anemone tenuifolia

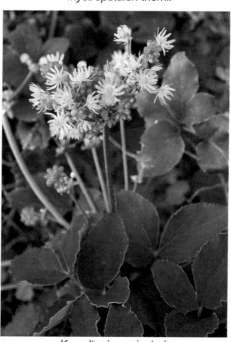

Knowltonia vesicatoria

179

LAURACEAE – The stinkwood family

Cassytha ciliolata   devil's sewing thread, devil's tresses, nooienshaar
A twining, rootless parasite with yellowish stems approximately the thickness of vermicelli, which attach themselves by means of disk-like pads to any host plant which presents itself sometimes building up to overwhelming tangles. The sessile, yellowish-white flowers, produced in clusters in the axils of the scale-like leaves, give rise to white, red or yellow berries which are eaten by birds. It occurs from Worcester and the Cape Peninsula to the Eastern Cape. (Flowers and berries all year).

♣ There are 16 species, 2 in South Africa, 1 in this area. It may be confused with dodder, *Cuscuta*, another total parasite with finer tangles of stems and flowers tiny pure white, star-like 5-lobed miniature convolvulus-like, of which two species occur here, both rare and not a pest like the exotic weeds of crop plants to our north.

Cryptocarya angustifolia   blue-laurel
An undistinguished shrub or small tree to 3m with narrow leaves, up to 11x1.2cm, slightly blue-green below, whose upper surface is conspicuously veined, and branchlets and buds covered with yellow hairs. The insignificant, whitish bisexual flowers (Nov) originating in groups in the axils of the leaves give rise to oval purplish fruits ca 2.3 x 1cm (Mar-Jul). It occurs in rocky river valleys from the Gifberg to the Langeberg and Swellendam.

♣ Elsewhere in the warmer parts of the world there are 200 species, many a source of aromatics and spices and valuable timber. In South Africa there are another six species in the summer rainfall region.

CARYOPHYLLACEAE – The carnation, catchfly and campion family

Silene pilosellifolia
An erect or sprawling softly hairy perennial to 70cm with narrow leaves broadening towards the tip. The flowers with a 10-20mm long calyx are borne facing more or less in one direction up a long flowering stem with white to purple notched petals. Found through out Africa. (Aug-Jan).

♣ Two more indigenous species are *S. crassifolia* of coastal sanddunes with fleshy felted leaves and white to yellow flowers with a c.13mm long calyx; and the glandular-hairy *S. undulata* up to 60cm high with 22-35mm long calyx and pink or white flowers. There are 2-3 further weedy exotic campions in our area.

BRASSICACEAE – The cabbage family

Heliophila subulata
A very finely-hairy annual or perennial to 50cm whose narrow leaves have stipules like resinous granular lumps. The blue, mauve or pink flowers have 4 petals regularly arranged and the fruits are narrow and up to 6cm long containing 24-42 seeds. It is widespread from the Cold Bokkeveld to the Eastern Cape on coastal slopes and flats. (Aug-Sept).

♣ There are 71 species confined to South Africa of which 5 annuals and 6 perennials occur in our area, They are identified by their seed pods as well as their habit.

Heliophila scoparia   sporrie
A tussock-forming often pleasantly scented perennial with striped branches to 1m tall has narrow leaves with minute stipules. The white, pink or purple flowers, borne in small groups on short side-branches, give rise to erect narrow 10-36-seeded pods. It is found on drier sandy slopes from the Gifberg to Genadendal and Hermanus. (Apr-Feb).

Cassytha ciliolata

Cryptocarya angustifolia

Silene pilosellifolia

Heliophila subulata

Heliophila scoparia

FUMARIACEAE

Cysticapnos vesicaria   klappertjies

A soft blue-green annual with bilobed leaves, branching and climbing to c. 1m by means of tendrils. The pink flowers, borne in racemes, are broadly winged and produce very distinctive and unmistakeable rounded, semi-translucent cherry-sized balloon-like fruits with 2 or more seeds. It occurs from Namaqualand to De Hoop on sandy flats and slopes. (Aug-Oct).

♣ *C. cracca* of damp slopes is distinguished by flattened fruits.

DROSERACEAE – The sundew family

Drosera cistiflora   sundew, doublom

A soft weakly erect perennial with an unbranched leafy stem to 20cm high. The leaves are 2-3cm long. The white, yellow, red, mauve or purple flowers have a dark green eye. It grows on sandy, often well-drained slopes or temporary seepages from Namaqualand to Port Elizabeth. (Aug-Sept).

♣ Three other sundews have leafy stems. *D. ramentacea* has a branched stem; *D. capensis* has leaves up to 15cm long with a well-defined leafstalk; and the sprawling *D. glabripes* of upper slopes has long erect hairs clothing the stem between the leaves, conspicuous tawny much-divided stipules, lower parts of the stem covered with reflexed withered remains of older leaves, and leaves like long-handled spoons.

Drosera pauciflora   little sundew

This small erect sundew has a rosette of reddish glandular-hairy leaves arising near the ground. 1-3 large pink or mauve flowers with a dark centre are borne on a leafless stem 10-15cm high, arising from the middle of the leaf rosette. Common in this area where it flowers most profusely after fire. (Aug-Nov).

♣ Four more rosette-forming species occur in this area: *D. aliciae* has a spike of pink flowers borne on a stem emerging from the side of the rosette while the similar *D. esterhuyseniae* has leaves without hairs on the upper surface toward the leaf base, and woolly below; and *D. slackii* resembles *D. esterhuyseniae* except for the leaves being only sparsely hairy below. *D. trinervia* has up to 10 flowers, most of them white at the end of the flower stalk.

Drosera hilaris   sprawling sundew

A very deep-rooted sundew with an unbranched sturdy stem up to 40cm high. The lance-shaped leaves with long stalks are up to 7cm long with dense rusty hairs underneath, and pale deeply fringed stipules. The pink flowers, c. 2cm across, are borne in a helicoid cyme arising out of the axil of a leaf: they open only in sunlight. It is found on sheltered, well-drained mountain slopes from the Cape Peninsula to Hermanus. In the latter area it is common about the contour path on Fernkloof but not higher. (Sept-Nov).

RORIDULACEAE – The Roridula family

Roridula gorgonias   vlieëbos

A woody, sparingly-branched shrublet to 1m or more whose narrow leaves, up to 12cm long, and crowded at the tips of the branches, are covered with sticky immovable tentacles. The pink flowers are 2cm across. A bug lives among the leaves, immune to the glue, living off the plant sap. Its droppings boost the fertility of the impoverished marsh soil immediately beneath the plant. It occurs in scattered colonies in damp places on the mountains from Stellenbosch to Swellendam. (July-Oct).

Cysticapnos vesicaria

Cysticapnos vesicaria John Manning

Drosera cistiflora

Drosera pauciflora

Drosera hilaris John Manning

Roridula gorgonias

183

CUNONIACEAE

Cunonia capensis butterspoon tree, rooiels

A large shrub or fire-resistant multi-stemmed tree to 30m whose glossy pinnate compound leaves have a serrated edge. The stipules are large paddle-like structures at the stem ends, enclosing the next pair of leaves and stipules and a dollop of creamy, rather sticky mucilage – hence the common name. Handsome creamy bottlebrushes of small tightly packed flowers arise at the branch ends. It grows in marshes, in streams and in damp forests from the Grootwinterhoek mountains to South Mozambique. (Mar-June).

♣ All other 16 species of *Cunonia* are confined to New Caledonia.

Platylophus trifoliatus witels

A tree to 30m with paired trifoliate, narrow, serrated leaflets and small stipules. The loose, long-stalked clusters of small, cream-coloured scented flowers arise in the axils of the leaves. It occurs in forest along streams from Betty's Bay to Humansdorp. (Dec-Feb).

♣ This is the only species in the genus.

CRASSULACEAE – The stonecrop and houseleek family

Adromischus caryophyllaceus nentabos

A branched succulent shrublet with tough, uniformly green, spoon-shaped or oval leaves 2.5-4cm by 1-2cm with rounded edges. The flowers, borne in spikes on stems up to 20cm long, are about 2cm long with petals joined to form a tube concealing the stamens. It is found on the coastal plain from Hermanus to Mossel Bay and inland areas of the Caledon district to Uniondale. (Oct-Mar).

♣ There are 26 species in South Africa with 2 in this area. *A. hemisphaericus* differs in having protruding anthers and spotted leaves.

Cotyledon orbiculata pig's ear, varksoor, kouteri

A hugely variable shrub to 1m with thick, fleshy branches and pairs of thick, waxy, green or grey leaves often with red edges, 5-10cm long by 2-5cm wide, widest in the upper third. The waxy red or pinkish flowers are up to 25mm long. Occurring widely in Namibia and South Africa and said to be poisonous, it may flower throughout the year. It is the only species in this area.

♣ There are about 150 species in Africa, Asia, Mexico and Europe, of which about 10 occur in the Cape Province. The leaves, scored, held in place on the foot and changed now and then, are quite effective in curing plantar warts.

Crassula fascicularis klipblom

A more or less branched succulent perennial with stems up to 40cm high bearing pointed, slightly fleshy leaves which are often hairy-edged. The jasmine-like flowers have petals up to 32mm long, white to pale cream or green, sometimes pink-tinged, which do not broaden towards the tips. It occurs from Vanrhynsdorp to Bredasdorp on lower fynbos slopes and is sweetly-scented in the evening. (Sept-Nov).

♣ There are about 300 species, mainly in Africa and India, with perhaps 30 in this area. Another large-flowered species is *C. obtusa* of mountain rock pools with narrow fleshy leaves and pale petals, flushed red, which broaden towards the tips.

184

Cunonia capensis

Platylophus trifoliatus

Adromischus caryophyllaceus   Anne Bean

Cotyledon orbiculata

Crassula fascicularis

185

Crassula capensis   cape snowdrop
A normally diminutive tuberous geophyte to 20cm tall it has pairs of delicate, disproportionately large round leaves with a scalloped edge. Clusters of snowy white flowers (occasionally pinkish), with 3-8mm long petals on stalks raised up above the leaves, make a pretty show in the shadows where they usually grow, often in damp places and under overhanging rocks. (May-Nov).

Crassula coccinea   red crassula, Kipblom
A succulent shrublet to 60cm with thick branches. It has overlapping, thinly fleshy, hairy-edged leaves 12-25mm by 10-15mm. The brilliant red (rarely white) flowers have 5 petals joined into a tube near the base. It is common in rock crevices and on ledges on sandstone from the Cape Peninsula to Bredasdorp. (Dec-Jan) and is pollinated by the Table Mountain Beauty butterfly.

BRUNIACEAE – The blacktips or Brunia family

The related genera *Berzelia* and *Brunia* differ in the former having one style projecting beyond the five petals of each small flower whereas the latter has two styles. All members of the family have leaves ending in black tips.

Berzelia incurva   klipknopbossie
A much-branched asymmetrical, open shrub to 1m with crowded, incurved, hairy-edged, flexible short-stalked leaves 6-7mm long, moveable on the branch. The flower heads are 6-7mm across and occur in groups of 1-3 on short twiglets near the tips of the branches, the flowers closely packed with the anthers projecting conspicuously from the mass. It is uncommon and confined to rocky upper slopes in the east of this area. (Jan-Mar).

Berzelia squarrosa   spiderbush
A resprouting erect shrub to 1.5m with soft-textured, spreading stalked leaves 10-15mm long and 1-2mm wide. Each flowerhead is 6-8mm across, growing singly on short stalks and grouped to form a flattish compound head at the ends of the branches. It occurs on moist slopes and stream-sides throughout this area except for the Kogelberg. (Aug-Sept).

♣ There are 12 species, endemic to the South and South Western Cape, 7 occurring in this area. In the Kogelberg occurs *B. dregeana* having flowerheads less than 5mm wide. Another similar species, *B. rubra* of the Klein River mountains, has flower-heads borne on cobwebby stalks and blooms in late summer.

Berzelia lanuginosa   kolkol, vleiknoppiesbos, kuikentjiebos
A finely-leafy reseeding shrub to 2m with short-stalked, soft-textured threadlike leaves on soft, drooping branches. The small cream flowers are grouped into heads c. 5mm across with characteristic red tissue at the bases of the stalks, and arranged in short axillary racemes clustered into terminal loose groups. A berry-like fruit is produced similar to *Brunia alopecuroides* which is a duller red. It is widespread in large populations from the Gifberg to the Bredasdorp mountain in seeps and on damp sandy slopes and streambanks. (Sept-Dec).

♣ 3 other species having larger flowerheads (>10mm) grouped to form a compound branch end head are: *B. ecklonii* of the Kogelberg with 3mm closely incurving leaves; 2 resprouters: *B. abrotanoides* on coastal sands and *B. intermedia* of upper slopes in the Hottentots Holland.

186

Crassula capensis

Crassula coccinea

Anne Bean

Berzelia incurva

Berzelia lanuginosa

Berzelia squarrosa

Brunia alopecuroides

A sturdy, erect shrub seen here in fruit, up to 1.5m tall with crowded, hairless, stalkless, stiff leaves about 4mm long covering numerous ascending slender branchlets. The flowers, with 2 styles each, are grouped in flowerheads about 5mm across, borne in short spikes on pale flowering stems, massed into large heads 15cm or more across at the ends of the main branches. The fruit of this species is far more distinctive than the flower. As the flowers fade the hard fruiting heads turn deep red. The tip of the plant grows on to produce the next season's flowers, leaving the fruits clustered among the leaves like miniature berries. They gradually fade to brown and may remain on the plant for a further season. It forms dense stands in marshy areas on mountain slopes throughout this area. (Sept-Jan).

♣ There are about 6 species confined to the fynbos area of South Africa, of which 5 occur in this area.

Brunia albiflora   coffee bush

A reseeding shrub to 3m with many side branches conspicuously more slender than the main axis, and several flushes of flowerheads persisting on the plant. The crowded, stalkless, spreading, very thin leaves are up to 12mm long and the flowerheads, borne singly on stalks about 4cm long, are up to 15mm across and form a pale, flat-topped group contrasting strikingly with the dark flowerhead stalks. It occurs in dense stands in rather damp places from the Hottentots Holland to Klein River mountains, and emits an elusive coffee scent. (Mar-Apr).

Brunia stokoei   rooistompie

An erect rigid resprouting shrub growing 1-2m high with hairless, stalkless, needlelike leaves 8-10mm long. The flowers are borne in heads about 15mm across with very imperfectly developed collars of bracts below, and is the only species with red flowers. It occurs at mid elevations in the Kleinmond and Betty's Bay areas. (Nov-Apr).

Brunia noduliflora   Stompie, fonteinbossie, volstruisies

A shrub to 90cm, resprouting from a persistent stump. The fairly hairy branches are covered with stalkless closely packed leaves 2-3mm long. The cream flowerheads, 10mm across and supported below by a sturdy collar of tightly packed bracts, are made fluffy by their long stamens. It is common on hills and mountain slopes from Piketberg to Jonkershoek, Hottentots Holland, Kogelberg through to Hermanus, and on to Uitenhage. (Mar-June).

♣ Another resprouter, B. laevis, has larger 15mm wide flowerheads and stiff overlapping leaves covered with fine short hairs that give it a grey appearance.

Nebelia paleacea   bergstompie

A dense rounded much-branched shrub to 1m or more, resprouting from a fire-resistant stump after veld fires. The leaves are 3-6mm long, almost without hairs, and held close to the twig. The flowers with 2 styles, immersed in long spiky bracts, are borne in groups of prickly heads up to 7mm across on branched shoots at the top of the main stem. It occurs in a diversity of soils and aspects from sea level to middle altitudes from Clanwilliam to Riversdale. (Mainly Oct-Feb).

♣ There are 6 species of which 2 others occur in this area. The more erect, N. fragarioides has round compound flowerheads 8mm across, crowded into dense heads 20-30mm across, which in bud have a lumpy appearance. The high altitude N. sphaerocephala is a massive hairy shrub with individual heads 20-30mm across, not collected into groups.

Brunia alopecuroides

Brunia albiflora

Brunia noduliflora

Brunia stokoei

Nebelia paleacea

Raspalia microphylla   false cedar
A much branched shrub to 90cm, with crowded, smooth round-backed scale-like leaves up to 1.8mm long. The single terminal whitish flowerheads are 3-4mm across. It grows on rocky outcrops at high altitudes from Paarl to Bredasdorp and Swellendam. (Sept-Jan).

♣ There are 16 species, mainly in the South Western Cape, of which 5 occur in this area, none of them common. Three more have small scale-like leaves, 2 with whitish flowers: The leaves of *R. virgata* are smooth but have a ridge down the back, *R. phylicoides* and *R. globosa* are white-hairy, the latter having magenta flowers.

Pseudobaeckia africana   streambush
A willowy slender branching shrub to 3m with hairy branchlets and needlelike leaves 10-35mm long. The small flowers, in short spikes, are crowded in clusters between the leaves. It occurs on mountain slopes near streams and on the edges of mountain pools from Clanwilliam to Caledon. (Sept-Nov).

♣ There are 4 species confined to the fynbos areas of South Africa, of which 3 occur in this area. The other 2 have broad leaves: *P. cordata* has dense spheres of flowers, 2-5mm across, at the tips of branches; the flowers of *P. stokoei* nestle in the axils of the crowded, overlapping hairy leaves.

Staavia radiata   altydbossie
An open shrublet with numerous short slender branches to 80cm, sprouting from a fire-resistant stump. It bears fairly crowded pointed leaves 4-7mm long, and daisy-like flowerheads 6-8mm across, either singly or in groups. It occurs at low to moderate altitudes on sandy flats and slopes from Malmesbury to Bredasdorp and on to Knysna It blooms all year round.

♣ There are 9 species endemic to the fynbos areas of South Africa, of which 2 more may be found in this area. *S. brownii* of the Kogelberg has 15mm wide whitish flowerheads with papery bracts. *S. capitella*, recorded from Houwhoek and the Klein River mountains, has pale flowers 1-2mm across and round-tipped leaves.

Lonchostoma purpureum
A densely leafy erect willowy shrub to 60cm with small, rounded, overlapping leathery leaves. The flowers, large and showy for this family, have a corolla tubular for a quarter of its length, and projecting stamens and stigma. It occurs on steep, marshy, upper mountain slopes from Bain's Kloof to Kogelberg, but only in rare scattered groups. (Aug-Jan).

♣ There are 5 species, but only one more in our area, *L. monogynum*, in wet places from the Cedarberg to the Klein River mountains, whose tubular flowers are white and the styles joined to and hidden within the corolla tube.

Thamnea massoniana
A twiggy shrublet to 30cm with slender branches and stubby, hard-textured round-tipped overlapping leaves closely pressed to the stems. The terminal solitary flowers have a long, pale to deep pink tube, clothed outside with a number of bracts, and 5 pale pink spreading petal lobes. It occurs in small isolated groups on high sandstone slopes from Du Toit's Kloof to the Hottentots Holland. (Dec-Apr).

♣ Of a total of 6 species, the only other in our area. *T. uniflora* of Sir Lowry's Pass northwards, has white solitary flowers and small rounded scalelike leaves.

Raspalia microphylla

Pseudobaeckia africana

Lonchostoma purpureum

Staavia radiata

John Manning

Thamnea massoniana

191

ROSACEAE – The rose family

Cliffortia ruscifolia
climber's friend, steekbos

A much-branched, spiny shrub to 1.5m or more with very hairy young growths and lance-shaped leaves, spine-tipped and 10-12mm long, each with 2 small pointed stipules, hallmark of the family, tucked between leaf and twig. The wind-pollinated male and female flowers open sequentially and are associated with shorter 3-toothed densely hairy leaves. They have a calyx of 3 lobes and no petals. The female (illustrated here) has long red feathery stigmas projecting well beyond the leaves, and the male has a group of c. 12 projecting stamens. It is common among rocks from Namaqualand to Humansdorp. The common name refers to its reliability as a holdfast in rock crevices, for it is exceedingly firmly rooted, and not ironically, to its extremely prickly nature. (Aug-Oct).

♣ There are about 120 species confined chiefly to South Africa of which 40 occur in this area. The very similar *C. multiformis* of the Klein River mountains differs in having hairless leaves.

Cliffortia grandifolia
grootblaarrysbos

Probably the tallest species at c. 5m of which only the male is known, with simple, coarsely toothed leaves 5-10 x 1.5-3cm. The male flowers with their dangling yellow c. 50 stamens are produced in the summer. It is found on the sides of steep kloofs at higher elevations throughout the Hottentots Holland and Kogelberg, often in dense impenetrable stands. It occurs from Du Toit's Kloof to the Langeberg mountains.

♣ Further tall species are the willowy *C. heterophylla* of Kogelberg, with willowlike leaves except those associated with the female flowers which are broad, wrap-around and overlapping; the 3m tall *C. phillipsii* of the Hottentots Holland mountains with spiny-toothed tongue-shaped 20-35 x 4-7mm leaves, and densely grey-hairy female flowerheads; *C. strobilifera*, widespread in moist places, with simple linear leaves, 10-15mm long, almost always carrying scattered conelike cherry-sized galls; and lastly, the widespread sprawling 1-2m tall *C. graminea* of damp places, with simple grasslike leaves up to 15cm long with a clasping base 30-60mm long remarkably similar to that of a grass leaf.

Cliffortia cuneata

A shrub to 2m with simple flat leaves 25-30mm x 5-7mm wedge-shaped below, cut off straight across at the tip and with a toothed edge. A distinctive peeling flaky reddish brown bark is characteristic of the genus. The dangling reddish stamens are borne separately from the female but on the same plant, one sex flowering first followed by the other. Common in the Jonkershoek valley it is found from the Cape Peninsula to Riversonderend. (Oct-Nov).

LINACEAE – The flax family

Linum acuticarpum

A half-woody shrub to 50cm with slender stems from a persistent base. The paired stalkless leaves are narrowly lance-shaped. A stipule transformed into a dark gland is visible on either side of the point of attachment of only the lower leaves. The flowers are in panicles with the styles joined together for half their length. It occurs on sandy slopes from Kogelberg to Hermanus. (Dec-Mar).

♣ *L. quadrifolium* of low mid-altitudes, is the only species with all leaves in whorls of 4; *L. thunbergii* has glands on most of the lower, sometimes 4-whorled leaves; in *L. africanum* the paired leaves have stipular glands throughout; *L. brevistylum* has styles free from the base; *L. thesioides* has flowerstalks sparsely hairy and some sepals have comblike edges. The latter 2 are similar to *L. thunbergii*.

Cliffortia ruscifolia

Cliffortia grandifolia

Cliffortia cuneata

Linum acuticarpum

FABACEAE – The pea family

Amphithalea virgata

An erect resprouting shrub to 30cm whose narrow, convex, simple leaves without stipules have edges strongly downwards-rolled (heathlike), are thinly hairy above, and silky, becoming rusty brown below when dry. The smallish stalkless flowers, crowded in 2's in the leaf axils forming a dense branch-end spike, are two-toned pink and dark pink, the stamens slightly joined and anthers of two sizes. An unjointed, cylindrical pod with one or two seeds is produced. It occurs on mountain slopes below 450m in the Caledon district. (May-Sept).

♣ There are 42 species, all Cape, of which c. 14 occur in our area; most have pink to red flowers, a few are yellow, white or blue-purple. The widespread, resprouting, 1m tall *A. ericifolia* found up to 1500m is similar but has entirely silky leaves. Two have small leaves with edges rolled upwards to conceal a silky surface, and smooth below: *A. oppositifolia* has paired leaves pressed close to the stem; the lowland *A. biovulata* with widely spaced alternate leaves has 2 blue-purple flowers at the end of side branches. The robust 2.5m tall resprouter *A. cuneifolia* of upper slopes has flat, open, rounded leaves and visible veins.

Amphithalea tomentosa

A willowy resprouting, open shrub to 1m with simple lance-shaped, grey-silky flat leaves and no stipules. The stalkless flowers are lemon-yellow, nod at the end of side branches and give rise to pods similar to those of *A. virgata*. It grows below 200m from Betty's Bay to Riversdale but not in Hermanus. (Apr-Sept).

♣ The sprawling resprouter, *A. bowiei* from Houwhoek to Kleinmond, has twisted, concave and incurved leaves, silky above, glabrous below and bright yellow flowers.

Argyrolobium lunare

A silvery weakly-stemmed shrublet often straggling through other plants, has 3-foliolate leaves, the middle leaflet larger than the other two and all folded along their length. Long-stalked clusters of bright yellow flowers, ageing brick red after pollination, each 15mm long, are borne well above the leaves. It is fairly common on lower slopes from Clanwilliam to the Riviersonderend mountains. (Aug-Feb).

♣ There are about 70 species in Africa, the Mediterranean and India. C. 3 others with groups of yellow flowers ageing red-brown occur here: *A. filiforme* is a dwarf tufted perennial with threadlike silvery leaves and terminal racemes of short-stalked flowers, resprouting after veld fires; the very rare (possibly extinct) silvery *A.splendens* of the Klein River mountains, a much-branched subshrub to 30 cm with 1-3 flowers on a long bare stalk; and *A. lanceolatum* with its 1-3 flowers borne on long peduncles of threadlike delicacy. Lastly, two have solitary flowers: *A. pachyphyllum* has stalked flowers and *A. argenteum* has stalkless flowers.

Rhynchosia ferulifolia

A prostrate, slender, almost hairless shrub with many stems to 1m long. The stipulate leaves are variably complex-compound from the simplest 3-leaflet condition as seen in the illustration, to many leaflets. The dense clusters of sticky yellow flowers are borne on 5-15cm stalks, and the leaves and calyx are gland-dotted. It is found on sandy flats from Piketberg and the Cape Peninsula to Humansdorp. (July-Jan).

♣ There are 200 species, cosmopolitan in the warmer parts of the world, of which 4 occur in this area, all with yellow flowers. 2 are climbers with 3-foliolate narrow leaves: *R. chrysoscias* with hairy stems, calyx and leaves; the leaves of *R. leucoscias* are densely white-hairy below. The prostrate resprouting twiner, *R.capensis* of river banks, has narrow leaves with conspicuous stipules.

Amphithalea virgata

Christine Wakfer

Amphithalea tomentosa

Argyroloblum lunare

Christine Wakfer

Rhynchosia ferulifolia

Aspalathus Cape gorse. There are about 278 species in South Africa, mainly in the Cape, of which some 49 occur in this area. All are shrubby, and without stipules. Some have simple leaves, like *A. cordata*, but in the majority of the species the leaves consist of 3 leaflets on axillary shoots in tufts, situated on a hard swollen leafbase. The leaflets may be flat as in *A. callosa*, channelled, or needle-like as in *A. retroflexa*. Of those in our area the majority have yellow flowers, but some are white, pink or blue. In some the flowers age red or brown. Most have only two seeds per pod. Many are prickly, having spines either at the base or the tips of the leaves.

Aspalathus cordata

An erect rather sparsely-branched shrub to 1m with sharply angled and winged branches, bearing simple, wrap-around oval leaves with a translucent prominent smooth edge, 11-21 veins from the base and a spiny tip. It is found on lower slopes of Jonkershoek, Hangklip and Houwhoek. (Sept-Dec).

♣ The similar *A. elliptica* has softer narrower leaves. *A. crenata* has scalloped leaf edges, even more prominently scalloped in *A. perfoliata* of Stellenbosch. *A. angustifolia* has sword-like pointed leaves.

Aspalathus excelsa

An erect, much-branched relatively short-lived non-spiny shrub or small tree to 2.5m whose compound leaves have narrow fleshy hairless leaflets, 6-15mm long. Groups of 5-15 bright yellow flowers up to 12mm long are borne on short, hairy stalks. It germinates abundantly and flourishes in the first decade after a veld fire, making a resplendent wonderfully-scented population, then dies off and leaves behind abundant replacement seed for the next fire. It occurs on sandy lowlands of the Klein River mountains near the coast. (Sept-Nov).

♣ The similar *A. carnosa* occurs in the Hangklip area and *A. fusca* of lowlands has variable grey-silky spine-tipped leaflets. The 60cm *A. callosa* has flat non-fleshy leaflets.

Aspalathus retroflexa

A sprawling shrub with branches to 1m long with compound leaves. The leaflets are almost round in cross-section and sometimes hairy. Usually one single flower is borne at the end of a lateral branchlet with long spaces between the leaf clusters as if on a flower stalk, and two-toned yellow with petals partly dark violet, purple or red. It occurs in mountain and lowland fynbos below 350m from the Cedarberg to Agulhas. (Sept-Mar).

♣ Other sprawlers are *A. biflora* with similar side branchlets ending with 1-5 flowers; *A. juniperina* has 1-5 flowers at the ends of side branchlets which are regularly leafy; *A. serpens* has a single flower at the end of a true long flowerstalk; and *A. hispida* has flowers scattered along the side branchlets and not crowded at the tips.

Aspalathus neglecta

A shrub to 2m with hairy needle-like spine-tipped leaflets. The single flowers, on short shoots nestling among the clumped leaflets, are bright yellow-orange or rust-coloured. It occurs in mountain fynbos between 240-830m from the Cape Peninsula to the Kogelberg. (Sept-Dec).

♣ *A. spicata*, in the north of our area, is very similar. The variable *A. ciliaris* has similar leaflets in our area with flowers sometimes forming groups at the end of branchlets. *A. aculeata* has a sharp spine at the base of the leaflets. *A. aspalathoides* has flat 3mm wide sparsely long-hairy leaflets.

Aspalathus globulosa

A shrublet to less than 1m with needle-like hairy leaflets. The branches end in a compact head of bluish violet flowers surrounded by white-hairy round leaves. Found in coastal fynbos from 110-180m where it is threatened by coastal development. (Oct-Dec).

♣ The sprawling rose to flesh-coloured *A. rosea* and the pale mauve-flowered mat-forming *A. argyrella* of lowland fynbos have similar heads. The round to spikelike heads of the 50-200cm tall *A. cephalotes* of mountain fynbos are pale violet or rose. The 70cm *A. nigra* and the spreading shrublet, *A. submissa*, both of renoster-fynbos scrub, are slate blue to violet.

Aspalathus cordata

Aspalathus excelsa

Aspalathus retroflexa

Aspalathus globulosa

Aspalathus neglecta

197

Aspalathus globosa

An erect shrub to 2m with rod-like branches, and needlelike leaflets clustered in dense groups on short shoots. The white woolly flowers form a compact group wrapped in distinct bracts, the tip of the upper petal darkening with age. It grows rapidly after fire and disappears from older veld. It is found mostly on richer clay soils from 300-700m in mountain fynbos from Jonkershoek to Kleinmond. (Aug-Oct).

Aspalathus forbesii

A variable shrub sometimes to 2m, with scarcely hairy 3-lobed cylindrical leaflets. The flowers, grouped at the branch tips, are white or cream-coloured, sometimes with a touch of pink. It occurs in fynbos in coastal limestone or marine sand from the Cape Peninsula to Stilbaai. (Jul-Apr).

Cyclopia genistoides   honey bush tea, heuningtee

A sturdy, densely rounded, resprouting, almost hairless shrub to 2m, with trifoliolate leaves, the finger-like leaflets having rolled-under edges. It bears showy clusters of bright yellow 10-15mm long flowers with free stamens and a several-seeded pod. It is widespread on flats and slopes throughout this area and extends eastward to Albertinia. A pleasant tea can be made of the young flowering twigs. (July-Dec).

♣ There are 23 species confined to South Africa, all very sweetly scented, of which 4 others occur in this area: the usually single-stemmed to 3.5m *C. maculata* is found beside streams on lower slopes; and *C. meyeriana* with conspicuous clasping bracts grows on the upper wet slopes. 2 resprouters occur on the upper slopes of the northern parts of this area: erect, robust *C. falcata*, with broad flat leaves; and sprawling narrow-leafed *C. alpina*. The sepals of all of them appear to have been pushed in from below to form a collar.

Dipogon lignosus   Cape sweet pea

A perennial climber whose 3-foliolate, rhombic leaves, blueish below, have stipules. Long-stalked, axillary, dense racemes of mauve to purple and pink pea flowers produce sickle-shaped 4-6-seeded pods. It grows in scrub and forest from Saldanha to the Eastern Cape. (Jan-Dec).

Bolusafra bituminosa   sticky tar-pea

A sprawling, twining or climbing, resinous-hairy, tar-scented perennial, woody at the base. The leaves have 3 leaflets, and the flowers, usually borne in racemes, are bright yellow. They give rise to cylindrical pods containing 4-6 seeds. It is common on mountainsides in mountain fynbos and alongside streams from Tulbagh to Caledon. (all year, mainly Aug-Jan).

♣ This is the only species.

Aspalathus globosa

Aspalathus forbesii

Cyclopia genistoides

Dipogon lignosus

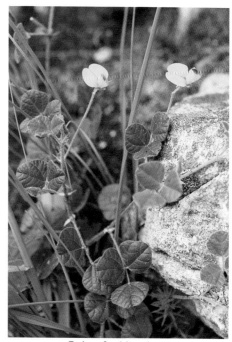

Bolusafra bituminosa

199

Hypocalyptus coluteoides
rooikeur

A willowy highly ornamental tree-like shrub to 3m with hairy young branches and almost hairless, blueish-green, stipulate, trifoliolate leaves with leaflets widest in the middle. The crowded elongated clusters of purple to bright pink flowers have sepals all the same size, but with the two at the top cut straight across the tips. The stamens are joined into a tube. Several seeds are produced in a hairless pod. It occurs at forest edges and along streams from Caledon to Humansdorp. (July-Nov).

♣ There are 3 species confined to the South Western Cape, all of which occur in this area. The similar *H. sophoroides*, a robust shrub to 4m, with leaflets widest at the tips may be seen in the northwest of the area.

Hypocalyptus oxalidifolius

A delicate, dense, wiry-stemmed sprawling shrublet to 50cm. The 3 rounded leaflets per leaf look very like the leaf of a sorrel, *(Oxalis)* as indicated by the specific name. Covered with masses of delicate sprays of lilac or pink to almost white flowers, it blooms profusely in the first season after a veld fire and thereafter hardly at all. It is locally and briefly common on sandstone slopes below 700m in damp, partly shaded places or alongside streams from the Hottentots Holland and Helderberg to Tsitsikamma. (Jul-Sept).

Indigofera glomerata

A prostrate, much-branched shrublet to 20cm with crowded overlapping 3-foliate softly white-hairy leaves and stipules longer than the leafstalks. Racemes of pink or purple flowers whose top petal is hairy, nestle in the leaves. It occurs in lowland and mountain fynbos up to 860m from the Cape Peninsula to Bredasdorp. (Aug-Nov)

♣ There are c. 720 species worldwide and c. 14 locally, usually easily recognised because, in most, the keel petals fall to expose the stamens early on. Most have 2-forked hairs[1] (visible with a 10x-magnifying glass). Two sprawlers have flowerheads on long stalks and simple leaves: *I. ovata* with round leaves, and *I. guthriei* whose narrower leaves have upturned edges. 3 have 3-digitate leaves; *I. incana* with coarse long leaf hairs, *I. gracilis* almost hairless and similar *I. sarmentosa*, with 3-5 leaflets, has smooth dark pods.

Indigofera digitata
sprawling pea

A resprouting much-branched sprawling hairy shrub, becoming distinctly woody at the base. The digitate leaves are roughly hairy with 7-9 leaflets at the end of a 4-7mm stalk. The flower stalks are at least twice as long as the leaves, with dense, elongating heads of rose to purple or brick red to orange flowers. The pods are hairy. It occurs from 30-830m on clay and sand from Tulbagh to Kleinmond. (Sept-Jan).

♣ Another with long flowerstalks is *I. filicaulis* with 3-9 digitate narrow stalkless leaflets; four have pinnate leaves: *I. alopecuroides* leaflets are densely hairy, *I. capillaris* leaflets are hairless below, and the similar *I. angustifolia* leaflets are felted below; *I. brachystachya* has silky grey leaflets and heavily scented bright pink flowers on short stalks, which retain their keel.

Indigofera filifolia
leafless pea

This erect, hairless, seemingly leafless shrub to 2m produces a few pinnate leaves when young, but the leaflets soon fall, leaving only the 7-13cm long stalk swollen at the base. The rose to purple flowers, 8-10mm long, are borne in loose racemes at the ends of stalks which are no longer than the leaves. The pods are rounded in cross-section with brown seeds. It is found at streamsides from the Gifberg and Cape Peninsula to George. (Dec-Apr).

♣ The flowerhead stalks of *I. ionii* of wetlands from the Cape Peninsula to Klein River mountains are twice the length of the leaves.

Hypocalyptus coluteoides

Hypocalyptus oxalidifolius Anne Bean

Indigofera digitata

Indigofera glomerata

Indigofera filifolia Charles Boucher

201

Indigofera cytisoides

A coarse, erect, grey-green reseeding shrub to 3m with a short trunk branching from near the base, and short-petiolate, (3)-5-foliolate leaves with large, finely hairy oval leaflets each 2-5cm long. Long racemes of crowded purple or pink hairy flowers with oval hairy bracts, are borne on short, sturdy stalks which project beyond the leaves of this spectacular plant. It occurs from the Cape Peninsula to Hermanus, on streamside or seepage slopes from 20-1300m. (Mar-July).

Indigofera superba

A willowy 1-3m tall grey-hairy shrub with 7-11 rounded leaflets per sessile or short-stalked leaf. The many pink flowers in dense racemes about as long as the leaves give rise to smooth pods. It occurs on lower moister slopes and streamsides of the Klein River mountains and is one of the fast-growing, probably short-lived post-fire pea species of young veld. (Dec-Apr).

Lebeckia carnosa

A yellow-flowered sprawling shrublet to 40cm with cylindrical leaves comprising one leaflet each, lacking stipules and having a joint on the leafstalk. It occurs in lowland and mountain fynbos up to 800m from the Cedarberg to Bredasdorp. (Oct-June).

♣ There are about 45 species in South Africa and Namibia, of which 3 more with unifoliolate leaves may occur in this area: *L. pauciflora* with unjointed leaves, a spirally twisted keel, partly purple standard, and bracts half as long or less; and the narrow-leafed, straggly, *L. wrightii* whose single axillary yellow flowers with ochre reverse become altogether orange also has a spirally twisted keel. *L. simsiana* leaves have a joint above the middle and yellow flowers in dense racemes at the ends of branches.

Lessertia frutescens (=Sutherlandia)   balloon pea, blaasertjie, kankerbos

A much-branched shrub to 1m whose stipulate leaves are pinnate compound with an odd number of leaflets: an unpaired one at the end. The leaflets are oblong and blunt-tipped with or without sparse hairs. The rather pendant red flowers, over 25mm long, are grouped into racemes in the axils of the leaves. The pod is strikingly inflated, reddened, hairless and translucent papery with many seeds. It is widespread from Namaqualand and the Karoo to the Eastern Cape. (Jul-Dec).

♣ There are 55 species in Africa, and 5 recorded in our area. The 40cm tall L.canescens of coastal sands has similar flowers and pods but differs in the notched tip of the silver-hairy leaflet. The others have flowers half as long: the prostrate dull red and pink *L. capensis* of mountain fynbos with compressed papery pods; the orange-red *L. miniata* has inflated leathery pods; the dull purple *L. prostrata* of Stellenbosch has broadly oblong compressed hairy pods

Liparia myrtifolia   mountain pea

A single-stemmed tree-like shrub to 3m with simple elliptic leaves and yellow flowers in groups of 4. It can be seen along the Hottentots Holland hiking trails in mountain fynbos and is distributed from the Hex River to the Outeniquas, including Kogelberg but not Hermanus. (Mar-June).

♣ There are 20 species of mountain pea, of which c. 14 occur in our area. The very rare, rather willowy 4m tall tree-like *L. rafnioides* of streamsides in the Kogelberg and Hottentots Holland has huge heart-shaped leaves and flowers in loose groups of 4.

Indigofera cytisoides

Indigofera superba

Lebeckia carnosa

Lessertia frutescens

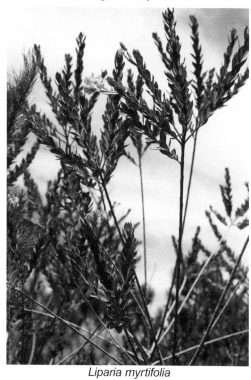

Liparia myrtifolia

FABACEAE

Liparia spendens ssp. comantha   mountain dahlia, klipblom, skaamblom

An almost hairless, coarse, stiff spreading shrub to 1m, sometimes dense and rounded, with oval leaves 3-5cm long. Numerous flowers are crowded into globose nodding heads 6-8cm across at the ends of the branches. It occurs on rocky mountain slopes from the Hottentots Holland to Albertinia.(Sept). Ssp. splendens only occurs on the Cape Peninsula.

♣ The small, single-stemmed, shrubby narrow-leafed rare *L. angustifolia* with yellow flowers clustered 3-10 in a raceme occurs throughout our area in damp lowlands. Three have flowers in 2 pairs of 2 and occur at high altitude: the creamy-green, single-stemmed *L. boucheri* is confined to the Kogelberg; the resprouting to 60cm *L. capitata* has leaves 3mm wide and is widespread; the low growing *L. bonaespei* is confined to the Hottentots Holland.

Liparia vestita (=Priestleya vestita)   mountain pea

A sturdy, multistemmed, sparsely-branched shrub to 2.5m, with densely-hairy silvery branches and broad, almost circular, cupshaped overlapping leaves which are sparsely- bristly above and shaggy on the reverse. The short-stalked yellow flowers are arranged 4 at a time in compact terminal heads, browning with age. It occurs on moist mountain slopes from Somerset West to Bredasdorp. (May-Feb).

♣ The very similar reseeding (single-stemmed) *L. calycina* differs in the leaves being longer than broad and more pointed.

Otholobium obliquum

An erect resprouting shrub to 1.2m bearing gland-dotted crowded leaves each with 3 hair-tipped leaflets 22-34mm by 6-8mm whose tips curve out and back. The lateral leaflets are very lopsided. The pale blue, pink or white flowers with hairy, densely glandular sepals nestle among the leaves on rather short stalks, and are followed by 1-seeded pods. Scattered plants occur on the mountain slopes from Piketberg, Paarl and Stellenbosch to Kogelberg. (Jun-Dec).

♣ 13 species occur in this area. They have scattered gland dots on all parts except the petals. The resprouting 1m tall *O. parviflorum* has elongated racemes of white flowers. The willowy 3.5m reseeder *O. spicatum* of coastal renosterveld and riverbanks has tight, elongated spikes of creamy-white or lilac flowers. Three have symmetrical lateral leaflets; the sprawling blue, white or violet clusters of flowers of *O. bracteolatum* nestle in the leaves; the trailing resprouter *O. virgatum* of marshes has pale pink flowers in 3's along the stems; *O. hirtum* of renosterveld has pale blue flowers and almost stalkless leaves.

Otholobium zeyheri

This resprouting shrublet with many stems to 40cm high arising from the ground, has 3-foliolate, lopsided lateral leaflets, undotted hairy leaves which become smooth, with only the leaf edges and stipules eventually long-hairy. The white and mauve flowers with a black-purple keel and black-silky calyx, crowded at the ends of slender leafless inflorescence shoots, are borne in masses after a fire. Found from Jonkershoek to Bredasdorp. (Aug-Mar).

♣ *O. pungens* of coastal fynbos-renosterveld has leaves with a sharp point.

Otholobium rotundifolium

The 20cm tall resprouting shrublet has 1-foliolate leaves, white-lilac flowers, a white-silky glandular calyx, oval to diamond shaped leaves and black-dotted stems. It occurs in mountain fynbos between 430-530m from Jonkershoek to the Klein River mountains. (Oct-Jan only after fire).

♣ Three further low-growing resprouting species, all similar and particularly responsive to veld fiires, have only one leaflet. The 40cm tall *O. thomii* of Highlands - Klein River mountains and Bredasdorp, has purple flowers, undotted hairy leaves, and a densely black- and white- hairy calyx; the 6cm tall *O. lanceolatum* of Shaw's mountain has white flowers and a densely white-hairy calyx; while the 15cm tall *O. sp "dreweae"* of the Klein River mountains has purplish-red flowers with short white and long black hairs on the calyx.

Liparia spendens ssp. comantha

carpenter bee

Liparia vestita

Otholobium zeyheri

Otholobium obliquum

Otholobium rotundifolium

205

Podalyria biflora

A resprouting, much-branched partly prostrate 30cm tall shrublet. The simple oval leaves, silky above, are silvery or golden-felted below and their stipules fall early. The flowers are bright pink and white with broadly oval to lance-shaped bracts, and the stamens are almost quite free from one another. It occurs on sandstone slopes up to 1000m from Clanwilliam to the Cape Peninsula and Mossel Bay. (Aug-Nov).

♣ There are 19 species in S.Africa, of which 6 occur in our area. *P. argentea* has broad silky leaves and rounded bracts with a sharp tip.

Podalyria calyptrata   keurtjie, keurblom, ertjieblom

A single-stemmed tree-like shrub to 5m, or multi-stemmed lax shrub to 3m, silvery silky, with the simple leaves characteristic of the genus, and 2-5cm long, have a pointed tip and the side-veins are clearly visible. The stipules fall early. The pink (occasionally white), sweetly-scented flowers, one of the pleasures of spring, are borne 1-2 per stalk in the axils of the leaves; they are followed by hairy, inflated pods, holding several seeds. The bracts form a unique hood or cap over the bud (= calyptra), which breaks away as the bud swells revealing the hairy calyx. It occurs in ravines or on moist hillsides at low and mid-altitudes from the Cape Peninsula to Garcia's Pass. (Aug-Oct).

♣ Three others having woolly, felted rounded leaves are *P. variabilis, P. hirsuta* and *P. cordata* with a heart-shaped base.

Podalyria oleaefolia (=P. speciosa)

A variable sprawling to erect resprouter to 1m. The lowest leaves are huge orbs, but the shape progressively narrows up the stem. The linear, 3-6cm long, upper leaves are distinctively glossy above but tawny-felted below, with edges which roll under to almost conceal the lower surface. The flowers are bright pink with a white eye. It occurs on the open montane sandstone slopes below 500m from Kogelberg to Sandbaai in rocky sand. (June-Dec).

Psoralea aphylla   fonteinbos, bloukeur

 A slender, resprouting or reseeding hairy shrub to 4m with apparently leafless green branches which arch downwards under the weight of their blooms. The black-hairy stalks of the flowers arise out of a cup-shaped structure which is characteristic of the genus. Some of the populations are sweetly scented. The scale-like leaves are 3-6mm long. It is found, often in dense stands, in marshes and along streams from Clanwilliam to Riversdale. (Oct-Feb).

♣ 130 species occur worldwide, 50 in Africa and c. 11 here. They have purple, blue or mauve flowers, are sprinkled with small dark or translucent gland dots and the calyx is often black-hairy within. Two are tree-like with 1-foliolate scale-like leaves and found at streamsides: *P. ramulosa* is a resprouter from the Hottentots Holland; *P.* pullata from the coastal mountains. Three are treelike and 3-foliolate of which two resprout: *P. fascicularis* of the coastal mountains; and *P. oligophylla* of inland streamsides. *P. aculeata* is a single-stemmed re-seeder with hook-pointed leaves.

Psoralea pinnata   fonteinbos, bloukeur, penwortel

An erect shrub or small tree to 4m with rather willowy branches, it is one of two psoraleas in our area with a leaf comprising 7-9 leaflets; these are needle-like and 20-30mm long. The lilac-blue and white flowers, sweetly scented in only some populations, are grouped in axillary clusters towards the ends of the branchlets. It occurs, often in dense stands, in mountain fynbos, forest margins or riverbeds from Cape Peninsula to Kogelberg. (Oct-Apr).

♣ The other species is the marsh-loving *P. affinis* with 5-9 leaflets, differing in a more erect build and occurring from Tulbagh to the Eastern Cape.

Podalyria biflora

Podalyria calyptrata

Podalyria oleaefolia

Psoralea aphylla

Psoralea pinnata

Anne Bean

207

Psoralea asarina

A prostrate, loosely trailing tangled shrublet with 1-foliolate spine-tipped, oblong 7-10mm wide, rounded leaves with heart-shaped base on hairy stems, and violet-blue flowers on threadlike stalks usually longer than the leaf. It occurs in mountain fynbos from the Cape Peninsula to Knysna. (Oct-Feb).

♣ 4 more (near-)prostrate species in our area with 1-foliolate leaves are the almost identical resprouting *P. monophylla* with narrower leaflets; weak, sprawling *P. laxa* with flowers on stalks shorter than the 2mm wide leaves, dotted and pointed at both ends; the marsh-loving, single-stemmed *P. restioides* with rush-like branches and thread-like leaves which pile up into a floppy heap, bearing stalkless flowers; and the sprawling resprouting *P. imbricata*, to 50cm high, with deep purple stalkless flowers nestled in hairy folded leaves. The trailing *P. repens* of coastal dunes is distinguished by its 3-foliolate leaves. All have purple, mauve or blue flowers.

Rafnia capensis ssp. pedicellata

As is universal in the genus, this is a resprouting, entirely hairless smooth shrub, often rather floppy in habit and blackening when bruised or dead. It grows to 50cm, with simple, smooth-edged, linear to round leaves, which are conspicuously larger low down on the plant. The 12mm long short-stalked flowers are grouped into terminal heads. It occurs on stony flats and slopes to 2000m from Stellenbosch to Hermanus. (Flowering irregular).

♣ 19 species occur from the Cape to KwaZulu-Natal, of which 6 occur in this area. The trailing *R. acuminata* with single flowers has rounded leaves that often clasp the stem. The rather floppy 2m *R. angulata* has the cleft between the upper sepals deepest and leaves that do not clasp the stem.

Rafnia triflora

An erect woody shrub to 2.4m with simple broadly rounded, usually paired leaves, the lowest largest at about 43-121 x 16-110mm, and yellow flowers three at a time in the axils of the leaves. It has been recorded from Clanwilliam to Humansdorp and throughout our area on stony slopes from sea level to 600m. (Sept-Mar).

♣ Two further erect-growing species occur in our area: the 60cm lowland *R. crassifolia* has flowers on long stalks and bright green, red-edged leaves; the broad leaves of the 1.2m tall, sparingly branched herbaceous *R. ovata* are tapered at the tip and its large flowers are 17-20mm long and carried 1(-4) at a time.

Tephrosia capensis   fish bean

A trailing, straggly perennial with sparse compound leaves on 2cm long stalks with a swollen base, each leaf consisting of 3-6 pairs of oval leaflets some 2cm long with a pointed tip. The sparse pink to rose-red flowers are followed by straight, opaque, woody, hairy pods with numerous seeds. It occurs from the coastal dunes to the high mountain slopes, on any kind of soil from the Cape Peninsula to the Eastern Cape and Transvaal. (July-Apr).

♣ There are some 400 species pan-tropical and sub-tropical, but this is the only one in our area.

Xiphotheca reflexa (=Priestleya guthriei)   silver pea

A multistemmed, prostrate or straggling shrublet to 50cm tall. Leaves simple, lance-shaped to ovate and silvery-silky, often bent back. Yellow flowers, crowded at branch ends, produce 5-7 seeded pods. It occurs in lowland fynbos below 300m from Piketberg to Bredasdorp. (Aug-Nov).

♣ 10 species occur in the Cape, 6 in our area. All have silvery, simple leaves and yellow flowers. *X. guthriei* is a single-stemmed shrublet to 30cm with narrow leaves, flowers crowded in stalkless head-like clusters, pods 2-3 seeded, limited to the lowland fynbos/renosterveld from Klein River to Potberg. Widespread *X. fruticosa* is a 2m tall single-stemmed or smaller multi-stemmed densely silvery-silky shrub with crowded stalkless flower-heads, on sandstone slopes to 1200m. *X. tecta* of mountain slopes above 500m is another resprouter to 1m tall with rounded leaves with its flowers in pairs along the stems. The flowerheads of the resprouting *X. elliptica* have short stalks.

Psoralea asarina

Rafnia triflora

Rafnia capensis ssp. pedicellata

Tephrosia capensis

Xiphotheca reflexa

209

GERANIACEAE – The Geranium family

Pelargonium cucullatum   tree pelargonium, wilde malva

A sturdy hairy shrub to 2m or more, woody at the base but with sappy new growth. The kidney-shaped aromatic, 45mm long leaves are cupped and pleated with irregular, sometimes reddish edges. The flowers are usually pink to purple, but a white form is sometimes found. The bright orange pollen on the 7 fertile stamens is usually conspicuous and the hypanthium channel is 5-12mm long, slightly longer than the flowerstalk. This form occurs on coastal flats and lower slopes from Gordon's Bay to Gansbaai and on the Cape Peninsula. A subspecies, *P. cucullatum ssp. strigifolium,* differing only in the harsher-textured leaf texture, is found further inland and at higher altitudes than the typical form. (Sept-Feb).

♣ There are c. 6 more shrubby, aromatic species in our area.

Pelargonium myrrhifolium

A soft hairy shrublet to 40cm with weak stems bearing very deeply divided leaves about 8cm long, including the long leafstalk. Up to 5 white or pale pink flowers, carried well above the leaves, have a shortish hypanthium channel 4-10mm long. The upper petals are much larger than the lower and have carmine nectar guides. Occurs from Clanwilliam to Willowmore and blooms all year.

♣ 11 more sprawling, soft-textured species occur in our area.

Pelargonium triste   night-scented pelargonium   kaneeltjie

This rather cryptic species is a geophyte whose tubers have a cracked woody bark. The prostrate leaves, 2-3-times divided, feathery and softly hairy, are produced from ground level, with minimal stems carrying the sturdy flowerstalks well above the leaves. Up to 20 rather inconspicuous pale yellow flowers with dark maroon to black markings are grouped in an open head. The hypanthium channel at 25-35mm long, the pale colour and the heady and powerful clove scent switched on at night hint at long-tongued moth pollinators. It occurs from Namaqualand to Albertinia on sandy flats and slopes. (Aug-Feb).

♣ There are c. 8 geophytic species in our area.

Pelargonium papilionaceum   butterfly pelargonium   rambossie

An erect, soft, unpleasantly scented shrub to 2m, with a woody main trunk, many softer shaggy branches and large leaves, 3-5 lobed lower down, heart-shaped on upper parts and c. 10cm across. The long-stalked flowers, grouped in clusters of 5-12, are 3cm across or more, with two large light pink to carmine petals, strongly marked in deep carmine and white, and three very small pale ones. Seven fertile stamens project strongly forward. The hypanthium is only 2-5mm long. It grows in partly shady kloofs and edges of forest from Stellenbosch to the Klein River mountains and on to Grahamstown, usually near streams. (Aug-Jan).

Pelargonium capitatum   kusmalva

A sprawling shrublet to 50cm or straggling to cover larger areas with heart-shaped, lobed hairy aromatic leaves c. 5cm diameter. The purple- pink flowers grouped up to 20 in a tight cluster are each 15-25mm diameter raised up above the leaves on sturdy erect stalks. The hypanthium channel is short at 3-8 mm long. It occurs on coastal sands, dunes and flats from Lambert's Bay to KwaZulu-Natal (Sept-Oct).

210

Pelargonium cucullatum

Pelargonium myrrhifolium

Pelargonium triste

Pelargium papilionaceum   Anne Bean

Pelargonium capitatum   Christine Wakfer

211

Pelargonium incarnatum (*=Erodium incarnatum*)   crane's bill, horlosies, vrouebossie

A sprawling perennial to 25cm with rough, long-stalked much-divided upper and heart-shaped, lobed, lower leaves. The distinctively marked flowers have 5 fertile and 5 infertile stamens and are 20mm across. The hypanthium is represented solely by a depression in the floor of the flower; there is no hollow tube. It occurs on stony hillsides in the Caledon, Worcester and Robertson districts, often in thick undergrowth or under bushes. (Aug-Nov).

Geranium incanum

A soft, prostrate perennial with a persistent taproot. The leaves are 3-7-divided to the base and further subdivided into a feathery structure on a sturdy leafstalk, densely white-hairy at least below. Symmetrical, flat-faced dark-veined pink, mauve or white flowers, 15-30mm across, are borne on long stalks raised above the leaves. It occurs on slopes and stony flats from the Cape Peninsula to Port Alfred. (Aug-Oct).

seeds being dispersed

♣ There are 260 species worldwide and 3 more in our area with leaves divided into 3-5 but not further divided: all having white or pink flowers. *G. caffrum* of damp places, with leaves divided to the base; white-flowered *G. canescens* of dry slopes and streambanks with leaves divided to the base; and *G. ornithopodon* of scrub and forest edges, forming clumps with a woody base and leaves divided more than halfway.

Monsonia speciosa   sambreeltjie

A soft, non-spiny herb with annual branches from a woody rootstock. The leaves are slightly to deeply digitately compound and more or less hairless. The solitary flowers are round, 25-65mm across, borne on strong stalks, and white to pink with deep pink reverse. It occurs on clay and granite slopes in renosterveld from Clanwilliam to Gordons Bay. (Aug-Nov).

♣ There are c. 40 species in Africa, Madagascar and south west Asia but only one more, *M. emarginata* of scrub and grassland, with hairy oval leaves and smaller cream to pink flowers on slender stalks, blooms in summer.

ZYGOPHYLLACEAE

Zygophyllum sessilifolium   witspekbos

A slender prostrate shrub forming large sparse mats about 75cm across, with soft branches bearing pairs of oval, harsh-edged, sharp-pointed, sessile bifoliate leaves. The white or yellow, usually purple-streaked flowers are borne on stalks longer than the leaves, and have pointed green sepals. The fruits are rounded and only slightly angled at first, but become angled and ribbed as they dry. It occurs on sandy flats and lower slopes from Clanwilliam to the Cape Peninsula. (Apr-Oct).

♣ 2 other spreading species have long 9-20mm stalked flowers: *Z. flexuosum* has succulent leaves and a single sticky seed per chamber; and *Z. fulvum* smooth hard-edged leaves. The coastal *Z. fuscatum* is an erect shrub with flowerstalks only 1-2mm long.

Pelargonium incarnatum John Manning

Geranium incanum

Monsonia speciosa John Manning

Zygophyllum sessilifolium Christine Wakfer

OXALIDACEAE – The sorrel family

Oxalis eckloniana

A stemless, dwarf plant with short hairy leafstalks bearing 3 rounded leaflets, hairy on midrib and edge and green or purple below. The flowers, 15-35mm long, with narrow-pointed shaggy sepals, are borne on unjointed hairy stalks up to 10cm long, which raise the flowers well above the leaves, and later curve downwards when the flowers fade. If a flower is forcibly opened up, the stamens spring outwards. A variable species, it is widespread in damp lowland places from Clanwilliam to Caledon. (Apr-June).

♣ There are c. 500 species mostly in South Africa and S.America with some 33 species in this area.

Oxalis luteola

A stemless, hairy, or smooth dwarf to 8cm. The leaves, with stalks up to 4cm long, are divided into 3 rounded leaflets, each with a shallow indentation at the tip and conspicuously veined be-neath. The yellow flowers are borne singly on jointed stalks which, after flowering, arch over to bring the developing seeds near to the ground. Occurring in sandy soils on flats and lower mountain slopes from Clanwilliam to Riversdale, it is the only yellow-flowered species in this area with a ground-hugging rosette of leaves. (May-Aug).

♣ The diminutive yellow-flowered *O. corniculata*, whose flowers are 7mm long, is a creeping, rooting, cosmopolitan weed of gardens.

Oxalis polyphylla   vingersuring

An erect plant up to 20cm high with many unbranched stems produced from a compound bulb, and leaves and flowers attached in a dense tuft at the top. The slightly hairy leaf-stalks are 1-5cm long, and bear 3-7 slender parallel-sided leaflets 1-3cm long, folded lengthwise. The rosy-pink, purple or white flowers are 15-30mm long often with dark-edged petals, and are borne on long stalks arising singly between the leaves. The hairy sepals have 2 orange dots at the tips. It grows in all kinds of lowland soil from Malmesbury to Port Elizabeth. (Mar-June).

Oxalis purpurea

A stemless tufted geophyte with a few leaves at ground level, each divided into 3 rounded leaflets. They are hairless above, but hairy and purple below, often with a visible fringe of white hairs around the edge, and liberally sprinkled with minute translucent dots and streaks, barely visible to the unaided eye, which blacken on drying. The single flowers may be purple, violet, rose, salmon or white with a yellow tube, on short unjointed stems which have 2 small bracts towards the base. It is widespread on flats and slopes from Namaqualand to Caledon at low altitude. (Apr-Sept).

♣ *O. obtusa* has darker veins on the flower and a jointed stem.

Oxalis tenuifolia

A slender plant with more or less hairy stems to 24cm tall, and small tufts of leaves along the length of the stem, with a larger tuft at the tip. The nearly sessile leaves are divided into 3 up-folded, very narrow, hairy leaflets 4-9mm long. The abundant white flowers, borne singly on unjointed hairy stalks, have hairy petals 10-25mm long with a striking purple edge. A common species of shady places from Paarl to Caledon, it blooms in the cooler months. (May-Aug).

♣ 2 are similar with white, purple-edged petals: the glandular hairy *O. multicaulis* has stalkless leaves and several long orange patches on the sepals; *O. versicolor* has leaves grouped on stalks at the top of the stem and 2 orange patches on the leaf tips.

214

Oxalis eckloniana

Oxalis purpurea

Oxalis luteola

Oxalis polyphylla

Oxalis tenuifolia

215

RUTACEAE – The citrus or buchu family

Acmadenia candida

A single-stemmed, slender sparsely-branched shrublet to 30cm with narrow leaves pressed to the stem. Groups of up to 6 white flowers, 4-5mm in diameter, terminate the stems. The flowers have a throat closed by the in-arching petals. The stamens and 5 much-diminished staminodes without anthers remain within the throat, and the horned ovary is 2-chambered. Rare: confined to a restio marsh at Landdroskop: observe from a distance but never walk into this marsh! (Feb-May).

♣ There are 33 species, all in the fynbos, but only 2 more in our area, the very similar, *A. nivea* of the Kogelberg, distinguished by its 3-4-chambered ovary; the sturdy, leafy, bright pink *A. obtusata* with 5-chambered ovary occurs on limy sands.

Adenandra brachyphylla

A lanky, moderately-branched shrublet to 80cm resprouting from a persistent stump after veld fires, with tiny heart-shaped leaves. The flowers are in clusters of 2-4 on long non-hairy stalks at the branch tips. The sepals are broad, blunt-tipped, often purple-spotted, with 9-12mm long petals, notched at the tip, and with a red reverse. Common on rocky slopes from Houwhoek south and east to the Klein River Mountains. (July-Nov).

Adenandra marginata ssp. serpyllacea   china flower

A shrublet to 30cm with many robust branchlets which, with the leaves, are at first hairy, maturing almost hairless. Leaves lance-shaped with rolled-under margins, with glands on the margins and sparse below. The groups of 4-12 flowers, borne on 8-17mm long stalks with 2 bracteoles raised high up on the flower stalk, are dark red in bud, opening intense white within with a red reverse, c. 7-16mm across, the 5 staminodes, 5 stamens and single stigma all dark-red tipped. It. occurs on the Hottentots Holland. (June-Sept).

♣ *A. marginata ssp. humilis* of lower mountain slopes of Houwhoek and Hermanus. has bracteoles near the base of the flowerstalk. Three other species have flowers on measurable stalks, the small-flowered *A. multiflora* of the Houwhoek area with flowers 4-7mm long in large groups; *A. lasiantha* of the Klein River mountains, with its hairy 4-18mm long flowerstalks and hairy 10-14mm long petals; *A. coriacea* from Kogelberg north to Bain's Kloof has hairless petals 8-12mm long.

Adenandra viscida

A branched shrublet to 50cm resprouting from a persistent stump after veld fires. The sparsely gland-dotted 6-12mm long leaves are pale beneath with a green midrib and thick edges. The almost sessile flowers are grouped in gummy heads with broad blunt-tipped purple-spotted sepals. The 8-12mm long petals have a pinkish reverse. It occurs on rocky hillsides or in coastal fynbos from Onrus east to Bredasdorp. (Aug-Dec). It is known to hybridise with *A. brachyphylla*.

♣ No other adenandras in this area have sticky flowerheads.

Adenandra villosa   china flower

An ascending shrublet to 50cm with narrow, sometimes hairy leathery, lance-shaped leaves 4-12mm long with slightly thickened edges, collecting into a dense involucre below the flowers. The short-stalked flowers in singles or compact clusters of 1-6 have 5 petals, china white within and pink on the reverse, alternating with the 5 stamens; the 5 staminodes are tipped with a reddish spoon-shaped gland and the 5-chambered fruit has no horns. It occurs from the Hottentots Holland to Kleinmond. (Oct-Dec).

♣ The 18 species are confined to the fynbos, with 9 in this area. *A. acuta* of the Hottentots Holland has a reddish knob on the petals and unthickened leaf margins. *A. uniflora* of lowland coastal areas has single short-stalked to sessile flowers with broad-tipped, 7-14mm long petals.

Acmadenia candida

Adenandra brachyphylla

Adenandra marginata ssp. serpyllacea

Adenandra viscida

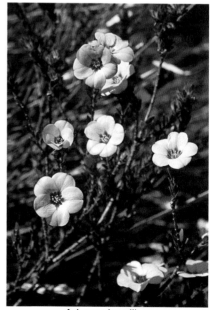

Adenandra villosa

217

Agathosma ciliaris

A dense, rounded shrublet to 45cm with oval, pointed hairy aniseed-scented leaves. White or mauve flowers in terminal clusters with bracteoles on the flowerstalk have 3-chambered ovaries, 5 sepals, petals, stamens and staminodes. It occurs on coastal flats and lower sandstone slopes and the basal shale band of the Table Mountain Group from the Cape Peninsula to Potberg. (May-Dec).

♣ There are about 145 species in South Africa of which 14 occur in this area, several having 3-chambered ovaries and small flowers in massed clusters at branch tips.

Agathosma crenulata commercial buchu

A single-stemmed densely leafy, intensely aromatic shrub to 2.5m with a clinging and pervasive scent. Leaves c. 30mm long including a stubby stalk, oval, finely scalloped, flat and glossy, with 1-3 starlike usually white (occasionally pale pink) flowers per leaf axil with flowerstalks apparently devoid of bracteoles (they are small and crowded at the base). The horned fruits are 5-chambered. It occurs on midslopes and valleys from Ceres to Swellendam, including Kogelberg. (June-Nov).

♣ The willowy 2m+ high *A. serratifolia* with similar flowers and similarly scalloped much longer leaf but a less strident scent, occurs on damp mountain slopes and kloofs; it has been used to bulk up the harvest of commercial buchu but has no medicinal value.

Agathosma juniperifolia stream buchu

A tall, elegant shrub to 2.5m with arching branches and needlelike leaves to 10mm long. The open clusters of long-stalked bracteolate purple flowers with short-stalked petals and threadlike sterile stamens, are borne on branch-tips and are followed by horned two-chambered capsules. It occurs near streams from the Cedarberg and Jonkershoek to Kogelberg and Riviersonderend. (June-Dec).

Agathosma odoratissima breëblaarbuchu

A resprouting densely rounded shrub to 1m, but becoming willowy and much taller where protected from fire, with leaves wonderfully and memorably citrus-scented when crushed. Flowers white, mauve or purple, grouped 1-2 in the upper leaf axils, with bracteoles only at the base of the flowerstalks. Fruits (3-)4(-5)-chambered with horns. Occasional on sheltered and damp upper rocky sandstone slopes, it occurs from Cederberg to the Langeberg including the Hottentots Holland. (Aug-Mar).

Agathosma tabularis stinkboegoe

A single-stemmed often willowy shrub to 1.5m with oval scalloped leaves which when crushed are at first foetid-pungent but almost immediately after, deliciously lemon-scented: few wait long enough to find this out! Drab, pale mauve flowers with narrow petals are produced in the leaf axils on the upper parts of the new growth on flowerstalks with basal bracteoles, soon succeeded by crops of 4-chambered horned fruits. Occurring at forest margins and in sheltered kloofs and much-favoured by summer veld fires which open up the thick fynbos characteristic of its habitat, it seems to be short-lived, making its best growth in the first years after a fire and then disappearing as it becomes overgrown. (Sept-Nov).

♣ Another intensely unpleasantly scented buchu is *A. rosmarinifolia*, a shrub to 50cm with dense heads of white flowers and 3-4(5)-chambered fruits which grows high up among rocks on the Klein River mountains summit ridges.

Agathosma ciliaris

Agathosma juniperifolia

Agathosma odoratissima

Agathosma crenulata

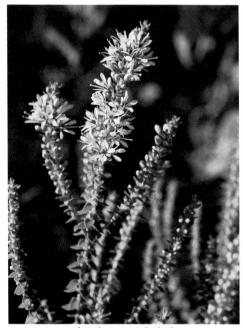

Agathosma tabularis

219

Coleonema album   confetti bush

A dense single-stemmed shrub to 1.8m branching from the base. The narrow, alternate leaves c.13 x 1.4mm taper to a sharp point with finely serrated edges and 2 rows of gland dots below, imparting a characteristic sweet scent. Fishermen are said to cleanse their hands of the smell of redbait and fish by scrubbing them with the leaves. The white flowers, 6-7mm across, are borne singly in the axils of the upper leaves. The 5 petals have a unique lengthwise groove in which a rodlike sterile stamen lies. A cup (the nectar disc) with a wavy edge tucks round the 5 stamen bases and the 5-horned ovary. It is a coastal plant of sandstone and granite, forming dense stands almost always within range of salt-laden winds, occurring at Saldanha, the Cape Peninsula to Gansbaai and Cape Infanta. It has abundant nectar and is probably pollinated by honey-bees and other short-tongued insects. (Aug-Oct).

♣ There are 8 species all in the fynbos and 3 in our area, all white-flowered. The resprouting *C. nubigenum* of Hottentots Holland above 900m has coconut-scented crushed leaves; the pine-scented *C. juniperinum* on mountain slopes from Banhoek to Hermanus is many-branched at the soil surface and has small flowers 3-4mm across and leaves 5-7mm long.

Diosma oppositifolia   bitterboegoe

A gently aromatic resprouting shrub to 1m or sprawling, with many tough stems. The neat rows of pairs of 5-10mm long, stiff, lance-shaped leaves, longer in post-fire re-growth, curve upwards and are slightly hollow above. Clusters of stalkless, white, starry flowers are open-faced to the sky, c.5mm across with short stamens, but lacking staminodes, and a knob-tipped style at first curved, later upright. The 5-chambered fruits are 5-horned. It occurs on well-drained sandy plains from near Saldanha to Quoin Point. (Sept-Jan).

♣ 28 species occur in the fynbos, but only 3 occur in our area. The resprouting *D.hirsuta* with narrow alternate leaves has an overwhelming buchu scent; the 1.8m tall single-stemmed *D.subulata* with pairs of awl-shaped leaves grows on coastal dunes.

Euchaetis elata

A slender erect to diffuse, single-stemmed, sparsely-branched shrub emerging above the surrounding vegetation with narrow, 6-8 x 1mm, pointed leaves tightly pressed to the stems. White flowers are borne in 3-flowered stalkless groups at the ends of branches, the stamens and style hidden by inward-pointing hairs which close the throat of the flower. The 5-chambered fruits have small horns. It occurs from the Slanghoek mountains south to the Kogelberg and the Palmiet on mid and upper slopes. (Flowering all year).

♣ Two other species occur in this area; *E. schlechteri* a resprouter with compact globose heads of white or pinkish flowers and narrow leaves up to 15mm long, on low-altitude clay soils from Sir Lowry's pass to Bredasdorp; and the single-stemmed *E. glabra* with about 12 white flowers per head and rounded leaves 4mm long growing in dense stands in dampish places on mid to upper slopes of the Hottentots Holland and Kogelberg.

Empleurum unicapsulare   false buchu

Willowy shrub or tree to 4m with narrow, resin-scented leaves 2-6cm long. Flowers solitary or paired in the leaf axils, greenish, producing single-chambered fruits topped by a scimitar-shaped horn. It occurs on streambanks and seeps from the Cedarberg to Port Elizabeth. (Apr-Sept).

♣ There is only one species here.

Coleonema album

Diosma oppositifolia

Euchaetis elata

Empleurum unicapsulare

221

POLYGALACEAE – The milkwort and butterflybush family

Muraltia heisteria

A sturdy erect shrub to 2m with hairy young growths. The spiny stalkless leaves are clustered and channelled above, usually with hairy edges and a long-tapering tip. The purple or purple and white flowers are short-stalked and borne in the axils of the leaves. The 2-chambered seedpods have two long tapering horns. It occurs on rocky sandstone slopes from the Bokkeveld mountains to Riversdale. (Oct-Dec), and is probably the tallest growing species in the genus.

♣ 115 species occur in Southern Africa, c. 20 here.

Muraltia vulpina

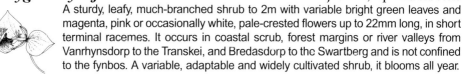

An erect shrub growing to 70cm with hairy younger parts. The stalkless narrow oval leaves are in bundles with long hairy edges and a pointed tip. The pink flowers on short stalks arise in the axils of the leaves and give rise to slender 4-horned seedpods. It grows on slopes from Jonkershoek to Kleinmond. (Nov-Jan).

♣ Two pink-flowered species both with stalkless flowers, are the similar but diffuse, 40cm tall *M. serpylloides* differing in its broader oval leaves that turn under at the edges, and the narrow-leafed common and widespread 40cm tall *M. ericoides*[1].

Polygala bracteolata

A lax or erect perennial to 1m, branching mostly at the base, with lance-shaped narrow leaves up to 30mm long. The pink, magenta or rarely white, 12-19mm long flowers, borne in crowded clusters at the ends of the main branches, have a white brush-like crest. The side petals are hairy below with a larger lower lobe. It is recorded from Vanrhynsdorp to Humansdorp from sea level to 900m. (Aug-Nov).

♣ There are c. 600 species, cosmopolitan, of which 88 occur in southern Africa and 9 in our area. 4 are sprawlers with flowers on side-branches at right angles to the stem: the pink *P. parkeri* of Helderberg with narrowly oval leaves has a tiny entire crest; the slender subshrubby purple *P. refracta* has narrow leaves. 2 have scale-like leaves and purple flowers: *P. pappeana* in the north of our area has a small crest and *P. nematocaulis* with a longer crest occurs in the southeast.

Polygala myrtifolia   blou-ertjieblom, septemberbossie

A sturdy, leafy, much-branched shrub to 2m with variable bright green leaves and magenta, pink or occasionally white, pale-crested flowers up to 22mm long, in short terminal racemes. It occurs in coastal scrub, forest margins or river valleys from Vanrhynsdorp to the Transkei, and Bredasdorp to the Swartberg and is not confined to the fynbos. A variable, adaptable and widely cultivated shrub, it blooms all year.

Polygala umbellata

A slender lax perennial to 40cm, with sprawling branches arising mainly near the woody base, and needle-like leaves up to 18mm long. The slender-stalked pink or magenta flowers are usually less than 11mm long and are borne in crowded more or less flat-topped terminal clusters. The 2 large side sepal lobes almost conceal the petals and purple crest within. It occurs on dry, lower, often rocky slopes from Ceres to Riversdale. (Aug-Oct).

♣ Two more with terminal flower clusters and narrow leaves are the closely leafy shrublet *P. meridionalis* of limey coastal sands, with hairy lower side petals that overlap, and the trailing *P. garcini* with white-crested flowers arranged in tapering loose racemes whose style is not bent in the middle.

Muraltia heisteria

Muraltia vulpina

Polygala bracteolata

Polygala myrtifolia

Polygala umbellata

John Manning

223

EUPHORBIACEAE – The rubber tree, spurge and milkweed family

Clutia alaternoides (=rubricaulis)
jeukbossie

A hairless, resprouting shrub to 70cm with sessile oval, blunt leaves with a fine point at the tip, and a fine-toothed edge. The cream-coloured female flowers, borne singly in the leaf axils, produce round hairless 3-chambered capsules, while the 4mm long clustered male flowers, borne on separate plants, emerge beyond the leaves. It occurs on coastal flats or lower slopes from Namaqualand to Paarl and through to Port Elizabeth. (June-Feb).

♣ *C. pubescens* has finely hairy branches and capsules, *C. laxa* has smooth capsules, both of Jonkershoek and Helderberg areas. *C. polifolia* has leaves with margins rolled under and clearly paler below. *C. pulchella* is recorded in forest margins and thicket in Kogelberg area.

Clutia polygonoides

A hairless shrublet to 60cm with many sparsely branched stems resprouting from a fire-resistant rootstock. The leathery, almost stalkless leaves are narrow, oblong and 12-18mm long. The flowers are yellow or orange, about 4mm long, with males and females on separate plants. The male flowers are in axillary clusters, whilst the female flowers, shown here, are solitary and followed by round hairless 3-chambered capsules. It occurs on the upper mountain slopes from Clanwilliam to Riversdale. (June-Oct).

♣ The similar *C. ericoides* has distinctly concave leaves, distinctive black axillary buds, and cream flowers.

Euphorbia silenifolia
melkbol

A dwarf, tuberous geophyte to 75mm with a basal rosette of annual leaves and flowering stems, and a milky latex. The clustered male and female flowers are on separate plants. It occurs at upper altitudes from Ceres to Grahamstown. (Apr-Nov).

♣ The very similar *E. tuberosa* occurs at lower altitudes and differs in having broader, more spreading leaves, usually with wavy edges.

Euphorbia erythrina
pisgoed

A perennial resprouting sparsely-branched hairless, leafy shrublet to 70cm with a milky latex. The crowded narrow leaves, 8-20mm long, have a short hard tip. The flowerhead stalks may be branched, and arise from a circle of leaves. It occurs from Ceres and the Cape Peninsula to the eastern Cape. (June-Oct).

♣ Three are similar: *E. foliosa* from the coast is half the size in most respects; *E. genistoides* with narrower leaves rolled under at the margins; *E. epicyparissias* has leaves bent downwards also with inrolled margins. *E. peplus* is a ubiquitous exotic small garden weed with rounded leaves.

AQUIFOLIACEAE

Ilex mitis
cape holly

A tree of variable size but up to 30m with a trunk diameter of 60cm or more, and a pale to nearly white bark. The shining dark leaves are alternate and mostly with a smooth but wavy edge, but a careful hunt will reveal a few with one or two teeth towards the tip; borne on short, usually conspicuously plum-coloured stalks. Clusters of small white sweetly-scented flowers appear in the axils of the leaves, single-sex male and female, (some said to be bisexual) said to be borne on separate trees, the females producing crops of brilliant red, round berries 4-6mm across, often so abundantly that the tree can be seen from a long way off, and much liked by birds. It occurs scattered in moist forest and along river verges from Table Mountain to Ethiopia and from KwaZulu Natal to Angola. (flowers Sept-Feb; berries c. Apr).

Clutia alaternoides

Clutia polygonoides

Euphorbia silenifolia

Ilex mitis

Euphorbia erythrina

225

ANACARDIACEAE - The poison ivy, pistachio, cashew and mango family

Heeria argentea
kliphout

A sturdy evergreen bushy tree with thick branches to 5m, a grey to brown mottled bark and dark green oval leaves, 2.5-5.5cm long with a silvery-white hairy reverse and conspicuous closely arranged, parallel veins. The single-sex small cream flowers are borne in clusters on separate trees, the females giving rise to oblong rough, yellow-green fruits. It grows among rocks on mountain slopes from Cedarberg to Kleinmond. (Fl. Jan-Jul, fr. Sept-Jan).

♣ There is only one species.

Laurophyllus capensis
iron martin, ystermartiens

A resinous, densely leafy, evergreen shrub or small tree to 6m, with oblong leathery leaves. The male and female flowers are borne on separate plants. The small white flowers of the female give rise to winged fruits, borne within overlapping, woody, distinctive coarsely-fringed bracts resembling diminutive antlers, which turn brown and remain on the plant for a number of seasons. It is recorded from streamsides and forest margins from the Hottentots Holland to Uitenhage, and is the only species. (Aug-Jan).

Rhus angustifolia
willowy korentebos

An evergreen dioecious shrub or tree to 4m with 3-foliolate leaves, pale below. The stalked leaflets are lance-shaped to narrow, and the clusters of yellowish female flowers produce elliptic short-hairy fleshy fruits. It occurs near streams from the Bokkeveld to Barrydale. (Oct-Nov).

♣ R. tomentosa has broad leaves, also pale velvety below and sometimes scalloped (Jul-Aug).

Rhus rosmarinifolia
rosemary, taaibos

A dwarf evergreen rather open shrub to 1m with 3-foliolate leaves, pale below, with stalkless linear, usually smooth-edged leaflets. Male and female flowers are borne on separate plants, the females producing elliptic, usually hairy fleshy fruits. It occurs on gravelly slopes throughout the fynbos. (May-Aug).

Rhus crenata
dune kraaibessie

An evergreen shrub or tree to 4m with 3-foliolate leaves. The stalkless rounded leaflets, broadest upwards, have a blunt, scalloped tip. The clusters of insignificant creamy flowers are unisexual, borne on separate plants, (dioecious), the female, shown here, producing fleshy dark blue-black/brown fleshy fruits. It occurs on the sandy coastal plain from the Cape Peninsula to KwaZulu-Natal. (Apr).

♣ There are about 250 species worldwide in the subtropics and temperate regions and over 60 in South Africa, of which 11 occur in this area. R. cuneifolia has deeply pointed scalloped leaves. R. glauca, a spreading bush and R. lucida, a cone shaped shrub both have glossy leaves with smooth margins. R. laevigata has leaf veins that appear somewhat transparent. R. scytophylla of rocky areas has deep red flowers and flowerstalks.

Heeria argentea (Female)

Laurophyllus capensis (Male)

Laurophyllus capensis (Female)

Rhus angustifolia (Female)

Rhus rosmarinifolia

Rhus crenata (Female)

227

CELASTRACEAE

Pterocelastrus rostratus
red cherrywood, kershout

A tree to 10m with alternate, leathery pointed leaves up to 9cm by 5cm. The tiny yellow-coloured fragrant flowers are borne in rounded clusters. Occurring in forests from Betty's Bay through to Mpumalanga, it blooms from April to June and produces its striking orange-brown fruits with many horns later.

♣ 5 species occur in tropical and southern Africa, but only 1 other occurs in this area. *P. tricuspidatus* of mountain forest and coastal thicket has blunt-tipped leaves, notched at the tip, 3-8cm long by 1-4cm wide and produces 3-horned orange-yellow fruits.

RHAMNACEAE

Phylica buxifolia
A rounded, velvety shrub or small tree to 4m, with leathery oval 15-25mm long leaves, grey-felted beneath and with margins curved inwards. The pale short-stalked unpleasantly scented insignificant flowers grouped in small stalked heads, give rise to three-seeded capsule fruits. Often associated with cliffs and boulders on lower mountain slopes, it is common from the Cape Peninsula to Caledon. (Apr-Aug).

♣ There are 133 species in the Cape with some 24 in this area.

Phylica ericoides
A much-branched, rather stiff neatly-rounded shrub to 90cm with crowded heath-like leaves 5-8mm long. The minute flowers are densely crowded above an involucre of small brown scale-like bracts, to form a posy head 4-7mm across. The heads are often massed towards the tips of the branches, especially in the coarser form shown here, found near the sea. On the mountain slopes a form occurs which is perhaps only 2/3rds the size in most dimensions. Widespread on dunes and lower coastal mountain slopes from Paarl and the Cape Peninsula to Port Elizabeth and south tropical Africa. (Blooms at any time of the year).

Phylica lasiocarpa
This low, spreading, many-stemmed, rather loose shrub to 60cm resprouts from a fire-resistant stump. The rough upcurved leaves, 6-12mm long, may be heathlike with edges tightly rolled underneath, or openbacked, almost flat and 3mm wide. The flowers may be grouped into dense, posy-like heads as here, or small, rather loose heads 5-6mm across. It is very common on the lower, drier slopes from Stellenbosch to Hermanus and Bredasdorp. (Dec-Apr).

♣ Many other species have this build, the variability and differences in their leaves and details of flowers baffling all but the expert.

Phylica spicata
A much-branched sturdy shrub to 2m with velvety branches. The sharp pointed leaves are up to 25mm by 12mm, shiny above and pale-felted below, with the edges tightly rolled under at the tip but progressively unfurled towards the base. The crowded flowers, attracting hosts of bees when open, are borne in woolly spikes which may vary in shape from being only slightly elongated to up to 75mm long. The spikes are borne singly or in groups at the tips of the branches. It occurs on mountain slopes from Clanwilliam to Worcester, Tulbagh to Hottentots Holland and Kogel Bay. (Apr-Aug).

228

Pterocelastrus rostratus

Phylica buxifolia

Phylica ericoides

Phylica lasiocarpa

Phylica spicata

229

Phylica pubescens featherhead,veerkoppie

A dense erect, moderately-branched shrub to 2m with shaggy, silky branches and younger leaves. The rather crowded mature leaves are 25-35mm long, spreading outwards and upwards. They may be open-backed with a pale felt-like undersurface, or tightly rolled underneath. The shaggy mophead-like single flowerheads are up to 5cm across. The flowers with tapering sepals enclose a hairy tube with petals and stamens attached to the wall. It is quite common on dry lower mountain slopes and flats in inland areas from Worcester to Stellenbosch and the Cape Peninsula to Riversdale. (May-Aug).

♣ The much shorter, similar but rusty-golden-headed *P. plumosa* with almost hairless branches and outcurving, rather shorter leaves, also occurs in this area.

Trichocephalus stipularis dogface

A resprouting shrub to 90cm with many stems from a persistent rootstock. The edges of the alternate, narrow leaves are rolled under and there is a pair of dry whiskery stipules at either side of the base. The pink flowers are tightly massed into woolly heads, and usually only three produce capsules in each head, giving it a vaguely foxy look. Note the flower mantid waiting to ambush visiting insects. It is common on sandy flats and lowland slopes from the Cedarberg to Knysna. (May-Sept).

♣ This is the only species.

MALVACEAE

Hermannia alnifolia dolls roses

A rounded grey-mealy shrub to 1m with hairy branches. The leaves are toothed towards the apex and mealy below. The small yellow flowers are clustered at the branch tips. It occurs on shaly or rocky slopes from the Bokkeveld mountains to George. (Jul-Oct).

♣ There are about 300 species of dolls roses in the dry tropics and subtropics of Africa, Australia and America, of which perhaps 8 occur in this area.

Hermannia angularis

A sprawling shrublet with branches rising to 60cm. The leaves are wedge-shaped to lance-shaped but broadest towards the tips. The red flowers have narrow throats but the petals flare abruptly out from the more or less hairless sepals. It is found on dry stony slopes from Hottentots Holland to Plettenberg Bay. (Sept-Oct).

♣ Another sprawler is the red to yellow-flowered *H. rudis* of coastal sands, with rounded terminal flower clusters and round flat, large papery sepals.

Hermannia salviifolia

A coarsely velvety much-branched shrub to 2m. The oval leaves, broadest towards the tip, are densely hairy and very sparsely toothed. The hanging flowers, crowded at the ends of branches, are yellow or orange tubes with flaring petal tips within a slightly ballooning calyx. It occurs on stony granite or clay slopes from the Cape Peninsula to Grahamstown. (mainly Sept-Oct; Dec-Apr).

♣ The 2m tall stiffly erect, twiggy *H. hyssopifolia* of stony granite and clay slopes has creamy or pale yellow flowers with an inflated calyx, in dense terminal groups.

230

Phylica pubescens

Trichocephalus stipularis

Hermannia alnifolia

Hermannia angularis

Hermannia salviifolia

231

Anisodontea scabrosa

An erect, harsh-textured, hairy, often sticky and aromatic shrub 2-3m tall with leaves variable in shape, the lower 20-70mm long but much reduced in size among the flowers. The hibiscus-like red to pinkish to off-white flowers occur singly or in small groups in the axils of the leaves, have the stamens gathered into a central column, and produce a 9-15 chambered fruit. Widely distributed in diverse soils, often in disturbed ground from Saldanha Bay to the Eastern Cape, mostly on the coastal plain, it blooms all the year round.

♣ There are 20 species from the South Western Cape to Lesotho and Namibia, but only 1 in this area.

Hibiscus trionum

A coarse, often straggly, harsh bristly annual up to 25cm or more. The leaves are lobed or deeply cut, and the yellow flowers with black centres are 25-40mm across. The calyx with its purple veins becomes inflated as the fruit ripens. It is a widespread and common weed of cultivation in the warmer parts of the Old World, often in damp places. (Sept-Feb).

♣ There are about 300 species worldwide of which 50 occur in South Africa and possibly 5 in this area. Two indigenous species have similarly coloured flowers: *H. aethiopicus* is a dwarf nearly prostrate resprouting perennial with oval serrated leaves and a staminal tube c.10mm long; the 2.5m tall *H. diversifolius* has prickly stems and a staminal tube c. 20mm long.

KIGGELARIACEAE

Kiggelaria africana   wild peach, spekhout

A resprouting tree to 17m with a smooth grey bark, bearing male and female flowers on separate plants. The simple, alternate, glossy oval leaves are very variable in shape, size, smoothness or serration, and are sometimes clearly paler below. The most consistent feature is the blisters, filled with hairs, in the angles between the main vein and its subsidiaries, clearly visible in the illustration[1], which provide a home for a mite. Male flowers, borne in clusters, have 5 sepals and petals and up to 10 stamens, while the long-stalked female flowers, borne singly in the axils of a leaf, have 5 sepals, petals and stigmas. The ovary matures into a rough-skinned cherry-sized fruit which splits to reveal bright orange-covered seeds beloved by African Olive pigeons and other birds. A rugged garden tree, it is sometimes defoliated without permanent harm by caterpillars of the clearwing butterfly. Common in forest patches. (Feb-July).

Anisodontea scabrosa

Hibiscus trionum

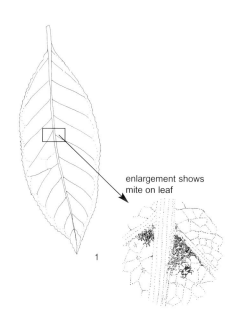

enlargement shows
mite on leaf

1

Kiggelaria africana

Kiggelaria africana

233

VIOLACEAE - The violet family

Viola decumbens
wild violet

A weak, sprawling perennial to 30cm with narrow leaves and blue-mauve or white flowers, sometimes yellow in the throat, typically violet-shaped and sometimes scented. It is quite common on lower mountain slopes in stony, rocky or sandy places from Bain's Kloof to Riversdale and throughout this area. (July-Dec).

♣ There are around 300 species mainly in the northern hemisphere. This is the only species in our area.

PENAEACEAE

Glischrocolla formosa

This single species is a densely leafy shrub to 1m with broad stalkless leaves. The tubular flowers in the axils of the uppermost leaves are white and enclosed below by bright red bracts. It is confined to high altitude moist kloofs and wet ledges on cliffs of the Hottentots Holland mountains where the slow-maturing populations are threatened by too frequent fires (Jan).

Brachysiphon rupestris

A stunted, gnarled, twiggy woody shrublet with almost stalkless, tough oval leaves. The flowers are two-toned pink, the paler sepals enclosed below by deeper pink bracts. It grows out of cracks in quartzitic sandstone rock cliffs in the Klein River mountains. (Sept-Oct).

♣ There are 5 species but this is the only one in our area.

Sonderothamnus speciosus

A sparsely branched resprouting erect shrublet to 60cm with broad overlapping 6-10mm long oval leaves neatly arranged on the upper stems, each with a round wart at the tip. On older plants the lower stems are naked. The crowded pink, 8mm long flowers are surrounded by fringed bracts. It is occasional on rocky and sandy mountain slopes in the Klein River mountains. (July-Oct).

♣ There are 2 species, both found in this area. The 35cm *S. petraeus*, with 5mm long flowers occurs in rock crevices of sandstone oucrops from Cape Hangklip to Kleinmond.

Saltera sarcocolla
vlieëbos

A rather untidy, resprouting sparsely-branched shrub to 1.5m with leathery, rounded, overlapping leaves and terminal flowerheads of 1-6 flowers surrounded by sticky bract-like leaves. The flowers are pink, often with white markings, but a less common white single-flowered form occurs in the Hangklip area. It is common on flats and slopes from the Cape Peninsula, inland to Franschhoek and along the coast to Bredasdorp. (Blooms mostly in the latter half of the year).

234

Viola decumbens

Glischrocolla formosa

*Sonderothamnus
speciosus*

Brachysiphon rupestris

Saltera sarcocolla
Hangklip form

Saltera sarcocolla

235

Penaea cneorum

A tall lanky hairless shrub to 2m or more whose oval stalkless leaves have straight points on the tips. The 10mm long flowers are borne in clusters at the branch tips. They are greenish-yellow, becoming brick red with age. It occurs in moist, often steep places from the Hottentots Holland mountains to Port Elizabeth and blooms throughout the year. There are two subspecies.

♣ There are 3 species confined to the fynbos, of which 1 other occurs in this area: the common resprouting *P. mucronata* of lower open mountain slopes and flats is a shorter, rounded plant with yellow flowers, somewhat incurved leaftip points and lightly hairy branchlets.

Stylapterus micranthus

A sparsely branched shrub to 1.5m with linear leaves which are grooved below. Tubular yellow flowers, ca 3mm long, have a short narrow style tipped with 4 small lobes, redden with age and have thin scimitar shaped persistent bracts. It grows at mid altitude almost undetectably among restios in the Kogelberg. (Sept-Oct).

♣ There are 8 species, two here: *S. barbatus* of the high damp sandstone slopes of the Hottentots Holland is a shorter growing shrublet with the leaves grooved beneath towards the base and 2mm long hairs in the axils of the leaves.

THYMELAEACEAE – The daphne or stripbark family

Gnidia penicillata

A shrublet to 40cm with pairs of narrow hair-fringed leaves and unusually wide open bright blue or pink flowers. These are clustered into terminal heads and have spreading sepal lobes and 4 hairy petal scales, each divided into 4 fleshy fingerlike lobes. Four of the stamens may be non-functional. It grows on marshy flats and lower slopes from the Cape Peninsula to the Caledon Swartberg and Kleinmond. (Aug-May).

♣ There are 150 species found mostly in Africa, 47 in the Cape and c.19 here. The similar *G. linearifolia* has large pink flowers and 4 membranous, deeply toothed scales; the flowers of the 3m tall *G. nana* are pale lilac to dull purple, sometimes cream, in groups of 3-5 with sepals bent back and fleshy petals in a continuous ring.

Gnidia pinifolia

An erect single-stemmed shrub to 1m tall with narrow, alternate, almost needlelike crowded leaves up to 16mm long. The hairy flowers, borne in groups of c. 10 or more at the branch tips, are sometimes pinkish in the bud, but open white. The tube is 12mm long and there are 4 fleshy fingerlike petals. Occurring on flats and low to middle slopes from Piketberg to the Eastern Cape and Transvaal, blooming any time of the year.

♣ Other 4-petalled species are the white-flowered *G. tomentosa* of marshes in the west of our area with alternate leaves; the cream to green-yellow, opposite-leafed *G. tenella* has flowers grouped 2-4 while *G. chrysophylla* of Kogelberg coast has flowers grouped 6-9.

Gnidia squarrosa

A much-branched willowy shrub to 2m tall, with narrow lance-shaped leaves 8mm by 1mm. The massed creamy-green to yellow flowers are pink-flushed with a fine-hairy, 7mm long tube and 8 fingerlike petals in the mouth. They are wonderfully scented at night. It occurs on limestone or sandy slopes near the coast from the Cape Peninsula to KwaZulu-Natal. (June-Oct).

♣ The similar densely-silky *G. anomala* also has 8 petals, but fewer flowers per cluster. Three have no petals: the shrubby yellow to brown flowered *G. laxa* with 4-8 flowered heads, the slender cream-flowered racemose, marsh and dune-loving *G. spicata*, and silky, white 1m tall *G. ornata*.

Penaea cneorum

Stylapterus micranthus

Gnidia pinifolia

Gnidia penicillata

Gnidia squarrosa

237

Gnidia oppositifolia

An erect slender shrub up to 3m tall with overlapping pairs of smooth oval, pointed leaves about 10mm long. The pale yellow hairy flowers, with a 16mm long tube, have 4 fleshy fingerlike petals in the mouth, and are in groups of 4-6 raised above the topmost leaves. Occurring in wet places and on stream-banks on mountain slopes from Clanwilliam to the Eastern Cape and Transvaal, it may bloom at any time of the year.

Gnidia juniperifolia

A hairless, sprawling or erect resprouting shrub to 50cm with scattered 10-12mm long narrow oval pointed leaves. The 6-8mm long hairless yellow flowers, borne singly or in pairs at the tips of the branches, have a long tubular calyx and 4 membranous petals visible in the mouth. This species is one of the few in the genus with almost solitary flowers. It is common on mountain slopes from Paarl, the Cape Peninsula to Riversdale. (Flowers any time of the year.)

♣ 3 more with hairless yellow flowers and 4 membranous petals may be found in this area: *G. galpinii*, *G. coriacea* and *G. simplex*. Two with hairy flowers are *G. humilis* of damp places in the west of our area, and *G. sonderiana* of Babilonstoring.

Lachnaea densiflora

This much-branched shrublet to 50cm has narrow pointed leaves up to 10mm long. The pink or cream flowers, each less than 5mm long, have a woolly calyx, no petals, and are borne in well-defined round heads. It occurs on sandy flats or lower slopes which may be seasonally damp, from the Cape Peninsula to Bredasdorp. (Sept-Jan).

♣ There are about 29 species in the southwestern Cape, of which 7 occur in this area. Others in our area have solitary cream or pink silky terminal flowers: the erect 40cm *L. filicaulis* of the coastal flats with curving branches; the resprouting, 1m tall compact *L. grandiflora* with large flowers; and loosely-open *L. laxa* of wet mountain slopes with 30cm spread.

Lachnaea macrantha   cape edelweiss, mountain carnation

An erect moderately branched shrub to 1.5m with rounded overlapping leaves below the magnificent flowerheads, which are sweetly scented, neatly circumscribed, posylike, white, occasionally pink or purplish tinged and 35-60mm across. It occurs in rocky outcrops at high altitude from Slanghoek to the Langeberg. (Sept-Jan).

♣ *L. eriocephala* of the lower slopes from Tulbagh to Sir Lowry's Pass has 20-55mm wide, posylike cream or mauve heads; *L. aurea* of lower slopes at Hermanus-Agulhas has 20-50mm wide yellow posies.

Passerina rigida   seekoppiesganna

A 2m tall robust wind-pollinated shrub with pendulous branches. Flattened stubby leaves are 2-4mm long and hairy on the back. The flowers, inflated below, have no petals, but 8 stamens which project beyond the mouth of the flower, which is closed by the mop-like stigma. It is one of two species which produce bright orange or red berries. It is found from the Cape Peninsula to KwaZulu-Natal.

♣ Another berry-making species is the 1m tall, willowy *P. ericoides* found between Blouberg and Hermanus. Both grow on coastal dunes. Two have dry fruits: *P. corymbosa* the small tree to 2.m, of sandy, often disturbed places, has small narrow leaves and reddish flowers; *P. paleacea* has cream to pale pink flower and grows on coastal sands from Saldanha to Agulhus.

Gnidia oppositifolia

Gnidia juniperifolia

Lachnaea densiflora

Lachnaea macrantha

Passerina rigida

239

Struthiola myrsinites

An open willowy shrub to 2m tall, often producing dense clusters of branches towards the top of the main stems. The stems are clothed quite closely with pairs of narrow, hairless, pointed leaves up to 12mm long and 5mm wide. The flowers, about 22mm long and arranged along the upper parts of the stems, pale to bright pink in bud, but opening up white or pale pink and richly fragrant at night. They are hairless on the outside and have 8 fingerlike petals projecting above a halo of pale bristles at the mouth of the flower. Occurring widely in sandy soil often near watercourses, from the Gifberg to the Eastern Cape, it can be found in bloom at any time of the year.

♣ There are about 40 species in Africa south of the equator of which c. 10 occur in this area. Four more have 8 petals: two have hairless flower tubes: the pinkish or yellowish flowered *S. salteri* of limestone from the Peninsula to Agulhas is distinguished by having leaves in 3's, occasionally 4's; the petal scales of the pink or white-flowered, 80cm tall *S. dodecandra* of lower slopes and flats nestle within its bristles. Two have hairy flowers: the 60cm tall cream or pink *S. confusa* is richly perfumed at dusk, as is the taller cream, pink or reddish flowered *S. ciliata* with its hairy white-woolly branches and flowers becoming more or less hairless.

Struthiola striata   katstertjie, roemenaggie, veertjie

A shrub to 1m tall, hairy when young but becoming hairless, with pairs of oval 10mm by 3mm, overlapping, ribbed leaves. The 10mm long cream, yellow or pinkish flowers are clothed with hairs outside and have 4 fingerlike petals surrounded by pale bristles. It occurs on coastal flats and lower slopes from the Cape Peninsula to Mossel Bay and on to the Eastern Cape. (Sept-June)

♣ Only 1 other, the reddish-flowered *S. tetralepis* of upper mountain slope has 4 petals.

Struthiola tomentosa   roemenaggie

A slender silvery-haired shrublet to 60cm with closely overlapping, paired oval leaves, silky when young. The sweetly-scented sessile cream to yellow flowers tinged with orange-red, emerging singly or in pairs from the leaf axils, are woolly on the outside with 12 fingerlike petals radiating from stiff golden hairs. It occurs on mountain slopes from Caledon to Swellendam and blooms all year.

♣ Two other species have 12 petals: *S. martiana*, of the upper slopes with hairy white or pink flowers, and the resprouting *S. mundii* of lower slopes, with hairless yellow flowers.

MYRTACEAE – The myrtle and Eucalyptus family

Metrosideros angustifolius   smalblad, Cape-gum

A shrub or small tree to 7m, with pairs of narrowly elliptic, simple leaves, 3.5-8cm long with the midrib visible but side veins obscure, lacking stipules. Creamy white flowers are borne among the leaves in crowded groups towards the ends of the branches. Each has a mass of central stamens and 5 short sepals and petals, scarcely visible in the illustration. The small rounded capsules remain on the branches for a few seasons and can be seen, mostly already open, in this view. It occurs quite commonly from the Gifberg to the Langeberg in the mountains along watercourses. (Nov-Mar).

Struthiola myrsinites

Struthiola striata

Struthiola tomentosa

Metrosideros angustifolius

ARALIACEAE

Cussonia thyrsiflora
cabbage tree, kuskiepersol

A shrub to small tree, often leaning on and through others, to 5m. The very large leaves are 5-8 digitate, the leaflets being slightly toothed towards the broadening apex. The short-stalked flowers are borne in crowded racemes, several racemes being clustered at the ends of stems, and give rise to purple berries. It grows in forest or coastal thicket and on dunes from the Cape Peninsula to the Eastern Cape. (Nov-Jan).

♣ There are 10 species in Africa, one in our area.

Centella triloba
varkoorties, pennywort

A sturdy sprawling hairless perennial usually forming dense cushions hanging from rocks, with woody older stems and ribbed branches up to 0.5m long. It bears tufts of wedge-shaped leaves, 2-5cm long, with up to 9 teeth at the apex and narrowing gradually below into leafstalks up to 6cm long, and insignificant flowers. It occurs on mountains from the Cape Peninsula to Agulhas and Robertson, from rocky coastal flats to the higher slopes. (July-Apr).

♣ About 50 species of Centella occur in southern Africa and 17 in our area. Only the hairy, stout and erect *C. difformis* has a similar leaf.

APIACEAE – The parsley and carrot family

Dasispermum (=Heteroptilis) suffruticosum
sea parsley

A hairless, branched, prostrate or erect perennial up to 50cm tall, with leathery, fleshy, divided, parsley-like leaves up to 8cm long, with a stalk half the length. The flowers are in clusters up to 30mm across, enlarging to double this width when in fruit. Occurring on dunes, flats and sandy slopes from the Cape to KwaZulu-Natal. (Dec-Apr).

♣ There is only 1 species.

Peucedanum galbanum
blisterbush, bergseldery

A resinous-scented, sturdy, branching shrub with hollow stems to 3m tall, and stalked compound leaves attached all along the stems, bearing diamond-shaped leaflets. The flowers are borne in a conspicuous compound umbel. It occurs from near sea-level to upper slopes, often in moist or sheltered places, from Piketberg to Riversdale. The flowering season is erratic. BEWARE OF THIS PLANT. It is known to provoke in some people, and in some conditions, quite savage blistering, characteristically delayed for a day or two. The worst reactions seem to arise when one is perspiring, and when the plant is bruised.

♣ There are about 170 species in Africa and Eurasia, of which some 7 occur in this area; none resemble this species and none other causes skin irritation.

Hermas villosa
tontelblaar

A robust shrub to 1m, with a group of very shiny, rigid, carrot-scented leaves at ground level. They have a densely white-hairy reverse, and are up to 15cm long and 6cm wide. The long, smooth, naked flowering stem bears globose flower clusters about 4cm across. It is extremely common on dry mountain slopes from the Cape Peninsula to Hermanus. (Dec-May).

♣ There are 9 species confined to the Cape, of which 7 others are found in our area. The resinous *H. gigantea* of the inland mountains has altogether woolly leaves double this size, and deep purple flowers. Two species are of similar proportions but have branched flower-stalks; *H. quercifolia* of damp places with rosettes of flannelly oak-like leaves; and *H. ciliata*, with eyelash-fringed, oval, long-stalked leaves. *H. quinquedentata* to 30cm has bright green leaves borne near the ground and an unbranched flowerstalk.

242

Cussonia thyrsiflora

Centella triloba

Dasispermum suffruticosum

Peucedanum galbanum   Anne Bean

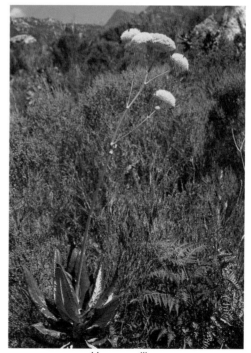

Hermas villosa

243

Lichtensteinia lacera
kalmoes

An edible-rooted perennial with large leaves, resembling a spiky form of rhubarb. The rigid branched flowering stems grow to 1,25m and emerge from a tuft of black fibres. The yellowish flower clusters are flat-topped. It occurs on the flats and lower slopes of Jonkershoek and the Cape Peninsula. (Jan-Mar).

♣ There are 7 species in South Africa, one other, *L. obscura*, is recorded from the Stellenbosch area.

Arctopus echinatus
platdoring, pokkiesdoring

A prickly perennial with underground stems, and a rosette of hair-fringed spiny leaves 4-10cm long and wide, pressed to the ground. The male flowers are pink or white, and the female yellow-green surrounded by 3-spined leafy bracts, borne on separate plants. It is common on flats and lower slopes from Namaqualand to Uitenhage. (May-Aug).

♣ There are about 4 species confined to the fynbos areas of the Cape of which 1 other occurs in this area, the rarer *A. monacanthus* with single-spined leafy bracts.

ERICACEAE – The heath family

Erica is a vast genus with c. 860 species in Africa and Eurasia, of which 771 occur in southern Africa and over 200 in the area of this book. The simple leaves are attached to the stem in 2's or circles of 3, 4, or more, each species having its own characteristic arrangement. The leaves are usually "ericoid": the edges of the leaves being rolled under to the extent of concealing the lower surface - but are sometimes open-backed. In our area most *Erica* flowers have 4 joined petals, 4-8 stamens opening by apical pores, and usually a 4-chambered ovary with many seeds, but departures from this pattern do occur. Features such as size, hairiness and position of the calyx and bracts are important for identification. The profusion of species and their propensity to vary will be the cause of uncertainties in naming heaths found in the region. Pollinators include butterflies, bees and other insects, birds or wind.

Erica cerinthoides
fire heath, rooihaartjie

An erect or short tufted shrub, occasionally to 1.8m when protected from fire, but now rarely seen so tall. It has relatively few branches arising from a woody fire-resistant stump known as a ligno-tuber. The leaves are 6-16mm long, and arranged in 4's. The flowers are 22-34mm long, inflated, hairy, sometimes sticky, crimson, rarely pink or white and borne in terminal clusters. The stamens and stigma are concealed within the tube. Occurring on sandy flats and slopes from Vanrhynsdorp along most of the escarpment mountains to KwaZulu-Natal and the Zoutpansberg and more or less throughout the fynbos area, it is one of the first plants in bloom after a veld fire, and may be found in bloom at any season of the year.

♣ In another tubular resprouting Erica with red flowers, *E. discolor*, the mouth may be yellow or white while the petals are hairless and the leaves in 3's

Erica mammosa

An erect slender-branched shrub to about 1.2m with narrow overlapping leaves in 4's, 6-10mm long. The drooping flowers, long-stalked, 24mm long, lopsidedly inflated and smooth emerge from the axils of the leaves and form a loose spike. It is very variably coloured, being found in white, orange, pink, purple and green as well as the commoner red form shown here. It is distinguished from all other species of similar habit by having 4 indentations at the base of the corolla tube. It is widespread throughout the Southern Cape from Clanwilliam to Caledon. (Dec-Apr).

Arctopus echinatus (Male)

Lichtensteinia lacera

Arctopus echinatus (Female)

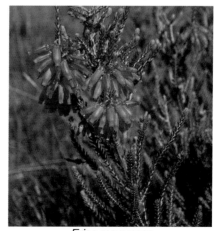

Erica cerinthoides

Erica mammosa

245

Erica viscaria ssp. longifolia (*=E. longifolia*) sticky heath

A compact to tall and willowy erect shrub to 90cm or more with open branches bearing crowded, rigid, overlapping leaves in 4's or more, up to 20mm long with a sharp point. The 12-22mm long flowers with a slightly flaring mouth may be green, white, yellow-green, red, pink and even bi-coloured. They are usually short-hairy and somewhat sticky, hence the name *viscaria*, and form a short whorl or spike near the tips of the branches. Common and widespread on mountain slopes from Mamre, Paarl and Worcester to Bredasdorp, its flowering time depends on the locality.

♣ The similar, narrow, densely crowded trembling leaves in 6's of the pink or white *E. vestita* makes it easily recognizable, while large bushes of *E. pinea* with dry, smooth, hairless tubular corollas in white or yellow may be seen on mountain slopes and plateaus in the northern Hottentots Holland and Kogelberg.

Erica abietina ssp. aurantiaca

A robust erect shrub to 1.5m with untidily arranged hairless incurved leaves up to 20mm long. The curved tubular flowers are borne singly in a spike on short shoots in the axils of the leaves. They are hairless, sometimes sticky, and up to 28mm long. The bracts and sepals are broad and green, tapering to a long point. The usual colour is orange-red, but a variant which grows at Jonkershoek is yellow. It occurs on the inland mountain slopes in the north of this area, and from Tulbagh to Riversdale. (June-Sept).

Erica pillansii

An erect finely hairy shrub to 1m with ascending branches crowded with bright red flowers in 3's and 4's at the branch tips. The leaves are in 4's and 4-6mm long. The velvety corolla is a 15mm long tube with stamens and style included. It grows often in large colonies in wetlands, for many months forming vivid sheets of colour on the lower slopes from Kleinmond to Kogelberg. (Jan-Jul).

Erica perspicua Prince of Wales heath

An erect shrub 2m or more high with willowy branches and tufts of very short usually hairy leaves in 3's or 4's. The softly-hairy tubular flowers, from less than 10mm to 16-25mm long, grow singly on short side-branches, forming a loose bottlebrush head. The colour varies from pure white, through rose to almost purple, usually with paler lobes, the colour being most intense at high altitudes. It occurs in damp places and swamps from sea level to upper mountain slopes from Kogelberg to Hermanus. (Sept-Apr).

♣ *E. dulcis* of the Hermanus area with more rounded, shorter tubed flowers has a noticeable sweet scent. The more robust *E. leucotrachela* of the Kogelberg has dry-textured velvety-hairy solitary red-tubed flowers with a white throat and lobes. Also hairy, *E. curviflora* has lobes folded well back.

Erica macowanii

A sturdy erect shrub to 1m+ becoming lanky with age, with rigid, incurved leaves in 4's. Stalkless flowers, hairy, hard-textured, varying in length to 30mm or so, flaring at the mouth and enclosing the anthers although the stigma projects, can be white, yellow, apricot, pink, red, dusky salmon or even two-toned red with yellow lobes as shown here, and nestle among the leaves. It occurs commonly on mid to upper slopes in the Kogelberg. (Aug-Mar).

Erica viscaria ssp. longifolia

Erica abietina ssp. aurantiaca

Erica pillansii

Erica perspicua

Erica macowanii

247

Erica thomae

An erect stiff shrub to 1m with incurving narrow leaves in 4's, bearing flowers 2-3cm long, short-stalked, curved, sticky, white pink, orange to reddish with tubes more than 10mm long, towards the ends of branches. The corolla has grooves along its length and conceals the anthers. Now incorporating *E. tenax* with green to yellow-green flowers and *E. porteri* with white-tipped red flowers, as this enlarged species it occurs only in the Kogelberg area. (Jan-July).

Erica sessiliflora   groenheide

An erect robust shrub to 2m high with narrow leaves in 4's or more, only 2-4mm long. The pale green tubular flowers grow in spikes near the tops of the branches. It can always be recognised even when not in flower by the unique fleshy sepals which turn reddish, increase in size around the fruits and remain on the plant for several years. This protects the enclosed seeds from fire damage until a fire kills the parent, whereupon the seeds are released in a mass. It is widespread in damp localities on coastal mountains and further inland often forming extensive populations, from Piketberg to Humansdorp. (Apr-Sept).

Erica ceraria

An upright stout non-hairy shrub to 90cm with lower stems bare and dotted with white leafscars, upper parts very densely leafy with leaves in 4's, 6-10mm long. Broadly tubular, sometimes curved, hairless green to yellow almost stalkless flowers approximately 15mm long, are borne 4-5 together at the ends of short branches. Their rigid wax-like texture is most distinctive, covered with a white bloom when young, becoming shiny and sticky-looking when mature. It is common on mid to upper open mountain slopes in the Kogelberg. (Apr-Nov).

♣ Other yellow, tubular-flowered species with clusters of blooms at branchlet tips are the very similar *E. nana* with stiff twisted sprawling branches making sheets of yellow hanging from cliffs, *E. galpinii* of the Hermanus area with hairy stems and stalkless flowers, and the rare *E. sacciflora* of Franschhoek with stalked yellow to orange flowers, with darkening lobes. The slender marsh-loving *E. campanularis* of the west of our area has single, honey-scented bright yellow bells. The very woody *E. brachialis* of coastal areas has hairy yellowish green flowers in 4's.

Erica patersonii   mealie heath

An erect plant to 1m with few branches and crowded overlapping leaves 8-12mm long in 4's. The dry-textured tightly-packed yellow flowers, 14-18mm long and almost stalkless, form a dense spike towards the ends of the branches. It is found on damp coastal sand flats at Betty's Bay and Kleinmond. It is also still to be seen at Cape Point, but has been exterminated at Hermanus due to overpicking and housing development. (Apr-Nov). It is seen here in an extensive stand of *Elegia filacea*.

Erica banksii *(incl. E. comptonii)*

A erect or sprawling woody shrub to 70cm, with the 4-8mm long leaves in 4's, crowded up the generally arching branch tips, from which the clusters of 3 flowers emerge, 2cm long and white, yellowish or rosy with contrasting tips, usually hanging downwards. The protruding two lobed anthers have a kink below. Preferring to grow among fire-protecting rocks over which it sprawls, it is quite common on the upper slopes from the Hottentots Holland mountains to Bredasdorp. A number of variants exist. (Apr-Oct).

Erica thomae

Erica sessiliflora Anne Bean

Erica patersonii

Erica ceraria

Erica banksii

249

Erica fastigiata　　　　　　　　　　　　　　　　　　four sisters heath

An erect or spreading shrub to 50cm with crowded hairless leaves in 4's. The flowers are borne at the branch tips in upright groups of 4, each with a narrow tube and 4 spreading lobes. In the Hottentots Holland form shown here, the usual darker central 'eye' is absent. It is found on flats and mountain slopes from Bain's Kloof to Caledon, and is very common in Hottentots Holland and Kogelberg. In the Hermanus mountains a variety has more sharply pointed petal lobes also without a dark 'eye'; at Franschhoek the flowers are slightly sticky. (Aug-Jan).

♣ All with similarly shaped flowers: *E. hendricksei* starting green but maturing pink is found in marshes on the northern slopes of the Klein River mountains; a creamy white variety grows in the same area. The white, cream, or pinkish carnation-scented *E. denticulata* grows on mountain slopes around Stellenbosch. The resprouting *E. transparens* has masses of 4mm long bright pink flowers with paler lobes.

Erica irbyana

An erect shrub to 45cm with wiry stems and narrow leaves in 3's, 4-8mm long. The sticky bottle-shaped flowers with spreading star-like lobes, 8-14mm long on stalks up to 14mm long, are borne in groups of 3 to 8 at the ends of the branches. This form occurs in Hermanus and at Onrus; further east it darkens until at Napier it is dark red to nearly purple. It is fairly common on lower slopes from Hawston to Bredasdorp. (Sept-Jan).

♣ *E.lageniformis* is paler with flowers perhaps twice as long, found on the Onrus mountains. (Dec.). *E. cristata* has lumpy, sticky, dark pink, umbels of tubular-urn shaped flowers while *E. curvifolia* has inflated grooved flowers. *E. trichroma* is sticky with 6mm purplish red flowers. *E. ventricosa*, the wax heath, has large urns in pale pink and 14mm long leaves.

Erica retorta　　　　　　　　　　　　　　　　　　bottle heath

Growing to about 45cm in height this shrublet has somewhat straggly branches. The tiny recurved leaves in 4's are thick and rigid and curve up at the tips, ending in a long bristle. The sticky flowers are variable in length, from 8-25mm, and occur in heads of up to 8 or more flowers on long stalks. Often a clear pink with darker pink lobes but varying from dark pink to white, it has woolly anthers. It is common on dry mountain slopes at Betty's Bay and Kleinmond. (Blooms all year).

♣ The smaller pale pink *E. lananthera* of the lower reaches of the Palmiet River has similar leaf bristles but the corolla is fluted, grooved and open-mouthed. (Oct-Mar).

Erica gysbertii

An upright, well-branched shrub to 90cm with long hairs on leaves, sepals and bracts, and leaves in 4's. The sticky flowers, pink, urn-shaped 10-15mm long, in groups of 3-4, constricted at the mouth and with spreading star-like lobes, may be almost hidden by the surrounding hairs. It occurs on lower slopes of the Kogelberg around Pringle Bay, usually associated with rocks. (Dec-Mar).

♣ Similarly hairy *E. intonsa*, confined to the Hangklip area, has longer rectangular leaves and a mixture of fresh and brown, dying flowers.

Erica aristata

An erect woody shrub to 60cm with stiff down-curved sharply-pointed leaves in 4's, 5-6mm long. The long tubular flowers 25-30mm long with darker pink stripes and short frilly lobes are extremely sticky and occur in groups of 4 at the ends of the branches. The styles just project. It is found only on the Klein River mountains. (Aug-Oct).

Erica fastigiata

Erica irbyana

Erica retorta

Erica gysbertii

Erica aristata

251

Erica massonii
Masson's heath

This magnificent sturdy erect shrub to about 1m with spreading branches becomes leggy with age. The closely overlapping leaves in 4's, are 6-10mm long and fringed with long hairs. Extremely sticky glossy red or orange 25mm long flowers with green tips in a whorl of up to 22 flowers per head make this an unmistakeable species. A form in the east of the Klein River mountains is orange with very little contrasting green and yellow. It occurs in dense stands on sandy or rocky slopes up to 1 000m, from Hottentots Holland and Hangklip to the Klein River mountains. (Oct-May).

♣ The similar *E. fascicularis* has pink, yellow-tipped flowers in whorls on 2m tall branches, and non-hairy shimmering leaves and sepals.

Erica plukenetii
hangertjie

A variable, erect shrub with stiff branches. The long-stalked flowers, with bracts towards the base, may be white, greenish, pink, red-orange or reddish-purple, and have a tubular corolla up to 18mm long. The anthers project in a tight cone which opens explosively when levered apart by the beak of a bird visitor, propelling the pollen onto its head. It is very common and widespread along the coast and mountains from Namaqualand to Mossel Bay. (all year).

♣ It is often confused with the sometimes resprouting *E. coccinea*, but the latter species has shorter leaves arranged in tufts up the branches, and flower bracts that are close to the corolla. *E. melastoma* has single inflated bulbous yellow corolla on a short leafy side branch; the resprouting *E. monadelpha* has sticky red flowers with a very short stalk and a characteristic kink below the anthers.

Erica holosericea
An erect shrub to 90cm, but usually much smaller, with few branches and narrow, sharp-tipped leaves in 2's, 3's or 4's, 10-16mm long. The soft, velvety flowers, mostly in groups of 3 on very short side branchlets, are 7-10mm long with sepals almost as long as the petals. As the petals fade the lobes darken and shrivel up to a point, whilst the conspicuous sepals remain colourful for quite a while longer. It is found on moist south-facing mountain slopes from the Kogelberg to Bredasdorp. (Sept-Dec).

♣ Many others in this area have conspicuous sepals of which *E. monsoniana* with papery white 17mm long flowers and *E. lanuginosa* with the corolla split to the base, are the most similar.

Erica corydalis
white petticoat heath

A twiggy, slender shrublet up to 60cm high, which often weaves through other vegetation. The leaves are 3-5mm long, in 3's. White or occasionally pink flowers, 4-5mm long and sweetly honey-scented, soon turning brown when damaged, have sticky sepals and bracts. They cluster in threes at the ends of short side branches. The corolla lobes flair broadly from a circular fold, exposing curiously crested anthers immersed in a pale hairy webbing, and a dark-tipped style included in the corolla cup. It occurs on cool, moist southerly slopes from Kleinmond to Sandy's Glen. (Oct-Jan).

♣ *E. lowryensis* of the Hottentots Holland to Pringle Bay slopes is very similar in appearance and habitat, but lacks the woolly covering on the anthers, while the style projects well beyond the corolla. (Sept-Nov).

Erica massonii

Erica plukenetii

Erica holosericea

Erica corydalis

253

Erica sitiens

An erect shrub to 80cm with leaves in 4's, 3-8mm long. Masses of pale to dark pink or white 6-8mm long flowers with or without white around the mouth are borne in small groups on 2mm long stalks, terminal on side shoots. The lop-sidedly inflated corolla makes it distinctive. A showy species, often in large stands from 300-1000m, it occurs between Stellenbosch and Hermanus. (Sept-Apr).

♣ *E. tenella* of Houw Hoek to Elim has a similar colour range, but lacks the pale mouth, and has a symmetrical, slightly shorter corolla, which is abundant above Hermanus in an intense pink form. (Nov-June) *E. lateralis* of the northern Hottentots Holland is rosy pink, the flowers projecting outwards on stalks twice as long as the flower. *E. autumnalis* has neatly packed tiers of pink flowers.

Erica hirta (=E. sphaeroidea)

An erect shrub to 50cm rising to 1.5m in some forms, with open light brown branches from a persistent rootstock. Stems and leaves are covered with bristly gland-tipped hairs giving them a soft slightly clammy feel. The leaves are spreading, usually oval and open-backed, in 3's and up to 10mm long. The flowers, oval, 3-7mm long, long-stalked, pink or white and somewhat sticky and usually covered with fine velvety hairs. They occur in groups of 3 at the branch-tips or scattered in the leaf axils. The stamens and style project slightly beyond the petals. It is frequent on lower and middle mountain slopes around Jonkershoek and Helderberg. (April to Aug).

♣ *E. racemosa*, which grows in the same areas, is similar but has much smaller, grey-green needlelike leaves and all the flowers are borne in the leaf axils.

Erica pulchella

A rounded many-branched fairly rigid 60cm tall shrub with narrowly lance-shaped overlapping 5mm long leaves in 3's. The tiny dark pink urns are smooth and firm-textured and about 5mm long, borne singly or in small groups on flowerstalks with short downcurving hairs, in the leaf axils crowded at the ends of the branches. The stigma and stamens are included within the flower. It occurs from the Cape Peninsula to Albertinia in open colonies on sandy flats and lower mountain slopes. (Dec-May).

♣ The very similar *E. longiaristata* of Hermanus to Bredasdorp differs only in shorter leaves, more lax growth and pale pink or white petals with a wider mouth.

Erica hottentottica

A compact shrub with erect branches to 2.5m, with short, flower-bearing side shoots, densely clothed in softly hairy 0.5-3.5mm long, oblong leaves in 4's. The urn-shaped flowers, pink, 3mm long, terminal, upright or pendant on 2mm long stalks, arise in groups of 1-4. While the stamens are included, the expanded stigma projects just beyond the petals. It occurs on the upper parts of the Hottentots Holland mountains. (Sept-Nov).

Erica curvirostris   honey heath

Smallish rounded shrublets to 30cm or more, with hairy branches and hairless leaves 4-6mm long, in 4's. The short-hairy-stalked flowers, sweetly scented, bell-shaped, open-mouthed and pink or white, out of which the curved style projects, are up to 4.5mm long and in groups on branch tips. It grows in almost pure stands on dry bedrock outcrops on mid to upper mountain slopes from Du Toit's Kloof to Kogelberg and the Klein River mountains. (Feb-Apr).

♣ *E. subdivaricata* of lower slopes is a quite sturdy shrub to 1m tall, with 2-4mm creamy-white, open-mouthed flowers, included straight style, in groups of 4 at the branch-tips, whose strong honey scent attracts bees. *E. turbiniflora* has 8 angled flowers and narrow sepals reaching to the flower lobes.

Erica sitiens

Erica hirta

Erica pulchella

Erica hottentottica

Erica curvirostris

255

Erica hispidula

A coarsely hairy erect, wind-pollinated, robust, much-branched shrub to 1.5m has leaves in 3's, and flowers, both about 1-2mm long. The sepals are occasionally sticky, and the corolla smooth, dirty white, pink or red. Often huge clouds of pollen are released, intercepted by conspicuous bright red plate-like stigmas which project well beyond the flowers. A common species occurring from Clanwilliam throughout the fynbos and as far as Uitenhage and the great Swartberg range, it often dominates the vegetation. (Jan-Dec).

♣ The very floriferous pink to mauve *E. copiosa* of the Stellenbosch area and on to Port Elizabeth differs in its longer style and rather less expanded stigma.

Erica imbricata   salt and pepper heath

An erect twiggy shrub to 80cm with crowded, shortly woolly leaves in 3's, 3-5mm long, often tufted on very short side branchlets. The usually white, but sometimes pale pink 3mm long flowers, which are sometimes slightly sticky, are in groups of 3 or more at the tips of the branchlets. Long sepals clasp the petals although the dark stamens project. It is extremely common on sandy flats and mountain slopes throughout this area. (Feb-Nov).

♣ The pink *E. placentiflora* with spreading calyx, *E. azaleifolia* and white to yellowish *E. penicilliformis* all have a very similar floral arrangement. In the red, frilly *E. spumosa*, white, purple blotched E. amphigena and white to pink *E. sexfaria* the three flowers form compact heads.

Erica jacksoniana

A sparingly branched shrub to 1.5m or more with crowded short side branches densely clothed in tightly packed small leaves in 3's. The leaves, stems and sepals are hairy. A profusion of 3mm long cup-shaped rosy pink flowers arising from paler sepals soon turn brown. Confined to the upper eastern slopes of the Hottentots Holland mountains above Somerset West it is frequent in marshes and wet slopes above 1000m. (Mar-May).

Erica intervallaris

A somewhat lax hairy shrub to 60 cm with leaves in 4's. The flowers, 4-angled, urn-shaped glossy purplish- to reddish-pink and 4mm long, with hairy sepals on non-hairy stalks, are borne along the branches. Occurring in masses in wetlands and along streams, they make bright patches on the mountainside of Hottentots Holland, Kogelberg and Caledon. (Jul-Jan).

♣ The hairy but otherwise similar *E. parviflora* has a more rounded flower and leaves in 3's (Sept-May) the 1,2m *E. hirtiflora* also has hairy flowers. Both grow in the same habitat.

Erica globiceps ssp. consors (=Simocheilus consors)

A low sprawling shrublet to 30cm with hairy stems and small hairy leaves in 4's. The very small tubular pink flowers cluster at branch tips. There are 3-4 hairy fringed sepals, petals and stamens, and style and stamens protrude. It grows from the flats to the upper slopes on the Riviersonderend and from the Klein River mountains to Agulhas. (Aug-Dec). This is one of what used to be termed the "minor genera" of the *Ericaceae* because of the reduced number particularly of its stamens and this subspecies is confined to the Hermanus area.

♣ Seven more with 4 stamens and notably hairy sepals: *E. eriocephala* has shaggy white hairs; *E. similis* has long hairs on joined calyx. *E. pilosiflora* has both corolla and anthers hairy. *E. niveniana* has a calyx joined 2/3rds. *E. ericoides*, the honey heath, has large clasping bracts and *E. labialis* of Paarl to Bredasdorp has a 2 lobed corolla with a thick green calyx sometimes 2 lobed. The latter is similar to the smaller flowered Hermanus endemic *E. ecklonii*. Another with hairless sepals *E. equisetifolia* (includes *E. parvula*) is a totally hairless shrub with the bracts at the base of a long flowerstalk.

Erica hispidula

Erica imbricata

Erica jacksoniana

Erica intervallaris

Erica globiceps ssp. consors

257

PLUMBAGINACEAE - The statice, plumbago and sea pink family

Limonium scabrum — sea lavender, brakblommetjie

A tufted, much-branched shrublet to 25cm with sandpapery stems and bluegreen lance-shaped to oval leaves, broadening towards the tip and up to 8 x 1cm in a tuft at ground level. The flowers are 9-12mm long and c. 5mm in diameter. Occurring from the Cape Peninsula to the Fish River near the sea, it is often temporarily submerged in estuaries and vleis. (Oct-May).

♣ There are about 350 species, 11 occur in southern Africa and 4 in this area. Two more have similar leaves: the mauve *L. depauperatum* with additional small leaf tufts on the flowering stems; and the white flowered *L. anthericoides*; *L. kraussianum* has needle-like basal leaves.

SAPOTACEAE

Sideroxylon inerme — white milkwood

A shrubby, dense-crowned tree to 10m high with a dense, billowing crown and milky sap. The dark green, simple leaves are leathery, blunt-tipped, and without stipules. The unpleasantly scented bisexual small flowers are greenish white with 5 sepals, joined petals, stamens and staminodes, and the fruits are fleshy, black and eaten by birds. They are an important component of coastal dunes and bush from the Cape Peninsula to tropical Africa. (Dec-June). This tree is protected by law.

OLEACEAE

Olea exasperata — dune olive

A shrubby tree to 7m with warty branches and pairs of simple, leathery, narrowly oblong leaves with leaf margins rolled under into a narrow ridge. The white flowers are borne profusely in terminal clusters and give rise to fleshy black fruits. It grows in coastal scrub on sand and limestone from the Cape Peninsula to the Eastern Cape. (Aug-Oct).

♣ Of the 35 species worldwide, two more forest forms occur here: the shrubby black ironwood *O. capensis*, and the large thick-trunked *O. capensis ssp. macrocarpa*. The resprouter *O. europaea* with narrower, greyer leaf, pale below is usually in more open country. Another relative in the family, *Chionanthus foveolatus*, with similar leaves, lacking the rolled edge but having distinctive leaf pits (see *Kiggelaria*), is a dominant in the coastal forests, such as Piet-se-Bos in Hermanus..

MENYANTHACEAE - The bogbean family

Villarsia capensis

A soft perennial with groups of long-stalked, oval leaves and 12mm long fringed yellow flowers borne on branched stems. Occurring in wet places or in open water from the Cape Peninsula and Worcester to Humansdorp; when growing in water the leaf and flowering stems elongate so that they reach the surface. (Oct-Feb).

♣ There are about 10 species mainly in Australia, with only this representative in South Africa.

Nymphoides indica — geelwateruintjie

An aquatic herb rooted in the mud, with round floating leaves, and groups of yellow or white flowers with fringed petals, arising just below the leaf blade. It occurs in permanent pools on flats, not in fast-running water, from Clanwilliam to Eastern Cape and throughout Africa, India and Australasia. (Dec-Feb).

♣ There are 20 species but only one here.

Limonium scabrum

Sideroxylon inerme

Olea exasperata

Villarsia capensis

Nymphoides indica

259

GENTIANACEAE - The gentian family

Orphium frutescens

sea rose

A spectacular, erect , usually hairy shrub to 80cm with soft, rather thick leaves about 5cm long. The stalked, markedly glossy, brilliant pink or occasionally white flowers, up to 3cm long, have coiled anthers and a 1-chambered ovary. It differs from *Chironia* by a fleshy thickened ring interposed between the sepals and the petals. It is common near the shore on sandy, often marshy brackish flats from Clanwilliam to George. (Nov-Feb).

♣ There is only 1 species. It is buzz-pollinated by carpenter bees. (see p. 205).

Chironia jasminoides

An erect non-sticky perennial to 90cm whose sparsely-branched 4-angled stems have narrow ridges at the angles, and bear pairs of narrow oval or oblong leaves 2-7cm long. The 24-38mm long flowers are borne on a flowerstalk 1-10cm long. The fruit is a 1-chambered capsule. It occurs on mountain slopes or damp coastal areas in sand or shale from Paarl to Riversdale. (Aug-Jan).

♣ There are about 30 species in Africa and Madagascar of which 7, all pink-flowered, occur in this area. *C. stokoei* is the only other non-sticky, upright species in this area, and is distinguished by a pair of sepal-like bracts attached to the flowerstalk immediately below the flower. *C. tetragona* of coastal sands and limestones is very similar but is distinguished by rigid, sticky branches and thick, rigid, wrinkled and often sticky leaves; the floppy non-sticky *C. decumbens* roots at the nodes and its stigma is broadly round and flattened.

Chironia linoides ssp. nana

A low shrublet to 20cm, with several slender branches from near the base of the stem, and narrow widely-spaced leaves up to 25mm long. The calyx is split to below the middle and at least one of the lobes stands away from the corolla tube. The flowers are 12-15mm long and are borne singly or in 2's or 3's at the branch tips, and are followed by dry capsular fruits. It grows on sandy or marshy flats and mountain slopes from Worcester to Bredasdorp. (Oct-Jan).

♣ *C. baccifera*, the Christmas berry, has similar flowers followed by a 1-chambered bright red berry; this is the only berry-making species.

Sebaea exacoides

naeltjiesblom, yellowwort

A short-lived, annual herb to 30cm with paired oval leaves. The flowers, large for this genus, are 5-lobed and cream or yellow with distinctive orange streaks in the throat, broad-winged sepals and a 2-chambered ovary. It is common in colonies in disturbed or burnt areas on sandy flats and slopes from the Bokkeveld mountains to Riversdale, and throughout our area. (Aug-Oct).

♣ Three more species have winged sepals and yellow flowers, of which the 15cm tall *S. sulphurea* is intensely yellow. They differ otherwise only in small details of internal flower structure.

Sebaea aurea

A short-lived annual to 30cm, with oval leaves. The flowers are 4-petalled with the tube shorter than the lobes, 2-6mm long, and yellow or white, with 4 keeled calyx lobes. It lives on sandy flats and slopes from the Pakhuis mountains to the Cape Peninsula through to Humansdorp. (Oct-Dec).

♣ There are 159 species in Africa, Madagascar and Australasia, with 53 in southern Africa and 8 in our area. Other 4-petalled species are *S. ambigua* whose calyx lobes are keeled only towards the tips and corolla tube is longer than the lobes; *S. minutiflora* with white flowers up to 2mm long, occurs on saline flats from the Strand and Kleinmond to Hermanus; and the white or yellow *S. schlechteri* with calyx keeled throughout and corolla tube longer than the lobes.

Orphium frutescens

Chironia jasminoides

Chironia linoides ssp. nana

Sebaea exacoides   John Manning

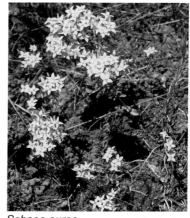

Sebaea aurea   John. Manning

261

APOCYNACEAE, incl. ASCLEPIADACEAE - The milkweeds

Gomphocarpus cancellatus
wild cotton, gansies, katoenbos

A rigid velvety shrub to 1m with milky sap, bearing leathery, paired leaves up to 50mm by 32mm, with a whitish reverse. Clusters of cream, brown and maroon flowers are borne on sturdy stalks in the axils of the leaves. They are followed by oval pods 5cm long or more, covered with finger-like projections and enclosing seeds which have silky parachutes to aid their dispersal. Occurring from Namaqualand to the Eastern Cape and Karoo, usually as isolated plants, it blooms most of the year.

♣ There are about 150 species in Africa, Arabia and America, with only 1 other indigenous to this area: the much taller more open *G. fruticosus*, with leaves several times longer than broad. The 2-3m tall balbos, *G. physocarpus* from tropical Africa, is a familiar weed in our gardens: all of these are food plants for the caterpillar of the African monarch butterfly.

Microloma sagittatum
heuningblommetjie

A sparsely branched quite delicate creeper without milky sap, to about 1m tall. The narrow, tapering, paired leaves are 7-35mm long. The cylindrical dull pinkish-red flowers 5-11mm long and at least partly hairy, give rise to a characteristically 2-forked dry fruit which splits to release a tightly packed cluster of seeds with silky parachutes. It occurs on stony or sandy slopes and flats from Namaqualand to Willowmore.(June-Oct).

♣ There are 10 species, only one other in our area: *M. tenuifolium* with shiny waxy urn-shaped flowers, 6-8mm long and narrow leaves 2-7cm long, occurs from the Gifberg to the Eastern Cape.

Oncinema lineare

A slender climber to 3m with a clear sap, pairs of narrow, short-stalked leaves and cream-coloured small flowers in lateral cymes or racemes which develop into long slender 'bokhoring' 2-forked pods. It twines through forest verge and river bank vegetation from Bain's Kloof to the Langkloof and in the Kogelberg. (Nov-Jan).

♣ There is only one species.

Orbea variegata
carrion flower, aasblom

A leafless succulent forming mats to 50cm diameter, with stems 5-10mm in diameter, the surface raised with conical points in 4 obscure rows. The hairless, 5-pointed, fleshy flowers, 5-8cm in diameter, cream to yellow spotted with liver-purple spots, have an interior floor ornamented by a complex thickened ring and petals surfaced with wrinkles or warts. The flowers exude a penetrating scent of carrion or manure obvious to flies and humans alike; the pollinators being blowflies deluded into visiting them to deposit eggs. It occurs on the coast on rocky outcrops of a variety of rock types from Lamberts Bay to Humansdorp. (Dec-Sept).

♣ This is the only species in our area, but there is a look-alike, *Stapelia hirsuta*, 'haasoor', of the north of the area and beyond, with finely hairy stems, sepals and flower stalks.

CONVOLVULACEAE - The bindweeds

Falkia repens
oortjies

Small herbs, rooting, running and mat-forming, with heart- or kidney-shaped leaves occasionally lobed at the base. Funnel-shaped white, pink or mauve flowers have 5 joined petals, 5 stamens and a 4-lobed superior ovary. It occurs on damp coastal flats from Darling to the Eastern Cape. (Oct-Dec).

♣ This is the only species in the area.

Gomphocarpus cancellatus

Microloma sagittatum

Oncinema lineare

Orbea variegata   John Manning

Falkia repens

263

BORAGINACEAE – The forget-me-not and borage family

Echiostachys ecklonianus
bottelborsel

A perennial with woody underground stems producing tufts of leaves and flowering shoots each year, which are seldom more than 36cm high. The lowest leaves are up to 12 x 1.8cm but are much smaller on the flowering shoot. The flowerhead can be up to 8cm long, purplish, reddish or pink and strongly scented. It grows in sandy or gravelly soil on the lower mountain slopes throughout this area and at Bredasdorp. (Aug-Dec).

♣ There are 3 species in the fynbos, with 1 other in this area: *E. incanus* has white or cream faintly-scented flowers.

Lobostemon fruticosus
agtdaegeneesbos, luibos

A rounded, rather harsh shrub to 80cm with densely hairy branches, and hairy leaves 15-60mm by 5-12mm. The funnel-shaped flowers are shortly hairy, up to 25mm long and in subtle shades of pink and blue, varying on the same plant. A white form is occasionally found. It grows in sandy places from Namaqualand to Uniondale. (Aug-Oct).

♣ There are 28 species in South Africa, mostly in the fynbos, of which 5 occur in this area. The pink-flowered 30-60cm *L. curvifolius* of Houwhoek-Highlands-Hermanus and Stanford has narrowish, grey-silvery leaves usually with recurved tips; and the possibly extinct similarly sized *L. hottentoticus* with white to pink flowers used to occur from the foot of Sir Lowry's Pass to Gordons Bay but too frequent fires may have eliminated it from that increasingly bleak mountain slope.

Lobostemon montanus

A sturdy shrub, at 1.2m one of the tallest in the genus, with silvery hairy stalkless leaves widening towards the tip. The nearly tubular, turquoise or blue flowers are hairy outside. It occurs on coastal sandstone from the Cape Peninsula to Hermanus. (Jul-Sept).

♣ The equally large tubular, red-flowered *L. regulareflorus* may still occur from Du Toit's Kloof to Hottentots Holland in wet places and cool shaded riverine scrub on granite slopes in the mountains.

STILBACEAE – The stilbe family

Campylostachys cernua

An erect shrub to 80cm with oblong leaves in whorls of 4's. The cream flowers, with sepals scarcely joined and 4, not 5, joined petals, are less than 12mm long. It occurs on sandstone and clay slopes from the Cape Peninsula to the Bredasdorp mountains. (Nov-Mar).

♣ A second white-flowered unnamed species occurs on the Riviersonderend Mountains.

Kogelbergia verticillata (=Stilbe mucronata)

A sturdy twisted shrub to 1m with 4-8mm long crowded leaves in whorls of 4-5, bending backwards when mature. The grey-mauve flowers with 5 more or less equal, hairy corolla lobes, four stamens and white hairs in the throat, are crowded into dense, rounded, white-woolly heads about 12mm across. It is occasional at mid to high altitude among rocks from this area to the Agulhas coast and Swellendam. (May-Oct).

♣ This is the only species in our area, *K. phylicoides* with leaves in 5-6's occurs in the Langeberg mountains.

Echiostachys ecklonianus

Campylostachys cernua

Kogelbergia verticillata

Lobostemon fruticosus

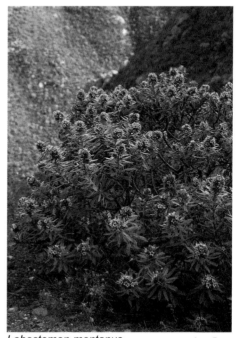

Lobostemon montanus

Anne Bean

265

Retzia capensis
heuningblom

A stiffly erect many-stemmed shrub up to 2m, but usually less, with a fire-resistant stump. Its stiff narrow leaves with edges tightly rolled under are dark green with rust-coloured flushes of new leaves as shown here. It is resplendent in full flower with the red and black tubular, 4cm long 5-petalled flowers. It is found on low to middle slopes of the mountains from the Hottentots Holland to Bredasdorp and is the only species. (Sept-Mar).

Stilbe albiflora

An erect, sturdy shrub to 1.2m with hard, point-tipped heath-like leaves in whorls of 4-6, and white flowers in a dense rounded spike at the top of each stem. Each flower has a stiff pale calyx, with a hairless 5-lobed petal tube with 2 large broad lobes and 3 narrow ones, 4 projecting stamens and a circle of white hairs in the throat. It occurs on sandy slopes from the Cedarberg to Swellendam. (Nov-Feb).

♣ There are 7 species confined to the Cape, 4 of which are found in this area: the very similar *S. vestita* has whitish petals with hairy margins, *S. ericoides* differs in its pink flowers and erect or straggling form; *S. rupestris* has crowded spikes of pink or white flowers and sprawls with somewhat reflexed leaves to 20cm from rock crevices.

LAMIACEAE – The sage family

Salvia chamelaeagnea
bloublommetjiesalie, afrikaanse salie

A much-branched rough-textured shrub to 2m with 4-sided stems. Pairs of simple, leathery, oval, almost hairless, gland-dotted leaves have smooth or slightly toothed edges. Distinctly 2-lipped blue, pink or mauve flowers with or without white markings have a gland-dotted calyx up to 28mm long, and are borne at the ends of leafless branchlets. It is widespread on sandy slopes and flats from Namaqualand to the Oudtshoorn area. (Nov-May).

♣ There are about 900 species worldwide, with about 40 in South Africa and 2 others in this area. The rather similar *S. africana-caerulea* has a calyx which enlarges greatly around the fruit.

Salvia africana-lutea
wild sage, strandsalie

A dense shrub to 2m with aromatic grey leaves and 2-lipped, 3-5cm long flowers of an unusual rich tan colour which appear to be made of suede. The anthers are concealed beneath the upper lip and swivel downwards when a visiting bird attempts to gain access to the copious nectar. The calyx remains on the plant, increasing slightly in size, after the flowers have faded. This once common and widespread plant, now becoming scarce because of the development of its habitat, is an essential food supply for sunbirds when the proteas on the mountains are out of flower, so should find a place in every bird-friendly coastal garden. It occurs in the coastal dune vegetation, and also further inland in dry fynbos, from the Gifberg to Port Elizabeth. (June-Dec).

Stachys aethiopica
katbossie

A straggling perennial with bristly 4-sided stems up to 50cm long and pairs of triangular leaves up to 24mm long with scalloped edges. The pink or white flowers have a 2-lipped corolla with a tube less than 12mm long and 4 projecting stamens. It occurs most often in shade in fynbos or forest from the Cedarberg to the Eastern Cape and on to tropical Africa. (Aug-Sept).

♣ There are about 450 species worldwide in temperate regions, of which 2 have been recorded in this area. *S. bolusii* of rocky outcrops, with mauve-dotted white petals, is a straggling softly hairy perennial with upper bracts exceeding the flowers in length.

Retzia capensis

Stilbe albiflora

Salvia chamelaeagnea   John Manning

Salvia africana-lutea

Stachys aethiopica

267

SOLANACEAE

Solanum guineense
An erect non-spiny shrub to 2m with smooth oval leaves up to 50mm by 28mm. The fruit is a yellow, orange or red berry some 25mm across. It occurs in forest margins, lower slopes and coastal dunes from Piketberg to the Eastern Cape. (Nov-June).

♣ There are two more spineless coastal species: the sprawling smooth-stemmed *S. africanum (=quadrangulare)* with purple terminal flowers and younger stems square in cross-section; and the bristly, sprawling *S. crassifolium* of the beach with woolly stems and sandpapery leaves. The spiny, stocky, yellowy-green spiny snake-apple shrub, *S. tomentosum*, with pale woolly leaves and orange berries may occur around Gordon's Bay.

SCROPHULARIACEAE – The snapdragon family

Dischisma ciliatum   basterslakblom
An erect spreading perennial with densely-leafy sparsely-branched stems to 40cm. It has narrow toothed leaves 6-25mm long, and 8-16mm long flowers in dense spikes. The calyx has two lateral lobes, free from the bract. The corolla has 4 lobes slit in front to resemble a small open upstanding hand, and the 2-chambered fruit has 1 seed per chamber. It occurs on slopes and flats from Nieuwoudtville to Port Elizabeth and the Karoo. (Aug-Dec).

♣ There are 11 species in southern Africa; 2 others occur here: the sparsely-leafy and much-branched greenish-flowered *D. arenarium* of dunes and flats, and the 10mm high *D. capitatum* with rounded heads of whitish flowers nestling in a rosette of long leaves. The very similar genus, *Hebenstreitia* represented by 5 species in this area, has a tubular, unlobed calyx (attached to its bract) and tubular 4-lobed corolla.

Halleria elliptica   bush honeysuckle, notsung
An erect shrub to 2m with pairs of oval leaves 12-36mm long and 6-22mm broad. The orange, red or purple tubular flowers which attract sunbirds are 10-17mm long, are borne in pairs in the leaf axils and are followed by berries. Often growing in colonies and spreading by means of an underground rootstock, it occurs in mixed bush on lower slopes or near streams from Worcester and Tulbagh to Swellendam. (Oct-Apr).

♣ There are 4 species from the South Western Cape to tropical Africa, of which 2 have been recorded in this area; *H. lucida*, the tree fuchsia, is a shrub or tree to 12m with similar leaves, flowers and berries.

Hemimeris racemosa   yellow faces
A weak-stemmed sticky-haired annual to 45cm with square stems and pairs of delicate, oval, toothed leaves 6-25mm by 2-15mm. The flower buds, clothed with sticky glandular hairs, open into yellow flowers up to 16mm across, growing singly in the leaf axils. The corolla is 2-lipped and slightly pouched at the base, there are 2 stamens, and the capsule has many seeds. It occurs on sandy lower slopes and coastal flats from Namaqualand to Knysna. (July-Oct).

♣ There are some four species in the Cape of which only one other has been recorded in this area, the yellow-flowered *H. sabulosa*, almost hairless and with lobed leaves.

Freylinia undulata   bell bush, klokkiesbos
An erect rigid shrub to 2m with long sparsely branched stems arising from an underground rootstock, and oval, stalkless 5-15mm long leaves with slightly crisped edges. Slightly pendant, 15-20mm long tubular white to purple flowers arise in racemes on the terminal portions of the stems. It is confined to shale slopes from Grabouw to Port Elizabeth. (June-Dec).

♣ The similar rare *F. longiflora*, of Arieskraal in the Elgin basin has elliptical 15-30mm long leaves. *F. lanceolata* of Stellenbosch and Helderberg has honey scented cream flowers fading brown.

Solanum guineense

Halleria elliptica

Hemimeris racemosa   John Manning

Dischisma ciliatum

Freylinia undulata

269

Manulea tomentosa

A densely-hairy sandpapery-textured perennial with sparsely-branched stems to 80cm, bearing stalked toothed leaves along their length. Each frosted flower, orange to brick-red in colour, has a short tube and 5 petal lobes which are folded along their length to resemble short fat fingers, the upper 2 folding over the others in bud. It is found on sand dunes and lower slopes from the Cape Peninsula to Bredasdorp. (June-Dec).

♣ Of c. 60 species, 5 occur in this area. 2 are perennials: *M. caledonica* with large basal leaves reducing in size up the 27cm stem, bears similarly coloured much-divided flowerheads of minute flowers; *M.rubra* of sandy flats near the coast becomes hairless. 2 are annuals: the 30cm *M. cheiranthus* with a basal rosette of glandular-hairy broad leaves and flowers with very long thin spidery petal lobes; and *M. exigua* has white flowers with black reverse.

Microdon (=Agathelpis) dubius   cat's tail

A soft branched perennial to 60cm becoming woody at the base, with very narrow crowded hairless leaves 6-18mm long. The flowers arise singly from dull-coloured bracts, 4-5mm long, which hide the tubular 5-lobed calyx and are joined to it. The tubular, pale yellow or deep red-brown curved corolla lacking an orange throat spot, with 5 small lobes concealing 2 stamens and a one-chambered ovary with one seed, gives off a penetratingly sweet scent at night. It occurs on flats and slopes from the Gifberg to the Cape Peninsula and into the Caledon district. (May-Dec).

♣ Of the 7 species, there is one more here: *M. polygaloides* of Helderberg and Jonkershoek has needle leaves, 4 stamens per flower, and dense white spikes sometimes branching.

Pseudoselago serrata   blouaarbossie

A striking erect or sprawling shrublet with stout angular branches to 90cm and crowded recurved hairless leaves about 12-25mm by 5-10mm overlapping like tiles. The bright mauve flowers with orange-yellow throat patch and stalked glands on the tube, are in dense heads up to 10cm across. At fruiting time the heads elongate into structures resembling very long, thin heads of barley, with 2-chambered ovaries each with one seed. It is widespread on mountain slopes from Clanwilliam to Knysna. (Oct-Feb).

♣ C. 150 species occur in Africa, with 7 recorded in this area. *P. pulchra* of Klein River mountains has leaves not recurved. *P. verbenacea* in wet areas has all leaves paired. The delicate *P. ascendens* (=*Selago incisa*) of the west of this area with white, cream or pale blue flowers becomes abundant after veld fires.

Pseudoselago spuria

A sparsely hairy perennial to 75cm with sturdy, thin stems. The narrowly lance-shaped leaves, massed below, are toothed towards the tip. The mauve flowers, grouped at the tops of much-branched flowering stems, have an orange patch. It occurs on flat and slopes from Tulbagh to the Klein River lagoon. (Aug-Feb).

♣ *P. gracilis* has leaves not massed below.

Manulea tomentosa

Microdon dubius

Pseudoselago serrata

Pseudoselago spuria Anne Bean

271

Nemesia affinis (*=versicolor*)   leeubekkie, weeskindertjies

An erect, simple or branched annual to 50cm with oval, stalked lower leaves and stalkless upper leaves 8-43mm by 1-15mm, with one main vein from the base. The very short-tubed flowers are some 11mm across with 2 velvety pegs in the throat and a finger-like nectar-containing spur at the back, as long as the petal lobes. It is extraordinarily variable in colour from blue, mauve or yellow to white with upper and lower petals often dissimilar in colour, and the reverse often dark-veined. All nemesias have 4 stamens and a 2-chambered, flattened ovary with many seeds. It occurs on sandy flats from Namaqualand to Knysna. (Aug-Nov).

♣ There are about 60 species in southern and tropical Africa, c. 10 of which occur in this area. The summer-flowering, slightly shorter *N. diffusa* of sandstone slopes with 3-5-veined leaves has lilac, darker-veined flowers with a raised velvety yellow throat. The white to cream *N. barbata* with blue to black lower lip and hairy throat is commonest after fire.

Sutera hispida

A much-branched bristly glandular hairy shrublet to 50cm with a coarsely toothed leaf edge. The pink to mauve flowers with yellow eye, sometimes in a cluster, arise in the axils of the leaves. Flowers tubular with 5 equal sepals and petals and 4 stamens, 2 projecting. It is found on rocky sandstone or limestone areas from the Cape Peninsula to Bredasdorp. (Jan-Dec).

♣ *S. revoluta* of shale soils has narrow leaves.

Teedia lucida   stinkbos

A pungent-scented hairless sprawling shrub to 1.2m with square branching stems and pairs of oval leaves up to 15cm by 5cm, but usually less. Clusters of purplish or mauve flowers 15mm long are followed by drab purple or yellowish-brown berries. It occurs as isolated plants often in rock crevices on mountain slopes in shade from Namaqualand throughout the Southern Cape to KwaZulu-Natal. (Sept-Jan).

♣ There are 2 species confined to South Africa, of which only this occurs here.

Zaluzianskya capensis   verfblommetjie

An erect slender usually hairy annual to 40cm with narrow stalkless leaves up to 4cm long. The 25-40mm long tubes of the flowers, containing 2 large and 2 small stamens emerge from a 2-lobed calyx, which is slightly joined to the bract. Each flower is about 5cm long, white with a red reverse, remaining tightly closed during the day but opening and becoming almost over-whelmingly scented at dusk. It is moth-pollinated and produces a many-seeded capsule. It occurs on sand dunes or lower slopes from Namaqualand to the Eastern Cape. (Apr-Dec).

♣ ß There are some 55 species widespread in southern Africa, of which 2 others have been recorded in this area: *Z. villosa* has hairs bending backwards, and corolla 10-25mm long, white or lilac often yellow-eyed with a purple reverse and deeply notched petals and 2 stamens; *Z. divaricata* of low gravely slopes has similar hairs, flowers yellow inside, brown on the reverse with a red eye, petals un-notched, and with 4 stamens, borne on a crowded spike.

Nemesia affinis

Sutera hispida

Teedia lucida

Zaluzianskya capensis

273

OROBANCHACEAE – The broomrapes

Harveya capensis   ink flower

A leafless branched or unbranched total parasite to 40cm with a raceme of white or pinkish flowers. It has a hairy calyx with narrow lobes divided to about half-way, and wide-spreading petals up to 45mm across which turn black if bruised. It is found on mountain slopes from the Gifberg throughout the Cape region to Port Elizabeth. (Oct-Feb).

♣ There are about 40 species, mostly in Africa but some in Madagascar with 3 more in this area: *H. tubulosa* is also pink or white to rose with paler markings but has very short broad calyx lobes; *H. purpurea* is purple or deep pink and *H. bolusii* has scarlet and yellow flowers.

Hyobanche sanguinea   snail flower, katnaels, wolwekos

A leafless fleshy total parasite with an unbranched stem to 15cm bearing crowded, velvety, water-melon-red flowers 3-5cm long. It is the curved anthers protruding from the flowers which give it the common name of "Katnaels". It is widespread on sandy places. (Aug-Oct).

♣ There are about 7 species widespread in southern Africa, of which only this is definitely recorded here. It could be mistaken for another curious red leafless fleshy 5cm tall parasite, *Cytinus sanguineus* of the family *Rafflesiaceae*, which also occurs in this area, but the latter has massive separate male and female flowers enclosed within orange, red to purple bracts emerging directly from the ground.

Melasma scabrum   witches foxglove

A soft, partly parasitic, unbranched or sparsely-branched perennial to 1m with pairs of lance-shaped, stalkless leaves up to 75mm by 35mm. The sweetly-scented funnel-shaped flowers are white or cream with a purple or brownish throat, with 4 hairy stamens and a long, briefly-coiled slender style visible in the throat. It is widespread as solitary plants throughout South Africa on marshy mountain slopes. (Nov-Mar).

♣ There is only 1 species in S.A.

DIPSACACEAE

Scabiosa columbaria   jongmansknoop, bitterbos, scabious

A rather soft tufted perennial to 80cm with variably shaped leaves up to 10cm long, mostly basal, lance-shaped and toothed, but the upper leaves are deeply-cut and comblike. The mauve or white flowerheads are up to 5cm across on long stalks, with involucral bracts in 1-2 rows. It occurs on sandy flats and slopes from the southwestern to the Eastern Cape and north to the Transvaal; it is also found in Europe and Asia. (Aug-Feb).

♣ The mauve *S. incisa* of coastal sands or limestone has leaves all more or less alike.

LENTIBULARIACEAE – The bladderworts

Utricularia bisquamata   bladderwort

A soft delicate annual to 12cm with one to a few irregular, nemesia-like flowers, often two-tone, white to lilac or yellow, borne on a slender stem. Tiny prey-catching bladders, attached to under-ground root-like stolons, suck in minute aquatic creatures. It grows often in fair-sized populations on acid seeps and bogs throughout southern Africa. (Sept-Jan).

♣ This is the only species in our area.

Harveya capensis

Hyobanche sanguinea

Melasma scabrum

Scabiosa columbaria

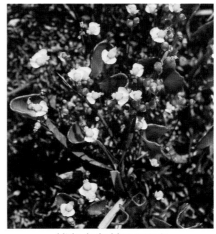

Utricularia bisquamata

275

CAMPANULACEAE – The bell flowers

Merciera leptoloba

A stiff, leafy, sprawling shrublet to 30cm resprouting after fire, with crowded 2cm long narrow leaves. Terminal on upcurving branchtips, the curry-scented white flowers with 8-15mm tube are crowded in spikes. The 1-chambered capsule has one seed. It grows on lower slopes and in disturbed places from the Cape Peninsula to Soetanysberg. (Dec-Feb).

♣ There are 4 species: on clayey soils: *M. brevifolia* from Bot River to Houwhoek differs in shorter leaves and flowers 6-8mm long. *M. tetraloba* of Gordon's Bay to Stellenbosch has a 4-lobed flower.

Merciera tenuifolia

A rigid much-branched shrublet to 30cm, resprouting after fires, with crowded bristly leaves to 3cm long. The almost stalkless flowers, 10-25mm long and blue to purple with narrow tubes, arise in the upper leaf axils. It grows in rocky or sandy places on midslopes from Franschhoek to the Klein River mountains. (Dec-Mar).

Prismatocarpus sessilis

A sprawling delicate subshrub to 60cm whose narrow leaves have edges rolled under. Small white or pale blue 5mm wide flowers arise 1-3 in axils, and produce fruits up to 15mm long. It grows on sheltered sandstone slopes and flats from the Cape Peninsula to the Klein River mountains.

♣ There are 30 species, of which 8 occur in our area. 3 more are dainty sprawlers of sheltered places: *P. nitidus* has oval leaves and 1-5 white or pale blue bell flowers, 8mm across, grouped together at branch ends; the similar *P. cordifolius* of Kogelberg has thinly hairy leaves and toothed bracts; *P. tenerrimus* has leaf edges thickened and prickly-toothed.

Prismatocarpus fruticosus

An erect or sprawling hairy shrublet to 50cm with tufted, hairy awl-shaped leaves. The flowers, borne in leafless groups on branch tips, are deep white cups with brown or purple reverse, and give rise to capsules up to 3cm long. It occurs on sandy flats and slopes from the Cedarberg to the Langkloof. (Nov-Apr).

♣ The similar *P. brevilobus* of rocky slopes differs in having short broad oval sepals; the hairy slender *P. schlechteri* of mountain slopes has broad prickly leaves and stalkless white 10mm wide bells in the upper leaves.

Prismatocarpus diffusus

A sprawling or rounded shrublet to 50cm resprouting after fire with strong basal parts clothed with needlelike leaves and more delicate leafy stems ending in open terminal leafless flowerheads. The petals of the almost stalkless 13mm long flowers bend sharply backwards on opening to reveal 5 free stamens and a long style. The elongated mature capsule splits into 5 lobes. (Nov-Feb).

276

Merciera leptoloba

Merciera tenuifolia

Prismatocarpus sessilis

Prismatocarpus fruticosus

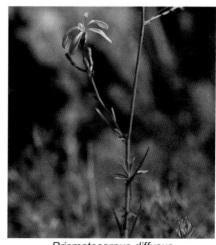

Prismatocarpus diffusus

Roella incurva

A variable sturdy, branched perennial with white-hairy stems to 60cm long. Narrow incurved spiny prickly 8mm long leaves, sometimes with a few hairs, are often in tufts. The regular white or blue flowers, often with dark blotches on the rim of the petal cup, are 2-3cm across and the petals are pointed. Arising from narrow bracts, they are grouped 1-3 together at branch tips. The smooth capsule is 2-chambered, the many seeds escaping via a hole at the top. It is common and widespread on sandy lower slopes from Tulbagh to Potberg. (Oct-Jan).

♣ There are 24 species: 9 are recorded here. Two more are large-flowered with narrow bracts and conspicuous spots: *R. ciliata* has rounded petals, white-hairy bracts and hairless ovary; *R. maculata* has a hairy ovary, calyx and bracts and dark spots between the petals. *R. triflora* has flowers 15-20mm across, 1-3 together and pale blue with a dark eye.

Roella prostrata

An erect or sprawling shrublet to 50cm whose narrow, spiny-pointed leaves may be in axillary tufts, and bracts are leaflike and sometimes prickly. The white or pale blue flowers, 10-15mm across, are borne singly at branch ends and lack markings. The ovary is hairy. It occurs on sandy flats from Hopefield to Potberg. (Dec-Mar).

♣ *R. arenaria* differs in spreading leaves and sepals strongly recurved and hairy; *R. dregeana* differs in the flowers being grouped 1-a few, and bracts having wire-like hairs; *R. compacta* of coastal rocks has similar flowers in terminal heads; *R. muscosa* on sandstone rocks is a diminutive mat-forming plant with single pale flowers 10mm across.

Wahlenbergia capensis

A roughly hairy erect annual 15-80cm high and branched in the lower parts whose stalkless oblong leaves 5-7 x 1.5-2cm, are usually wavy, with a few teeth. The single, dull blue 1cm long flowers with a dark eye, have stalks up to 20cm long and a densely hairy 5-chambered ovary, the capsule opening by 5 lobes. It grows on sandstone flats and slopes from Clanwilliam to Knysna. (Sept-Dec).

♣ There are c. 200 species (now including *Lightfootia*) with c.150 in southern Africa and 14 recorded here. Other species with long-stalked flowers are: *W. cernua*, with 1 to a few flowers, white or blue with a dark eye, oval toothed leaves and a smooth ovary, and the flowers of the similar *W. obovata*, without dark eye, but with projecting glands below the stigma, are borne on a much-branched flowering stem.

Wahlenbergia tenella

An erect or sprawling shrublet to 80cm whose strongly recurved oval leaves have a thick margin and sometimes minute teeth below. Regular white, purple or blue flowers 5-8mm across with narrow spreading petals are clustered in upper axils or on a flowerhead stalk. It occurs on coastal flats and slopes from Mamre to the Eastern Cape. (Nov-May).

♣ Another sprawler with reflexed leaves: *W. parvifolia*, of streambanks has white flowers, 5cm across, in terminal groups; the mat-forming *W. procumbens* has single white, blue or mauve flowers 8-10mm across; another sprawler, *W. rubioides*, has axillary stalked white flowers; the tangled *W. capillaris* with leaves sometimes reflexed, has the small white flowers with a dark reverse. *W. longifolia* of coastal sands has flowers in open branched racemes.

Roella incurva

Roella prostrata

Wahlenbergia capensis

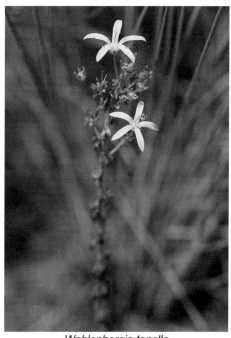

Wahlenbergia tenella

279

Wahlenbergia subulata
An erect or sprawling shrublet to 30cm with opposite or alternate narrow, rigid, often toothed leaves. The stalkless axillary flowers, white or blue fading yellow and 6mm across, have pouched swollen sepal bases and a half-inferior hairy or smooth ovary. It occurs on lower, stony slopes from the Gifberg to the Potberg. (Oct-Feb).

♣ 5 more species have clusters of small flowers, and diverse vegetative forms.

Siphocodon spartioides
A tangled, wiry, harsh-textured unobtrusive perennial with few minute leaves pressed against the branches. Tubular blue or purple flowers with a green calyx are borne on a simple or branched flowering stem. It grows on sandstone slopes from Franschhoek to the Langeberg mountains. (Dec-Apr).

♣ The only other species, *S. debilis*, differs in being less coarse in growth, and with bell-like violet to white flowers which open towards midday.

LOBELIACEAE

Cyphia bulbosa   bergbaroe
A geophyte with annual unbranched or sparsely-branched leafy stems to 40cm with deeply palmately lobed leaves basically triangular in shape, decreasing in size upwards, the longest being 5-6cm long. The showy, white or mauve irregular flowers are 8-13mm long. It is common on coastal flats and slopes from Clanwilliam to the Eastern Cape. It is most noticeable after veld fires. (Aug-Oct).

♣ Of 60 species, 8 occur in our area. 3 more are non-twining with flowers in the same colour range: *C. phyteuma* with its basal tuft of leaves has flowers 16-20mm long; the tufted *C. incisa* has pinnately lobed leaves and flowers 10-14mm long; the sometimes weakly twining *C. linarioides* has narrow leaves and 7-9mm long flowers all facing to one side.

Cyphia digitata
A twining tuberous perennial whose leaves are 3-7 digitate with narrow leaflets. The white, pink or mauve flowers, borne in the upper leaf axils, are laterally slit and the 7-14mm petals are almost free. It occurs on sandstone and clay slopes from Namaqualand to Port Elizabeth. (Jul-Oct).

♣ 3 more twiners with narrow leaves are: *C. volubilis* with showy white to purple flowers 10-26mm long, and narrow or digitately lobed, toothed leaves; the flowers of C. crenata are 9-11mm long, borne 1-3 in the upper axils, and the leaves may be short-lobed; the flowers of *C. zeyheriana* in the north of our area are showy and cream to mauve often with a darker reverse and 10-18mm long.

Monopsis lutea   yellow lobelia
A straggling bristly perennial with narrow leaves, borne on thin stems to 60cm long. The hairy sulphur-yellow flowers, resembling *Lobelia*, are 2-lipped and split down the back, but differ in forming a funnel-shaped tube. It occurs on damp flats and lower slopes from Clanwilliam to the Peninsula and Caledon to Riversdale and the western Karoo. (Nov-Apr).

♣ There are about 18 species in tropical and South Africa, with 3 in this area. Both others have purple flowers: The annual prostrate or ascending *M. simplex* has an irregular dark-eyed flower borne on a long stalk with bracts at the base; the almost regular flower of the tufted *M. debilis* is without bracteoles.

Siphocodon spartioides

Wahlenbergia subulata

Cyphia digitata

Cyphia bulbosa

Monopsis lutea

281

Lobelia chamaepitys   wild lobelia

A tufted 30cm tall perennial with a simple or branched densely leafy stem, the leaves being narrow, toothed and about 20mm long. The leafless wiry flowering stems are light brown in colour, with 1 or 2 bright violet blue hairless flowers 10-16mm long. The corolla is split down the back with the column of stamens arching through. It is frequent on mountain slopes from Stellenbosch to Swellendam. (Sept-Apr).

♣ There are about 300 species worldwide, 70 in southern Africa and c. 15 in this area. Other erect very similar species occur here: the blue, violet or pink *L. tomentosa* has harshly hairy leaves; the purple-blue and white, occasionally pink *L. coronopifolia* has green flowering stems; *L. comosa* has long flowerstalks bearing linear forked or toothed leaves and flowers crowded at the top. The 20cm *L. stenosiphon* of high altitude from Kogelberg northwards after fire has long 20mm narrow rose to purple flowers facing upwards.

Lobelia jasionoides

A low-growing mat-forming annual with small, almost hairless leaves 10-22mm by 1-10mm (broadest in shady places), and very small lilac and white flowers grouped into crowded heads. It occurs at upper altitudes from Vanrhynsdorp to Swellendam. (Oct-Feb).

♣ An even more diminutive, sprawling, 15cm, pale-blue-flowered *Lobelia sp. (=Unigenes humifusa)* occurs in shady damp places in the west half of our area.

Lobelia pinifolia

An erect, untidy well-branched sturdy shrublet to 50cm with narrow, crowded, pointed, smooth-edged leaves, 1-2.5cm long but only up to 2mm wide. The racemes of 3-10 crowded flowers arise in the axils of leaves or terminal, and may be blue or purple, occasionally pink or white. It occurs or rocky slopes and flats from Ceres to Riversdale. (Mainly Dec-Apr but sporadically throughout the year).

Lobelia pubescens

A soft sprawling, often hairy, perennial with spoon-shaped irregularly-toothed leaves, the lower up to 2cm long, but becoming progressively smaller and narrower upwards along the stem. The white or pale blue flowers, which may have blue or white markings respectively, are 11-17mm long and have narrow petal lobes which are very delicately hairy. It occurs from Tulbagh and the Cape Peninsula to Humansdorp, often in shady places or sprawling on damp rocks. It blooms throughout the year.

♣ *L. erinus*, the wild progenitor of our ubiquitous garden and hanging basket cultivar, is blue with a white spot in the throat, but in cultivation all shades of blue, pink or white. *L. humifusa* is another of a group of soft sprawling species found in sheltered dampish places; the similar *L. anceps* with axillary blue or white flowers on the coast; the 60cm tall *L. valida*, perhaps our coarsest herb in the genus, has branches curving out and up from the base with handsome bright blue flowers towards the tips, occurs occasionally in coastal areas.

Lobelia linearis

An erect, wiry sparsely branched shrublet to 70cm with scattered very narrow leaves to 2cm long, the lowest sometimes pinnately divided. The blue or purple flowers are borne on an open branched raceme. The ovary is tapered to the base and usually hairless. It occurs on the lower dry stony slopes from the Cedarberg to Langkloof. (Sept-Mar).

♣ Another broomlike species is the tufted and sprawling 60cm *L. setacea* with hairy ovary, rounded below.

Lobelia chamaepitys

Lobelia jasionoides

Lobelia pinifolia

Lobelia pubescens

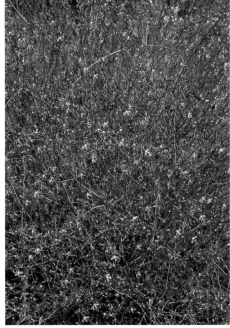

Lobelia linearis

ASTERACEAE - the daisy family

Brachylaena neriifolia   waterwitels

This tallest daisy in our flora, and very atypical indeed, is a coarse aromatic shrub or tree to 8m with rusty-velvety, lance-shaped, leathery, slightly toothed, short-stalked leaves. The insignificant whitish discoid flowers are unisexual and borne in clusters on separate plants. It is widespread along waterways from the Gifberg to Humansdorp.

♣ 15 species are distributed in Africa and Indian Ocean islands, and 4 in southern Africa, but only one here.

Gerbera tomentosa   tontelblaarbossie

A perennial with a tuft of leathery leaves at ground level, up to 20cm long and 5cm wide. They are at first covered with dense woolly hairs, but the upper surface becomes bald and glossy green later. The ivory-coloured flowerheads, about 8cm across, are borne singly on almost leafless, ivory-hairy stems up to 60cm tall. Occasional on dry stony south-facing slopes from Paarl to Bredasdorp, it blooms mostly after veld fires. (Jan-Dec).

♣ There are about 100 species in Africa and Asia, c. 30 in South Africa and 4 in this area. *G. linnaei* has leathery, much-lobed leaves; *G. crocea* has leaves similar to *G. tomentosa*, but cobwebby scaly flowerhead stems; and *G. piloselloides* has flowers half the size and leaves with very short stalks.

Oldenburgia intermedia   kreupelbos

A coarse, hard cushion-forming shrublet to 30cm, from a thick woody rootstock. The simple nar-rowish leaves are leathery with edges rolled under to the woolly reverse. Single, tan-coloured capitula rise up on strong, white-woolly stalks and open with white florets. It grows in rocky places above 1000m from the Cedarberg to the Hex River and Hottentots Holland mountains. (mainly Feb-Mar).

♣ *O. paradoxa* is the only other species in our area out of a total of 4, it has a stalkless capitulum.

Capelio caledonica   fire daisy

A thinly woolly open shrublet to 1m with sparsely toothed, oval leaves, the same colour above and below, broadest towards the tip, with edges rolled under. Long bare rather open branched flowering stems have single yellow, radiate heads with thinly woolly bracts. It occurs on coastal sandy slopes on the Palmiet River mountains. (Sept-Nov).

♣ There are 3 species, but only one more here: the more robust *C. tabularis*, with stalked leaves clearly paler below than above, mostly after fire, from the Cape Peninsula to Betty's Bay.

Brachylaena neriifolia

Gerbera tomentosa

Oldenburgia intermedia

Capelio caledonica

Athrixia heterophylla
boesmanstee

A cobwebby shrublet from a woody rootstock (a resprouter), to 45cm high, the leaves largest nearer the base, lower leaves oval, becoming narrowly linear upwards, with edges rolled in and often sandpapery above, but densely felted below. The flowerheads are radiate, the ray florets are pink or magenta and the central disk florets are yellow. It grows on rocky slopes from the Cape Peninsula to the Eastern Cape. (Aug-Dec).

♣ There are 14 species but only one more, *A. capensis* with linear, sharp-pointed leaves, in our area.

Dolichothrix ericoides
the mossy clubmoss daisy, kliprenosterbos

One of very few of our plants which are alpine in habit, being dwarf, hugging the substrate and forming a domed, dense shrublet occasionally to 70cm with white-felted branches and scalelike twisted linear, pointed, stem-hugging leaves. The ray florets, almost immersed in the leaves, are pale with purple bands. It blooms in such profusion that, when in full flower, it is an unforgettable sight. It clings to exposed rock at high altitudes on high rock ridges from the Cedarberg down to the Kogelberg. (Nov-Feb).

♣ There is only 1 species.

Metalasia erubescens

A white-woolly shrub to 1m with half-twisted narrow leaves 2-18mm long, often in axillary tufts. Each capitulum has 3-4(5) florets, and several capitula are grouped into a larger flowerhead with erect pink occasionally white inner petaloid bracts. It occurs on sandy flats from Kleinmond to Agulhas. (Sept-Feb).

♣ There are about 33 species in South Africa, with 17 in this area. The slender *M. seriphiifolia* of Hermanus is similar but has needlelike leaves twisted once or twice. The to 30cm *M. quinqueflora* of the Kogelberg has capitula with 5 florets and leaves sometimes tufted.

Metalasia muricata
blombos, witsteekbossie

A much-branched densely leafy shrub to 3m, with tufts of needlelike half to fully twisted, hooked leaves 2-9mm long with a woolly upper and woolly or naked lower surface The flowerheads of numerous discoid capitula with 4-5(6) florets each, are free from one another and are surrounded by several tightly-enfolding rows of bracts, the outer ridge tipped, all clustered rather loosely on a much-branched flowerhead stalk. It is widespread in the Western to Eastern Cape and confined to the coastal areas where it can form dense thickets.

♣ Also with free capitula: the common, variable *M. densa* has straight spreading leaves with a half twist and the lower bracts ending in a slender point; the pink flushed flowerheads of *M. lichtensteinii* comprise 8-13 florets; *M. brevifolia* has shorter densely tufted 5mm leaves; *M. humilis* and *M. tenuifolia* are Houwhoek endemics.

Metalasia cephalotes
rooiblombossie

A variable stiffly-branched erect or spreading shrub to 1m with matted-woolly branches and scarcely twisted needlelike leaves up to 10mm long, bent downwards and borne singly or in tufts. Each capitulum has several rows of white or pink petaloid bracts, and several capitula are tangled together with matted wool into a compound flowerhead. It occurs on flats and mountain slopes throughout this area and from Worcester to Bredasdorp. (Aug-Nov).

♣ Other species with tangled-matted heads are: *M. confusa* of the Kogelberg with almost hairless, almost un-twisted flattish lance shaped leaves; the 2.5m tall riverine white or green-woolly shrub *M. riparia* with 3-4 florets per capitulum; the 60cm tall *M. cymbifolia* of the Klein River mountains with strongly incurved but untwisted leaves and white or pink heads; and *M. inversa* with downward curving leaves.

Athrixia heterophylla

Dolichothrix ericoides

Metalasia erubescens

Metalasia muricata

Metalasia cephalotes

Disparago ericoides (=D. lasiocarpa) basterslangbos

A densely-leafy, sometimes woody, cobwebby shrublet to 30cm with slightly twisted, curved, needle-like leaves to 6mm long. The flowers form dense, rounded stalked clusters of flowerheads up to 14mm in diameter, the sterile pinkish conspicuous ray florets in 2's between dry papery bracts, and the disc florets with densely woolly ovaries. The outer involucral bracts are leaflike, the inner papery. It is widespread in sandy and stony places on lower slopes from Piketberg to Riversdale. (Nov-Mar).

♣ Of the 9 species, 4 are in this area. The similar *D. laxifolia* has white florets and widely spaced spreading leaves. The ray florets of the larger, white or pink *D. tortilis* make seeds. *D. anomala* occurs on coastal sands and limestone.

Stoebe aethiopica knoppiesslangbos

A rigid, densely leafy grey-hairy to almost hairless shrub to 1.5m, and like most stoebes prickly to handle. The needlelike, down-curved leaves are twisted with edges rolled upwards, and sharp pointed. The dense, crowded flowerheads consist of 1-floret capitula with conspicuous sturdy white florets. It occurs on sandy slopes from the Bokkeveld mountains to the Langkloof. (Sept-Nov).

♣ There are 34 species in southern and tropical Africa, with 11 in this area. Others with conspicuous florets: the wiry *S. capitata* has dense rounded pink or white flowerheads on branch tips; *S. fusca* to 30cm has open flowerheads; the sparsely hairy *S. cyathuloides (= S. humilis & S. phaerocephala)* has lance-shaped leaves with upcurved edges and white sometimes pink florets; *S. prostrata* has dense mauve flowerheads.

Stoebe spiralis

An erect greyish shrub to 60cm whose needlelike, twisted recurved leaves have upcurved edges. The rounded to oblong flowerheads are composed of 1-floret capitula, with inner bracts dry and translucent and the outer ones yellow and shorter than the yellow flowers. It occupies damp sandstone slopes from Elandskloof to Robinson Pass. (Mar-May).

♣ *S. incana* has brown bracts, longer than the flowers, giving it a spiky appearance. The sprawling white-woolly slangbos, *S. plumosa*, has granular, tufted leaves and flowerheads of tapering golden bracts grouped in small heads along the branches; while the green-woolly ericoid leaved *S. cinerea*, has purplish grouped flowerheads arranged long and spike-like at branch ends.

Elytropappus glandulosus

A distinctive, fairly stiff, wonderfully aromatic, slightly woolly erect shrub to 1m with narrow, curved, twisted leaves with uprolled edges and many conspicuous glandular hairs. The capitula have 2-6 pink or mauve discoid florets with tawny bracts collected into long axillary spikes. It occurs on sandy slopes from the Cedarberg to the Klein River and the Riviersonderend and Langeberg mountains. (Feb-June).

♣ There are 10 species. *E. longifolius* is very similar, but sandpapery in texture. *E. gnaphaloides* has a few stout glands on the leaves and flowerhead clusters of capitula on short stalks along the branch ends; the renosterbos, *E. rhinocerotis* is dark grey-green with tiny adpressed, glandless leaves and is the defining plant of renosterveld.

Phaenocoma prolifera everlasting

An erect, stiffly-branched woody shrub to 60cm with densely woolly stems and scale-like leaves. The large showy flowerheads have many rows of glistening pink papery 'petals', which are in fact bracts, surrounding the many tiny florets within. A taller white form occurs on the lower north slope of Maanschynkop at the back of the Klein River mountains. The pink bracts gradually fade with age, remaining on the plant for many months and said to protect the fruits from fire. It occurs in coastal or mountain fynbos from Ceres, Worcester, Ladismith and the Cape Peninsula to Bredasdorp. (Sept-Apr).

♣ There is only 1 species.

Disparago ericoides

Stoebe aethiopica

Stoebe spiralis

Elytropappus glandulosus

Phaenocoma prolifera

289

Syncarpha gnaphaloides
vlaktetee

An erect, white-felted shrublet to 30cm whose narrow, ascending leaves have upcurved edges. The fragrant, reddish-brown single heads on long stalks are about 10mm across with long-tapering sharply backward bent bracts. It differs from *Helichrysum* mainly in the fruit having a feathery parachute, whereas that of *Helichrysum* is bristly. It occurs on sandstone slopes from Tulbagh and the Cape Peninsula to the Outeniqua mountains. (Oct-Dec).

♣ There are over 25 species in southern Africa with about 10 in this area.

Syncarpha speciosissima
Cape everlasting

A sprawling white-woolly shrublet to 60cm with erect annual stems. The capitula are discoid, solitary on long stalks and 3-4cm across. The bracts are ivory-coloured. It grows on sandy slopes from the Cape Peninsula to the Langeberg. (Jul-Jan).

Syncarpha (=Helichrysum) vestita
Cape snow, sewejaartjie, tontelblom

A robust, much-branched woolly shrub to 1m, with narrow crowded leaves 80cm or more in length, becoming smaller towards the top of the plant. The flowerheads are borne few to several in loose clusters on white woolly stalks with dry membranous bracts becoming more crowded towards the top. The tiny purplish florets in the centre are surrounded by several rows of papery white pointed bracts, each head being about 5cm across and 35mm long. It is quite common to the most conspicuous element in the veld in the first years after a fire on flats and middle slopes from Paarl and the Cape Peninsula to Knysna and on the Swartberg mountains. (Nov-Jan).

Syncarpha (=Helipterum) zeyheri

A sturdy shrublet to 20cm, with upright stems closely clothed with rather narrow felt-textured leaves up to 5cm by 6-8mm, becoming smaller upwards. A few flowerheads are grouped terminal on stems, each head with small scattered rosy bracts which become larger and more crowded upwards. The colour fades to white as the flowers open. Occurring from the Cape Peninsula to Hermanus on grassy and rocky flats and slopes. (Aug-Oct).

♣ The pink 25-35mm wide flowerheads of *S. canescens* are mostly single on the grey-felted sparsely branched 50cm plant.

Atrichantha gemmifera

A densely leafy silvery-woolly shrub to 60cm with lance-shaped leaves broadest at the base and margins folding upwards. The discoid flowers with white papery bracts tinged pink and maroon at the base are grouped in clusters at the end of branches. Uncommon in moist areas above 900m in the Hottentots Holland and Kogelberg Mountains. (Oct-Jan).

♣ This is the only species in the genus.

Syncarpha gnaphaloides

Syncarpha speciosissima

Syncarpha vestita

Syncarpha zeyheri

Atrichantha gemmifera

291

Anaxeton asperum

A straggly shrublet with grey-woolly branches and harsh, almost prickly, narrow leaves 5-35mm long, glossy, shiny green above and white woolly below. The flowerhead, up to 35mm across, consists of numerous individual posy-like groups each surrounded by a few outer buff-coloured hairy bracts. They appear deep red in bud, but open a dirty white. It occurs on sandy or stony mountainsides throughout this area from near sea level to 1 200m. (Jan-Dec).

♣ There are 10 species confined to the fynbos of which 5 more, all white-woolly, occur in this area.Two are from high altitudes: *A. ellipticum* of Hottentots Holland has heart-shaped leaves; the edges of the oval leaves of *A. nycthemerum* southward in the Kogelberg are rolled under; *A. laeve* has smooth needlelike leaves and a woolly seed; *A. lundgrenii* is a Klein River mountain endemic with only 2 male florets; *A. virgatum* is a sparse shrub with spreading leaves and an almost hairless seed.

Edmondia sesamoides   sewejaartjie

A sparsely-branched single-stemmed white-woolly shrublet to 30cm. The lower leaves are linear and spreading with the edges up-rolled, those above short and pressed against the flowerstalks. The solitary flowerheads are yellow with involucral bracts papery white, or yellow or pink. It grows on rocky flats and slopes forming white fields in the first few years after fire. It is found from the Cedarberg to Mossel Bay. (Aug-Dec).

♣ There are 3 species, all in our area, *E. pinifolia* the resprouting of higher altitudes is a more robust plant; the upper leaves of *E. fasciculata* soon dry at the tips and the involucre is bright yellow.

Helichrysum retortum

A straggling, densely leafy, silvery shrublet to 50cm with overlapping, oblong, recurved, hooked hairy leaves. The top-shaped white or pink-tinged flowerheads without rays nestle in the leaves. What appear to be rays are actually bracts. It grows in coastal sands and cliffs from Blouberg strand to Stilbaai. (Aug-Dec).

♣ There are 500 species in Africa and Madagascer, c. 245 in South Africa and c.30 species in this area.

Helichrysum pandurifolium   kooigoed

A straggling, grey-woolly shrublet the base of whose oval, grey-woolly leaves are broad with ears clasping the stem, and densely wavy-serrated edges. The creamy 6 X 8mm capitula are few to many in flat-topped flowerhead and involucre is of pointed bracts. It occurs on sandy flats and slopes from Bain's Kloof to the Kouga. (Oct-Jan).

♣ There are 81 species in the Cape. Others include the similar *H. patulum* which is distinguished by its round-tipped bracts; in *H. petiolare* the leaves have stalks; the bracts of the white-woolly *H. crispum* are opaque white and wavy, spreading above, the leaves broadest towards the tip and the capitula are 3-6 x 3-4 grouped into clusters; *H. diffusum* is like *H. crispum* but has larger flowers and leaves elongated with a broad clasping base.

Lachnospermum umbellatum   rooiblombos

A stiffly erect shrub to 30cm with woolly stems and minute hard ericoid leaves in tufts resprouting from a woody underground base after fire. The tubular shaped capitula at the end of branches lack ray florets but have pink, reflexed bracts encased in woolly hairs, pink bristles surrounding the florets and dark purple petals. Found from the Cape Peninsula to Hermanus. (Nov-Feb).

♣ There are 4 species with only this one occurring in our area.

Anaxeton asperum

Edmondia sesamoides

Helichrysum retortum

Helichrysum pandurifolium

Lachnospermum umbellatum

Heterolepis aliena   rotsgousblom

A spreading rounded shrub to 60cm high and more across. Crowded narrow leaves 25-37mm long have the edges rolled under nearly to conceal the pale woolly lower surface. The 6cm yellow flowerheads on sand-papery leafless stalks are often so profuse as to cover the plant, obscuring the leaves. The involucral bracts are distinctive in 2-3 rows, the outer being smaller and narrow, the inner larger, oblong, and membranous edged, all joined near the base. It occurs on rocky slopes and in crevices from the Cedarberg and throughout this area. (Sept-Jan).

♣ There are 3 species in the southwestern Cape, 1 other, *H. peduncularis* occurs here in drier parts. It has yellow flowerheads 3cm across on stalks 6-10cm long and fewer leaves.

Haplocarpha lanata   brandbossie

A perennial with basal leaves sometimes 20cm long, but often less, sandpapery in texture above and pale and felt-like below. The single capitula are borne on leafless woolly stalks about 15cm long, arising from among the leaves at ground level. They are surrounded by many rows of free bracts, the outer small and leafy, the inner rounded and membranous. The white or yellow flowerheads with red or purple reverse can be up to 35mm across. It occurs throughout this area and is most frequently observed in recently burnt veld. (Mar-June).

♣ There are 8 species in Africa, of which only 1 occurs in this area.

Berkheya barbata

A rather rigid erect, resprouting shrublet to 60cm with the spiny leaves characteristic of the genus arranged in pairs. They are dark above but strikingly paler and woolly below, up to 6cm long and 25mm broad, leathery and with the edges rolled under. The solitary flowerheads, c.10cm across, are surrounded by several rows of long spiny leaflike bracts. It is found from the coast to the lower coastal mountain slopes, from Gifberg to Bredasdorp. (Aug-Jan).

♣ There are about 150 species, mostly in Africa, with 3 others in this area. The rosette *B. herbacea*, with rather smaller clustered flowerheads and alternate leaves, is similar to *B. armata* on clay and granite of Stellenbosch, and the 1m tall *B. rigida*, with clusters of very many flowerheads not more than 35mm across, and alternate, much-divided leaves some 8mm wide.

Gazania pectinata

A soft perennial to 20cm with tufts of short-stalked leaves. They may be narrow and strap-like or pinnately divided (sometimes on the same plant), green and smooth or bristly above, and pale and woolly below. The solitary yellow or orange flowerheads are borne on hairy stalks up to 30cm long and are up to 9cm across. They arise from a firm, smooth or bristly cup of several rows of bracts, the innermost tapering, slightly papery-edged, all joined for less than half their length. It occurs commonly in sand or fine gravel at low altitudes. (Aug-Nov).

♣ There are about 16 species in Africa, of which 5 occur in this area. The common and widespread *G. krebsiana* has flowerstalks rarely longer than 15cm and the bracts are non-hairy.

Oedera capensis

A straggling prickly shrublet to 30cm, with rather rigid narrow leaves about 15-25mm long, having rough glandular spines on the edges. Terminal flowerheads up to 4cm across with several irregular rows of radiate florets enclose distinctive small circles of discoid heads, this whole false capitulum surrounded by a few rows of bracts, the outer leafy and inner translucent. It occurs on dry flats and slopes from the Cape Peninsula to the Eastern Cape. (June-Dec).

♣ There are 18 species. *O. imbricata* growing on the same slopes but usually associated with rocky outcrops, has broader more rounded leaves but an identical flower structure.

Heterolepis aliena

Haplocarpha lanata

Berkheya barbata

Charlie Boucher

Gazania pectinata

Oedera capensis

295

Chrysanthemoides monilifera   boneseed bush (Australia), bietou boetabessie

A dense shrub to 2m with leaves up to 45mm by 25mm with a smooth or toothed edge. The flower-head is 20mm across, and the fruit is a purple berry, (here still green) which distinguishes this species from nearly all other daisies. The berries are beloved by birds and the seeds are widely dispersed in their droppings. It grows in the coastal districts from the southwestern to the eastern Cape and on to tropical Africa, and blooms all year. It has also been introduced into Australia and America and in the former country it has become a serious pest plant, invading huge areas of natural vegetation.

♣ There are 2 species; the other, *C. incana*, a straggling shrub of coastal dunes and inland sandy slopes, is spiny and grey-leaved.

Euryops abrotanifolius   geel margriet

A robust erect shrub to 2m, single-stemmed and sparsely-branched above. The leathery to slightly fleshy leaves are blueish-green, usually crowded, up to 9cm long, deeply divided, and with the segments scarcely 1.5mm wide. The solitary, occasionally clustered flowerheads, 3-5cm across, are sometimes reddish on the reverse and have a single row of bracts united into a smooth cup. This typical member of the fynbos, found from Calvinia to Riversdale on sandy and rocky slopes from sea-level to 1 800m is often a pioneer after veld fires. (Jan-Dec).

♣ There are about 100 species in Africa, all yellow-flowered, with 4 in this area. The 40cm tall *E. tenuilobus* grows on clay hills. The other 2 are uncommon.

Ursinia paleacea   geelmargriet

An erect almost hairless perennial to 90cm, branched at the base, with leaves 2-6cm long, divided into long narrow segments. Slender, single, relatively leafless, long flowerhead stalks, gracefully arched over in bud, straighten as the yellow flowerhead with a dark reverse, opens. There are 6-7 rows of dark-edged bracts, the innermost longest with very pronounced papery tips. It is common on damp mountain slopes from Tulbagh to the Cape Peninsula and east-wards to Humans-dorp. (Oct-Feb).

♣ There are c. 38 species, mainly in southern Africa, with 8, all perennial, in our area. Three more are 50cm tall shrubs with long unbranched flowerhead stalks; 2 have a coppery/reddish reverse: the leafy *U. dentata* of Lebanon and Kleinmond with heads c. 40mm across; *U. nudicaulis* with narrow, divided leaves bunched below and heads 15-30mm across, and the very similar *U. tenuifolia* with undivided leaves. *U. pinnata* is the only species in our area with open branched flowerstalks. All of these prefer wet places.

Ursinia quinquepartita

An erect, single-stemmed shrublet to 40cm, the upper stems densely-leafy with divided thread-like segments, the lower parts with persistent flattened leafstalks. Each stem has a single short-stalked yellow flowerhead, sometimes with brown reverse, and enfolded below by 5 rows of dark-edged bracts, the innermost tipped with large papery flaps. It occurs most frequently in damp places on mountains from Stellenbosch to Caledon. (Nov-Apr).

♣ Two with very short flowerhead stalks and narrowly lance-shaped leaves, broadest above, and often terminat-ing in 3 teeth are *U. eckloniana* in marshes of Fernkloof and Palmiet River mouth area, and *U. caledonica* of moist upper mountain slopes of the Kogelberg and Stellenbosch.

Chrysanthemoides monilifera Anne Bean

Euryops abrotanifolius

Ursinia paleacea

Ursinia quinquepartita

297

Osteospermum polygaloides

An erect rather leggy, sparsely-branched shrub to 2m with tufts of wool in the axils of the leaves. The alternate, sessile, lance-shaped bluegreen leaves decreasing in size upwards have a point at the tip. The unbranched or branched flowerhead stalks are densely clothed with glandular hairs, as are the several loose rows of soft green bracts. It occurs on the slopes of the Klein River mountains. (Oct-Dec).

♣ There are about 70 species, mainly African, of which some 14 occur in this area. *O. rotundifolium* of the Klein River mountains is superficially alike but for broadly oval leaves.

Hymenolepis (=Athanasia) parviflora   basterkaroo

A sturdy densely leafy shrub to 1.3m with pinnately-branched needlelike leaves up to 7cm long. The flowerheads, emerging from slender branches among the uppermost leaves, can be 10cm across. Each head is made up of a multitude of flower clusters each 5mm long by 1-2mm wide, and surrounded by many rows of horny bracts. The flowers have a strong sickly-sweet scent. The species is widespread on flats and mountains from Namaqualand to Uitenhage. (Nov-Dec).

♣ There are 7 species.

Hippia frutescens   rankals

An aromatic, erect or straggling, weakly-branched shrub to 60cm with hairy branches bearing rather crowded, pinnately-divided leaves up to 6cm long. The discoid flowerheads, each seldom more than 6mm across, are grouped in dense or open clusters at the ends of the branches, and are surrounded by 2 rows of green bracts with papery edges. It occurs most frequently in damp places from sea level to 2 000m from Piketberg along the Cape mountains to Uitenhage and also in the Transvaal. (Aug-Jan).

♣ There are 7 species in South Africa, mostly in the fynbos regions, of which 2 have been recorded in this area. The young buds of the rather sprawling *H. pilosa* of shady places on sandy slopes often have long russet hairs.

Othonna dentata

A succulent hairless shrub to 70cm with thick fleshy partly-woody stems. The smooth, hairless leaves, borne towards the tips of the branches, are 37-50mm long and half as wide, with edges which may be quite smooth to sharply or coarsely toothed. It has 1 or more branched almost leafless flowering stems bearing heads about 2cm across, with a single row of joined bracts shorter than the flowers within. It occurs in fissures in rocks on the coast and mountain slopes from the Cape Peninsula to Hermanus. (May-Dec).

♣ There are about 145 species in South Africa, of which 10 have been recorded from this area.

Othonna quinquedentata

A short-lived erect shrub to 2m, single-stemmed or sparsely-branched from near the base, with the lower stems becoming woody with age. The slightly fleshy, smooth, hairless leaves are clustered untidily on the lower stems and are often streaked and spotted with red. They are 5-15cm by 1-5cm, broadest in the upper half, often with a toothed edge (hence the specific name: 5-toothed). The flowerheads are borne on almost leafless branched stems, each up to 3cm across, and have a single row of joined bracts shorter than the flowers. Occurring in damp places on lower slopes and flats from Worcester and the Cape Peninsula to Mossel Bay and the Swartberg mountains, it becomes abundant as a pioneer plant in disturbed places, especially after veld fires, dying off after a few years but lingering on as rather gawky skeletons above the regenerating fynbos. (Jan-Dec).

♣ The 2m *O. parviflora* has heads in dense clusters and leaves somewhat clasping at the base.

298

*Osteospermum
polygaloides*

Hymenolepis parviflora

Hippia frutescens

Othonna dentata

Othonna quinquedentata

Osmitopsis asteriscoides swamp daisy

A robust leggy camphor-scented shrub to 2m with lower stems leafless, exposing the cracked naked bark. The upper stems are well branched, with crowded velvety leaves up to 80mm by 18mm. The flowerheads are about 35mm across and borne on short side branches, but not at the tip of the main stem. Its soft, green bracts are in several rows. Dense stands are indicators of swamps and seeps from the Cape Peninsula and Paarl to Caledon and the Riviersonderend Mountains. (Jan-Dec).

♣ There are 9 species in the Western Cape of which 6 occur in this area.

Osmitopsis parvifolia

A hairless shrublet to 40cm with crowded, toothed leaves, neatly spiralling up the stem, becoming clearly smaller towards the top. The flowerheads, 20-25mm across, are borne singly at the ends of the branches and are surrounded by several rows of soft green bracts. It occurs among rocks on mid and upper slopes from Sir Lowry's Pass to Kleinmond. (Sept-Feb).

♣ *O. afra* of the Kogelberg is a similarly sized resprouter with densely felted leaves.

Polyarrhena reflexa wild aster

Superficially very similar to *Thaminophyllum* and *Felicia*, this is a straggling, bristly, perennial undershrub to 1m with broad-based, recurving leaves about 10mm by 4mm with barbed edges. The single flowerheads, about 18mm across, are white above and reddish-purple on the reverse. It forms large dense mats especially in moist places on lower slopes, and occurs from Paarl and the Cape Peninsula to Caledon. (June-Sept).

♣ There are 4 species, all confined to the South Western Cape of which 1 other, *P. stricta*, occurs in this area, distinguished by its straight, less recurved, leaves with roughened margins.

Thaminophyllum mundii

A silver silky shrublet to 60cm or more, with silky branches and narrow, spreading leaves. The flowerheads, each with only 2-6 white ray florets, are grouped several together at the branch tips. It occurs on sandstone but favours deep clay soils from Kogelberg to Caledon Swartberg. (Jul-Nov).

♣ There are 3 species all found in our area. All have rather wide, well-spaced rounded "petals". The other two have 1-3 flowerheads per branch tip: the silvery-silky *T. multiflorum*, up to 1.5m, also with white rays, is otherwise very similar and grows from Viljoen's Pass to Houwhoek. The sprawling *T. latifolium* has rather broader leaves with recurved edges and pink or white rays, and grows on the Klein River mountains.

Dimorphotheca (=Castalis) nudicaulis ox-eye daisy, witmargriet

A perennial with variable usually toothed leaves 10cm long by 15mm wide, mostly crowded at the base of the stem. The flowerheads are about 6cm across, borne singly on a harsh leafless hairy stem. They are white with a purple or coppery reverse, and the involucre comprises 1-2 rows of narrow pointed bracts. The fruits are of two sorts, those of the ray florets are 3-angled and winged, those of the disc florets[1] flattened and 2-winged. It is quite common on mountain slopes from Clanwilliam to Uniondale. (Aug-Sept).

♣ There are 9 species in South Africa, but only one more here, the glandular-hairy annual *D. pluvialis*, the reënblommetjie, purple centred with white rays, darker on the reverse.

Osmitopsis asteriscoides

Osmitopsis parvifolia

Thaminophyllum mundii

Polyarrhena reflexa

Dimorphotheca nudicaulis

Senecio speciosissimus

A magnificent robust shrub to 2m with sturdy woody stems and sparsely sharp-toothed leaves up to 9cm by 2cm. The showy flowerheads, up to 4cm across, are borne in groups on cobwebby stalks and have 2 rows of woolly or hairless bracts, the outer shorter than the inner and alternately papery-edged. It occurs on wet mountain slopes near rivers or in seeps, in the Kogelberg area. (Sept-Jan).

♣ There are over 2 000 species worldwide with about 250 in South Africa and c. 30 in this area. The similar *S. glastifolius* is a completely hairless shrub.

Senecio hastifolius *(= S. cymbalariifolius)*

An erect, hairless perennial to 40cm with tuberous roots, and very variable leaves mostly at the base of the plant and often purple below. The lower ones are on long stalks, with much smaller, stalkless upper leaves partly enfolding the flowering stems. The flowering heads, purple or yellow with purple or white rays, about 3cm across, have a single row of loose narrow bracts, alternately papery-edged. Occurring on lower to midslopes from the Cedarberg to the Cape Peninsula and Caledon, it blooms profusely after fires. (Aug-Dec).

♣ Two more smallish species have rosettes or tufts of rounded or broad, pointed leaves but yellow flowers: *S. cordifolius* of moist sheltered slopes has delicate leaves often purple beneath, borne on branches which may become trailing; the sprawling *S. arniciflorus* of coastal sands has leathery leaves with a woolly reverse.

Senecio elegans   wild cineraria, strandblommetjie

A purple-flowered glandular-hairy annual to 1m tall with variable leaves 35-75mm long with rounded or finely divided lobes. They are often slightly clammy to the touch and those growing on the seashore are somewhat fleshy. The flowerheads are 25mm across and are clasped below by 2 rows of smooth green bracts with brown tips. It is a very common and colourful constituent of sandy coastal flats and lower slopes from Namaqualand to the Eastern Cape. (July-Mar). The yellow flowers belong to spiny *Berkheya barbata*.

♣ Another purple-flowered species of the seashore is *S. arenarius*, which has hairy bracts.

Senecio triqueter

A hairless sparsely-branched shrublet to 30cm with leafy branches bearing needlelike leaves 8-15mm long. Stems with scale-like leaves arise at the tips, bearing single creamy flowerheads about 18mm across with only disc florets (discoid). They are enfolded below by a double circle of greenish bracts, the length of the inner approximately double that of the outer and alternately papery-edged. It occurs on slopes from the Cape Peninsula to Caledon. (Jan-May).

♣ Other discoid species: *S. paniculatus* has flowers on lax branched racemes; 2 have fleshy leaves: round spindle-shaped in *S. crassulaefolius* and flattened spindle-shaped in *S. serpens*.

Mairia coriacea   uimaster

A hairy, tufted perennial to 12cm with leathery leaves in a basal rosette, oval but widest above and usually with broad teeth and thick edge, at first silky below but becoming bald. The solitary capitula are purple with a yellow centre. It is recorded from Rooiels to Potberg on rocky slopes after fires. (Nov-Mar).

♣ There are 5 species with 2 more in our area, both flowering after fire: the 30cm tall *M. hirsuta* is softly woolly with mauve-pink rays; the 15cm *M. crenata* has pink, mauve or white rays and leaf margins with many small teeth.

Senecio speciosissimus

Senecio hastifolius

Senecio elegans

Senecio triqueter

Mairia coriacea

303

Felicia aethiopica
wilde aster

A dense leafy shrublet to 50cm or more, often rooting at the nodes, with harsh oval to tongue-shaped almost sessile leaves 2-5mm wide. The blue flowerheads with a yellow eye, some 30mm across, are carried well above the foliage on long harsh-textured naked stalks. They have two rows of free bracts. It occurs on flats from the Cedarberg to the Eastern Cape and KwaZulu-Natal. (Jan-Dec).

♣ There are about 85 species, all African, with 7 in this area, the majority with blue-rayed flowers.

Felicia tenella
astertjie

A dainty annual to 20cm with simple ericoid leaves up to 25mm long. The flowerheads are about 10mm across and may be pink, pale blue or mauve with 3 rows of involucral bracts. They are borne singly on almost leafless unbranched stalks. It is found in moist sandy areas on flats or coastal dunes from Nieuwoudtville to Riversdale and blooms throughout the year. (The orange daisy is a *Gazania*.)

Corymbium africanum
heuningbossie, plampers

A variable clumped perennial to 30cm whose very narrow harsh leaves up to 20cm long have a tuft of woolly hairs at the base. The single flowers are usually grouped together in flat heads and may be purple, pink or white with purplish style, each with 5 rough and sticky bracts, the inner 2 longer than the outer. It is found from the coast to 1800m from the Cedarberg to the Langkloof and Swartberg and seldom blooms except after veld fires, when it is profuse. (Oct-Jan).

♣ There are 9 species confined to the fynbos, of which 6 occur in this area. *C. villosum* differs in 1cm wide ribbed hairy leaves.

Corymbium glabrum
This tufted perennial has smooth, broad, strongly-veined sword-shaped leaves, and smooth stems and bracts. The flowers are pink or white. It occurs on rocky sandstone slopes throughout the area. (Nov-Jan).

♣ *C. enerve* of Hangklip is white or pink with sandpapery stems and narrow smooth unveined leaves. The ivory *C. cymosum* throughout our area has very narrow leaves, smooth to slightly rough stems and smooth bracts.

Corymbium congestum
vingerhoed

This tufted perennial to 30cm has sandpapery sticky stems bearing mauve to pink branching racemes of flowerheads. The leaves, 15-25mm wide, are sandpapery and silky at the base. The bracts are sandpapery and sticky, the inner as long as the flowers. A montane species above 700m it occurs on damp sandstone slopes from the Cedarberg to the Hottentots Holland and Houwhoek. (Nov-Feb).

Felicia aethiopica

Felicia tenella

Corymbium africanum

Corymbium congestum

Corymbium glabrum

305

Involucral bracts of ASTERACEAE

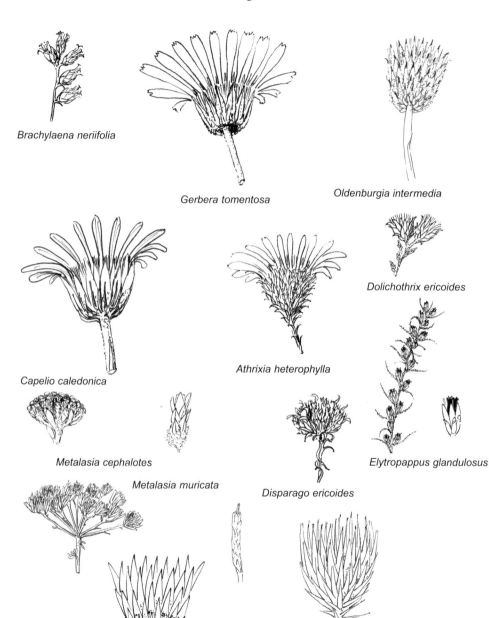

Brachylaena neriifolia

Gerbera tomentosa

Oldenburgia intermedia

Dolichothrix ericoides

Capelio caledonica

Athrixia heterophylla

Metalasia cephalotes

Metalasia muricata

Disparago ericoides

Elytropappus glandulosus

Phaenocoma prolifera

Syncarpha vestita

306

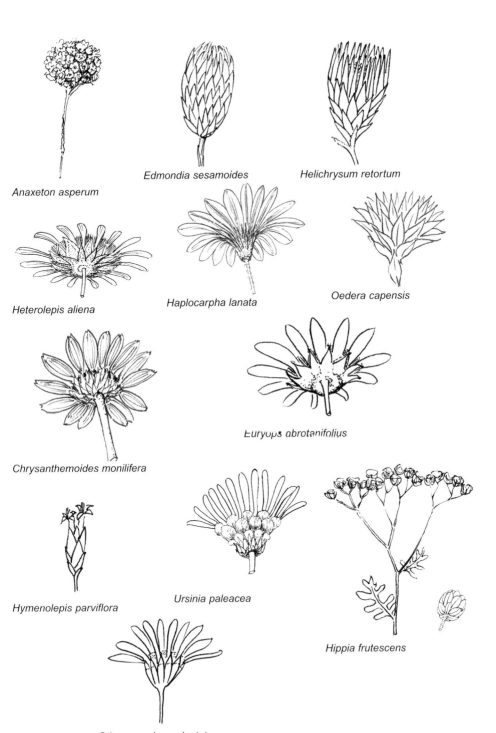

Anaxeton asperum

Edmondia sesamoides

Helichrysum retortum

Heterolepis aliena

Haplocarpha lanata

Oedera capensis

Chrysanthemoides monilifera

Euryops abrotanifolius

Hymenolepis parviflora

Ursinia paleacea

Hippia frutescens

Othonna quinquedentata

307

Polyarrhena reflexa

Dimorphotheca nudicaulis

Senecio elegans

Mairia coriacea

Felicia aethiopica

Corymbium villosum

Glossary

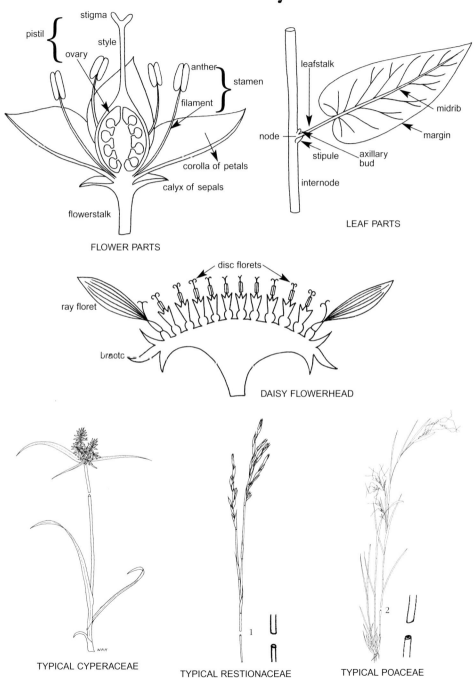

FLOWER PARTS

- pistil
  - stigma
  - style
  - ovary
- anther
- stamen
- filament
- corolla of petals
- calyx of sepals
- flowerstalk

LEAF PARTS

- leafstalk
- node
- stipule
- internode
- midrib
- margin
- axillary bud

DAISY FLOWERHEAD

- disc florets
- ray floret
- bracts

TYPICAL CYPERACEAE

TYPICAL RESTIONACEAE

TYPICAL POACEAE

actinomorphic – Regular: of a flower with its parts arranged in a ground plan like that of a wheel, so that it can be divided into two equal halves through many axes.

adpressed – Of a leaf or bract, but also other plant parts like anthers or petals, when it lies closely touching another part.

alien plant – Plant from another land growing wild in our area.

alternate – Leaves attached one at a time on the stem.

apical pore – A circular or oval opening usually at the top of an anther out of which pollen escapes.

archaic – Deriving from an ancient line of ancestry.

awn – A barb or whisker attached to the back of a bract or leaf.

axil – The angle between a stem and its subtending leaf.

basal – Of leaves, arising from ground level.

bifoliate – A leaf with two leaflets.

bract – A leaflike structure associated with a flower.

bracteolate – Flowerstalk bearing bracteoles.

bracteole, bracteolate – A small, usually leaflike, organ, usually reduced in size, attached to a pedicel or flower stalk; having bracteoles.

bulb – A swollen subterranean storage organ formed from the fleshy bases of previous leaves as in an onion (compare corm).

bulbils – Diminutive bulbs attached to the base or stem of a mother plant.

buzz pollination – Effected by carpenter bees which project a stream of air under pressure into the anthers, causing pollen to be squirted out.

callus – a hump or wartlike projection of solid tissue.

calyx – Outer usually leaflike and green circle of parts of a flower.

capitulum – A head of a daisy or other flowerhead with tightly packed flowers.

capsule – A dry fruit containing several seeds, splitting open to release the seeds.

carpel – A single unit of an ovary, e.g. a pea pod consisting or a stigma, style and ovary.

catkins – A dense spike-like flowerhead of unisex flowers without petals.

cladodes – Stems flattened to resemble leaves.

compound leaf – A leaf divided into subordinate lobes called leaflets.

compound palmate – Leaflets attached like rays of a fan, or fingers on a hand.

corm – A swollen subterranean storage organ formed from the base of a stem and usually enclosed by dried persistent leaf bases.

cormlets – Small axillary subsidiary corms below or above ground.

corolla – Second circle of broad attachments of a flower, usually brightly coloured.

corona – The crown-like structure between the petals and stamens.

corymb – A flat-topped raceme with the flowers all ending up at one level.

diaphanous – Translucent; veiled.

dichotomous branching – Of a stem or vein, splitting into two equal subdivisions.

dicotyledon – A seedling having two embryonic, first leaves.

digitate – Leaflets arranged in a fan or like the fingers of a hand.

dioecious – Having the male and female parts of the flower on separate plants; the sexes on separate plants.

disc florets – The central flowers of a daisy, with 5 equal but small petals.

discoid – Having a flowerhead made up of only discoid florets.

eliaosome – A waxy growth/deposit on a seed or fruit, attractive to ants.

endemic – Having evolved, that is, arisen, in the area being discussed and being confined to it in nature.

310

epiphyte – A plant growing on but not parasitic on another plant.

ericoid – Leaves like Erica, narrow and small with edges rolled beneath.

evergreen – Retaining leaves for more than one year.

exotic – Originating and evolved from outside the area.

fibrous roots – Mass of roots without a single main leader root.

filament – Stalk of an anther.

florets – Small flowers, grouped together into heads as in most proteas and daisies.

foliolate – a leaf with several lobes or leaflets.

foliolate-bi- tri – a leaf with 2 or 3 lobes or leaflets.

frond – The leaf of a fern.

fruit – The matured ovary containing one or more seeds. It can be dry, as in capsules, or fleshy as in berries.

geophytic – A plant having an underground food store such as a bulb, corm or tuber usually produced to carry the dormant plant through a difficult season.

glandular – Of hairs: having knoblike tips; or in tissue, patches or dots of contrasting colour or transparency, secreting aromatic oils, etc. They are small structures best seen with a handlens.

Gondwana – Ancient continent, a huge southerly land mass incorporating Africa, South America, Australia, India, Antarctica, New Zealand, Madagascar and associated islands, breaking up and diverging into its constituent modern continents commencing c. 150 mya, parts continuing to move to this day but the major rifts complete about c. 30 mya.

granite – A non-sedimentary rock upwelling as a molten mass from deep within the earth's crust, intruding into other pre-existing rock and often forming domes and rounded boulders when exposed; visibly consisting of a variety of differently coloured components.

habit – Overall appearance of the plants.

habitat – The total environment within which a living organism grows and lives.

helicoid cyme – A branch carrying flowers on one side only, with the youngest at the top, the whole structure rolled up like a watch spring.

herb – A non-woody, soft-bodied usually short-lived or annual plant.

hypanthium – The portion of a flower below the insertion of the sepals and petals, enclosing or partly enclosing the ovary.

hysteranthous – Of geophytes, flowers appearing before the leaves or at a different time from the leaves.

indusium – The covering over a patch of spore-bearing bodies in a fern.

inferior – Of the position of the ovary in a flower, being below the point of insertion of the other flower parts.

involucre – The modified leaves just below and to some extent enfolding the flowerhead in proteas, daisies and some other plants.

irregular – Of a flower with its parts arranged in a ground plan so that there is only one line through which it can be cut to yield two equal halves: = zygomorphic; compare actinomorphic, regular.

keeled – With a central lengthwise ridge like the upturned keel of a boat.

leaflet – One of 2, 3 or more subdivisions of a leaf.

legume – A member of the pea family, (Leguminosae or) Fabaceae.

lignotuber – A woody, largely subterranean base of a long-lived shrub or tree.

ligule – A structure, of hairs or membranes mostly, between the wrap-around and the free portion of a grass leaf, and lying against the stem, therefore on the inner curve of the leaf.

limestone – A chalky rock, originating in the sea, usually pale in colour. A drop of vinegar on its clean surface will cause it to fizz.

linear – Very narrow leaves with parallel sides.

lobe – A flap or projection from a petal or leaf, usually rounded or oval.

membranous – Thin, soft, flexible, more or less translucent.

mimicry – An evolutionary change in the form of one organism leading it to resemble another.

monocotyledon – A great group of plants whose embryo and seedling has only one first leaf.

monotypic – A genus consisting of only one species eg. *Witsenia maura.*

montane – Pertaining to a mountain.

mucilaginous – Slimy or gelatinous.

multi-stemmed – Having several main branches arising from below ground level.

mya – million years ago.

naturalised – Evolving elsewhere, but now growing and surviving here.

node – A joint in a stem marking the attatchment point of a leaf and either a bud or its grown-out side branch.

palmate – Of a compound leaf whose leaflets all arise from one point and spread out like a fan.

pappus – A ring of fluff, bristles or hairs on daisy seeds between the flower parts and the ovary, often serving as a parachute.

perennial – A plant growing from a seed and living for several years.

perianth – The outer parts of a flower, either sepals and petals, or tepals.

petaloid – In the form of or serving the function of a petal.

petaloid bract – A bract in the form of a petal, hence usually brightly coloured.

petals – The inner of the two circles of flower parts, the outer being the sepals.

 pinnate – Of a leaf, the arrangement of leaflets equally on either side of the mid stalk, like the flight feather of a bird.

pistil – The female part of a flower, consisting of ovary, style and stigma = gynoecium.

plumose – Feathery.

pollen – The usually powdery cells arising within an anther, containing the male reproductive nucleus.

 raceme – Stalked flowers arranged up a stem with the oldest at the bottom. See spike.

radiate – Branching out from a central point like spokes of a wheel. In daisy flowers, a head containing ray florets. See discoid.

radiate – Branching out from a central point like spokes of a wheel. In daisy flowers, a head containing ray florets See discoid.

ray florets – A daisy floret some of whose petals are much elongated to one side to form a petal-like lobe.

receptacle – The expanded, flattened top of a flowerhead stalk on which the florets are arranged; seen well in dry Protea flowerheads whose florets have dropped.

receptacle – The expanded, flattened top of a flowerhead stalk on which the florets are arranged; seen well in dry sunflowers or Protea flowerheads after the florets have dropped.

reclining – Of stamens, lying on the floor of the tube of the flower.

recurving – Curving smoothly outwards and downwards.

reflexed – Of leaves, usually, which are bent sharply downwards on their long axis (compare recurved).

regular – Of a flower whose ground plan allows the flower to be divided into two equal parts along many axes: see actinomorphic.

renosterveld – A scrubland on clay soil in the winter-rainfall region of the Cape, whose components lack the typical heaths, proteas and restios of fynbos, but consist very largely of grasses, members of the daisy family and characteristically, a diversity of geophytes in season.

resprouting – Of a shrub, having an underground fireproof woody stump from which new growths can shoot after a fire.

resupinate – Bent back; upside down.

rhizome – The fibrous or woody horizontal underground stem of a plant, bearing roots.

rhombic – Diamond shaped.

rootstock – The rooted portion of a plant.

sandstone – A coarse rock of uniform structure laid down in layers under water.

seep – A place where soil water oozes out onto the surface and runs very gently to maintain a local wetland area.

sepals – The outer circle of parts of a flower, usually green.

serotinous – Of a seedhead, its ability to persist for more than one season on the mother plant, and, with its contents of live seeds, to withstand a bush fire.

sessile – Lacking a stalk, usually of a leaf or flower.

shale – A fine-grained sedimentary rock of uniform structure, in layers, derived from clay or mud.

sheath – A structure which wraps around and encloses another structure.

shrub – A many-stemmed woody plant living many years.

simple leaves – Leaves consisting of only one lobe or flat part.

single stemmed – A plant with only one main stem arising from the ground, but which may be well-branched above-ground.

sori/ sorus – A patch of spore-bearing structures (sporangia) on the underside of the leaf of a fern.

spadix – The central column of flowers in an arum lily.

spathe – The usually brightly coloured large leaf-like structure enclosing the flowers, the spadix, in an arum, but often less conspicuous. In the restios it is the large bract subtending the flowerhead.

 spike – Stalkless flowers arranged up a stem with the oldest at the bottom, youngest at the top. Compare raceme.

spikelet – The smallest unit of a flowerhead in a grass, restio or sedge.

sporangia – The small usually stalked boxes within which the spores of a fern develop.

sprouter – See resprouter.

spur – An outgrowth from a flower, usually to contain nectar or oils.

ssp – subspecies.

stamens – The stalked boxes which manufacture pollen in a flower.

staminode – A sterile stamen.

stellate – Starlike in shape.

sterile stem – A stem which does not produce flowers.

stigma – The tip of a pistil built to receive pollen and allow it to grow down to the seeds.

stipules – A pair of usually small leaflike structures on either side of the attachment of a leaf, clearly seen in Pelargonium, but present in many other plants.

stolons – A subterranean stem growing out from the base of a mother plant, usually rooting as it goes, and sending up shoots into the air some distance away.

stomata – Gas exchange openings on the surface of green parts of the plant.

style – The stalk of a pistil, supporting the stigma in a position appropriate to receive pollen.

subterranean – Below ground.

succulent – Fleshy, storing water.

superior ovary – An ovary positioned within a flower so as to be above the point of attachment of sepals and petals or tepals. It is then visible from above if the flower is gently opened.

tepals – The outer parts of a flower, usually 6 in number, in a monocotyledon, in function acting as sepals and petals, but in only one circle.

 trifoliolate – A leaf comprising 3 leaflets.

tuberous – A geophyte with surplus food stored in a swollen underground stem, like a potato.

two-lipped – Having the petals grouped into an upper and a lower half, the lower often serving as a landing platform for a pollinator.

 umbel – Having the flowers arising from one point at the top of a shared stalk, as in an amaryllid or parsley.

unifoliate – A leaf comprising one leaflet, the others having not developed.

zygomorphic – See irregular; of a flower with a ground plan permitting the flower to be divided into two in only one plane.

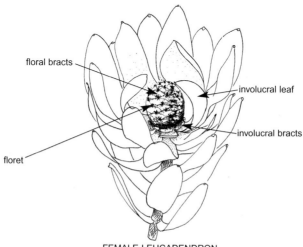

floral bracts

involucral leaf

involucral bracts

floret

FEMALE LEUCADENDRON

BOTANICAL INDEX

Species names printed in bold are both illustrated and described in the book, the remaining are described species only. Synonyms are given in italics.

A

Aandblom   110, 118
aandpypie   116
aardroos   160, 178
aasblom   262
aasuintjie   124
Acmadenia candida *I.Williams*   216
Acmadenia nivea *I.Williams*   216
Acrodon subulatus   *(Mill.)N.E.Br.*   174
Acrodon parvifolius *Du Plessis*   174
Acrolophia bolusii *Rolfe*   136
Acrolophia capensis *(P.J. Bergius)*   136
Acrolophia lamellata *(Lindl.)*   136
Acrolophia micrantha *(Lindl.)*   136
Acroanthes teretifolia *Eckl. & Zeyh.*   174
Adenandra acuta *Schltr.*   14, 216
Adenandra brachyphylla *Schldl.*   22, 216
Adenandra marginata *(L.f.)Roem. & Schult.*   216
Adenandra marginata *(L.f.)Roem. & Schult.* ssp serpyllacea *(Bartl.)Strid*   216
Adenandra obtusata *Sond.*   216
Adenandra uniflora *(L.)Willd.*   22, 216
Adenandra villosa *(Berg.)Roem. & Schult.*   216
Adenandra viscida *Eckl. & Zeyh.*   216
Adenandra   14, 22, 59
Adromischus caryophyllaceus *(Berm.f.) Lem.*   184
Adromischus hemisphaericus *(L.) Lem.*   184
Aeropetes tulbaghia   33, 98, 128, 140
afrikaanse salie   266
AGAPANTHACEAE   46, 102
Agapanthus africanus *(L.)Hoffmanns*   102
Agapanthus walshii *L. Bolus*   102
Agathelpis, see **Microdon dubius**   270
Agathosma ciliaris *(L.)Druce*   218
Agathosma crenulata *(L.)Pillans*   14, 218
Agathosma juniperifolia *Bartl.*   218
Agathosma odoratissima *(Montin) Pillans*   218

Agathosma rosmarinifolia *(Bartl.)I.Williams*   218
Agathosma serratifolia *(Curtis)Spreeth*   218
Agathosma tabularis *Sond.*   218
Agathosma   14, 31
Agtdaegeneesbos   264
AIZOACEAE   46, 174
Aizoon sarmentosum..L.f.   176
Albuca canadensis see **Albuca flaccida**   94
Albuca cooperi *Baker*   94
Albuca echinosperma *U.Moll.-Doblies*   94
Albuca flaccida *Jacq.*   94
Albuca fragrans *Jacq.*   94
Albuca juncifolia *Baker*   94
ALLIACEAE   46, 88
Aloe haemanthifolia *A.Berger & Marloth*   84
Aloe mitriformis see **Aloe perfoliata**   16
Aloe perfoliata *L.*   84
Aloe plicatilis *(L.)Mill.*   15, 84
Aloe succotrina *Lam.*   84
Aloe   15, 16, 48
Altydbossio   190
AMARYLLIDACEAE   46, 98
Amaryllis belladonna *L.*   98
Amphithalea biovulata *(Bolus)Granby*   194
Amphithalea bowiei (Benth.)A.L.Schutte   194
Amphithalea cuneifolia *Eckl.& Zeyh.*   194
Amphithalea ericifolia *(L.)Eckl. & Zeyh.*   194
Amphithalea oppositifolia *L.Bolus*   194
Amphithalea tomentosa *(Thunb.) Granby*   194
Amphithalea virgata *Eckl. & Zeyh.*   194
ANACARDIACEAE   47, 226
Anapalina nervosa see **Tritoniopsis antholyza**   128
Anapalina triticea see **Tritoniopsis triticea**   128
Anaxeton asperum *(Thunb.)DC.*   292
Anaxeton ellipticum *Lundgren*   292
Anaxeton laeve *(Harv.)Lundgren*   292
Anaxeton lundgrenii *Nord.*   292

317

319

325

337